ROUTLEDGE LIBRARY EDITIONS:
EARLY WESTERN RESPONSES
TO SOVIET RUSSIA

Volume 13

THE CITY OF THE RED PLAGUE

THE CITY OF THE RED PLAGUE
Soviet Rule in a Baltic Town

GEORGE POPOFF

Routledge
Taylor & Francis Group
LONDON AND NEW YORK

First published in Great Britain in 1932 by George Allen & Unwin Ltd

This edition first published in 2018
by Routledge
2 Park Square, Milton Park, Abingdon, Oxon OX14 4RN

and by Routledge
711 Third Avenue, New York, NY 10017

Routledge is an imprint of the Taylor & Francis Group, an informa business

© 1932 English Translation George Allen & Unwin Ltd

All rights reserved. No part of this book may be reprinted or reproduced or utilised in any form or by any electronic, mechanical, or other means, now known or hereafter invented, including photocopying and recording, or in any information storage or retrieval system, without permission in writing from the publishers.

Trademark notice: Product or corporate names may be trademarks or registered trademarks, and are used only for identification and explanation without intent to infringe.

British Library Cataloguing in Publication Data
A catalogue record for this book is available from the British Library

ISBN: 978-1-138-04993-2 (Set)
ISBN: 978-1-315-11072-1 (Set) (ebk)
ISBN: 978-1-138-08515-2 (Volume 13) (hbk)
ISBN: 978-1-138-08521-3 (Volume 13) (pbk)
ISBN: 978-1-315-11144-5 (Volume 13) (ebk)

Publisher's Note
The publisher has gone to great lengths to ensure the quality of this reprint but points out that some imperfections in the original copies may be apparent.

Disclaimer
The publisher has made every effort to trace copyright holders and would welcome correspondence from those they have been unable to trace.

THE COURTYARD OF THE CENTRAL PRISON

After the massacre carried out by the fleeing Bolshevists on the last day of their rule

THE CITY OF THE RED PLAGUE

SOVIET RULE IN A BALTIC TOWN

BY

GEORGE POPOFF

TRANSLATED BY ROBIN JOHN

ILLUSTRATED

LONDON
GEORGE ALLEN & UNWIN LTD
MUSEUM STREET

FIRST PUBLISHED IN 1932

All rights reserved
PRINTED IN GREAT BRITAIN BY
UNWIN BROTHERS LTD., WOKING

CONTENTS

CHAPTER		PAGE
	INTRODUCTION	9
I.	THE EVE	17
II.	A TOWN BY THE BALTIC	33
III.	THE ENTRY OF THE MUSCOVITES	42
IV.	"THE BEGINNING OF A GLORIOUS NEW ERA"	55
V.	THE ATTACK ON THE HOME	72
VI.	THE TERROR BEGINS	87
VII.	WAR ON RELIGION	99
VIII.	ABOLITION OF MONEY	113
IX.	SOVIET SOUP FOR ALL	132
X.	THE CITY OF THE RED PLAGUE	149
XI.	THE FEAST DURING THE PLAGUE	165
XII.	A SIGN IN THE SKY	180
XIII.	THE FIRST RESISTANCE	194
XIV.	THE MASSACRE IN BICKERN WOOD	210
XV.	A VISIT FROM ANOTHER WORLD	222
XVI.	THE TRIUMPH OF THE MUSCOVITES	237
XVII.	"BOURGEOIS TO THE FRONT!"	252
XVIII.	AT THE LAST GASP	266
XIX.	RESURRECTION DAY	282
XX.	OUR SAVIOURS	291
XXI.	THE FLIGHT OF THE MUSCOVITES	305
XXII.	SHATTERED IDOLS	322
	EPILOGUE	337
	BIBLIOGRAPHY	341

ILLUSTRATIONS

THE COURTYARD OF THE CENTRAL PRISON	*Frontispiece*
GENERAL VIEW OF RIGA	*Facing page* 40
COMRADE PETER STUTCHKA	64
"GUNWOMEN"	160
ROUGH MAP OF LATVIA AND THE NEIGHBOURING COUNTRIES	*page* 196
THE RED DEMONSTRATION ON THE ESPLANADE	248
SKETCH-MAP OF THE CENTRAL PART OF RIGA	288
THE STORMING OF THE LÜBECK BRIDGE	304
SOME OF THE RIGA CLERGY KILLED BY THE BOLSHEVISTS	320

INTRODUCTION

The political and economic crises of the past year have created such an alarming situation in Europe that many continental countries seem at the present time to be again seriously threatened by the spectre of revolution. The Soviet leaders in Moscow are, in addition, doing their utmost to aggravate still further the difficult economic situation of Europe and to accelerate the outbreak of disturbances. Communist activity in most continental countries is being carried on with increased intensity. Particularly is this true of Germany, where, owing to the recent considerable Communist gains, an attempt on their part to seize power is seriously thought to be possible.

Now, if their efforts should one day be successful, if violent upheavals on a large scale should again take place in any country of Europe, if the Communists succeeded in attaining to power in any particular place and setting up Soviets in the heart of Europe—what would be the outcome? Would things in a Western European land, thus subjected to Soviet rule, resemble the conditions already in force in Russia, or not? And if so, in what degree, and how?

These questions can, in my opinion, be answered with a greater measure of certainty than is generally supposed. In two European countries—in Hungary and in Latvia—the Soviets have, since the war, already held the reins of government for a period of several months. Unfortunately, the instructive history of Soviet rule in Hungary has been forgotten all too soon; and with regard to Latvia I am even prepared to assert that the incredible actions perpetrated by the Muscovites in that country have remained up to the present day entirely unknown to the general European public.

The present period of crises and unrest appears to me a particularly appropriate time to remind wider circles of this memorable attempt on the part of Moscow to apply the Soviet system in a country other than Russia, and to inform people of the full details concerning that remarkable experiment; and this, moreover, is a task which I feel all the more capable of performing as I have not only considerable personal experience of Russian Bolshevism, but have also lived throughout the entire period of this Soviet domination, established for a short time *outside Russia*.

The events described in this book took place in Riga, the capital of the present democratic republic of Latvia, in the period between January 2nd and May 22nd of the year 1919. They are all, without exception, true occurrences. Further, all the political figures appearing in the book, as well as the other characters, are people who really existed, many of whom are still alive to-day. And with the exception of some few of my most intimate friends and acquaintances (whose names I felt bound to alter for personal reasons), all those mentioned in the book are called by their real names.

Nevertheless, the experiences of individuals, my own included, interesting as they sometimes were, have not appeared to me to be the most important part of the book, and I have treated them only *en passant*. The main theme of the book, to me, is the fate of the town and its population, who were the defenceless victims of a real Bolshevist invasion and of a forcible attempt at Sovietization.

This point, together with certain other special reasons, led me to consider this case particularly worthy of public attention and detailed recapitulation.

1. The history of Soviet rule in Riga may be described as an *entirely clean-cut, easily surveyed Soviet experiment* outside Russia. For five months (i.e. in a period sufficient for any Government to reveal its true character) Moscow attempted here to set up a Soviet State exactly modelled on the Russian prototype. The imitation extended to every sphere of public and private life. Therefore the "attack on the home" which the Reds carried out, and which is described in this book in especial detail, will perhaps make its nature clearer to the reader than any number of more general, or purely political, treatises on the Soviet system.

2. In the case of the Republic of Latvia, this Bolshevist experiment was introduced into a country in which the conditions of life *more nearly resembled those of Western Europe than those of Russia*. The old Hanse town of Riga, situated on the Baltic, hundreds of miles from Moscow, is far more like—in respect of the character and manner of life of its population— the German, Scandinavian and Dutch seaport towns than the inland cities of Russia. For a Western European, therefore, the "case of Riga" should be no less instructive than the history of Russian Bolshevism itself.

3. Everything stated in this book concerning Soviet rule *can be fully and completely proved.* This circumstance is of special importance. One of the chief objections to most of the reports about Bolshevism is, as is well known, the fact that on account of the Terror reigning in Russia they cannot be irrefutably proved. Here, now, we have a case in which this argument cannot possibly be advanced. Riga to-day is free from all Soviet control. But of its present population approximately half, like myself, lived through the period of Soviet domination. These 150,000 people, now living in a free, democratically governed State, can always bear witness to the truth of all that is described in this book. Moreover, a large number of foreigners of all nationalities, including many Englishmen, were living in the town then under the heel of the Soviets. Finally, the originals of the most important official documents and the proclamations, decrees, articles, etc., printed in the Soviet newspapers are available. All these sources, as well as numerous statements by eye-witnesses, are freely employed in the text, their origin being always quoted, and, taken together, may be regarded as absolutely irrefutable evidence of the truth of the narrative.

This episode of Bolshevist invasion in Europe and of its ultimate defeat has also a special interest for English readers. The principal force that then was primarily responsible for the final triumph over the Bolshevists (The Baltic Volunteer Corps) was later commanded by a distinguished British officer, Colonel the Hon. H. R. Alexander, Irish Guards, who is a brother of the present Earl of Caledon; and a second

INTRODUCTION

Englishman—Brigadier-General Alfred Burt—was at the head of an Inter-Allied Commission which, after the departure of the Bolshevists, created a new order in the Baltic States.

Finally, I would like to say that this is not a political book in the ordinary sense. It makes no claim to be a theoretical or scientific work. It does not advocate or condemn any particular social order. Least of all is it directed against Socialism as such. It describes simply and solely the *methods* which the Soviet leaders employ in their efforts to carry through their system in other countries, and its basic intention is to open the eyes of those who have as yet no clear idea of what these methods are.

Among such persons, in these days of grave crises, are a considerable number, in every country of Europe, who turn their eyes towards Moscow in search of help, and hope to find a solution to all their economic troubles in the acceptance of Communism. These people, who dream of a "Soviet Germany," of a "Soviet Austria" or even of a "Soviet Europe," naturally do not realize what this involves. They do not pause for a moment to consider what Soviet rule represents in practice and what such a régime, Eastern in its origin, would necessarily mean to any civilized country of Western Europe. For them, more than anybody else, may this story of a Bolshevist experiment outside Russia serve as a deterrent and an example.

Only those who, like the author, have had personal experience of Bolshevism know what a grim reality hides behind this word. They know that the main principle of the Bolshevist system is brutal force. They know that the gospel preached by the Moscow leaders is not a Communism by persuasion, but a Communism by force only. They know that, in all the years that have passed, there has been practically no change in the Soviet methods. And, as the result of all their experiences with the Soviets inside and outside Russia, they have not the slightest doubt that Soviet rule in any other European State would assume a form, if not identical with, at any rate very similar to, the phenomena which we experienced in Latvia and which may still now be observed in Russia on the most extensive scale.

LONDON
October 1931

THE CITY OF THE RED PLAGUE

THE CITY OF THE RED PLAGUE

CHAPTER I

THE EVE

During that memorable winter of 1918–1919, when the last weary year of the Great War had drawn to its close and the first year of peace was beginning, I was in Riga, the town I regarded as my home.

It was just at this time, while the rest of the world was at last able to look forward to a peaceful future in which to recover from and forget the horrors and destruction of war, that the old Hanse town of Riga was fated to pass through the worst period of trial and bloodshed that it has known in the course of its seven centuries' history.

In the first days of January 1919 there approached the defenceless city, coming from the east and leaving ruin and desolation in their path, innumerable hordes of Bolsheviks. They were coming to establish in our town, by blood, iron and fire, their Muscovite rule of violence and terror.

The only defenders which the town possessed were the force of Baltic Volunteers, a good many of them little more than boys. The German troops of occupation had all been withdrawn, except for a few details. The newly formed Government of the democratic republic of Latvia had fled to Libau a few days earlier. The Volunteers had hurled themselves heroically against the Red hordes, only to be overwhelmed by them, beaten back, and finally forced to retire, having suffered heavy losses, to the west of the town.

Nearer and nearer came the ominous, regular booming of the enemy's big guns. Then there came a pause. The Reds were now camped outside the city, preparing to make their entry.

It was the 2nd of January. The whole country was in the grip of the bitter northern cold. The town itself was plunged in a death-like, almost awe-inspiring silence, like the breathless pause before some great historical event. Now and then there floated on the clear, cold air the sound of shots fired somewhere in the distance—one did not know by whom.

On that strange day, the town, abandoned by its defenders, but still unoccupied by the invaders, was in the peculiar position of belonging to nobody. There was no authority to look after public order and safety. Here and there, as dusk fell, disorderly mobs were forming. Bands of evildoers, eager for loot, began to bear down on the shops and warehouses. Already, wantonly or out of carelessness, they were setting fire to some of the deserted houses. The old German theatre was in flames. The red glow of the burning buildings lit up the dark winter sky.

The people of the town had hoped against hope to the last moment that help would arrive from somewhere. They would not believe until compelled to do so that their Volunteer army, composed of their own brothers and fathers and sons, and the German troops would depart so easily and abandon them to their fate.

Hitherto, the presence of some Inter-Allied Missions

and a few British destroyers (since the conclusion of the armistice) had reassured them. They thought: "After all, we are not living in the age of the migration of peoples. In our day the horrors of a Vandal invasion are unthinkable. Even though our own troops and the Germans may not be strong enough to save us, the Allies, with Great Britain and her Navy, have taken us under their wing. Whether they are Germans, English or French, they are at least Europeans, and surely no European nation is going to stand by and watch this city, an old centre of European civilization, being plundered and devastated by Asiatic hordes."

Yet this incredible thing had come to pass.

The inhabitants of Riga could scarcely believe it at first. But when they saw their late protectors, the German troops, daily retreating in masses towards the west; when they discovered that the various Allied Missions and the bourgeois Lettish Government had made off from the threatened town; when, one morning, they awoke to find that even the proud British fleet had vanished from their harbour; when that fateful day passed without a sign of help—then, as the truth at last burst upon them, as they saw that the outrage was really to be committed, that they themselves were to be its victims, they were gripped by a deathly fear.

The Red Terror was known only too well in our town. About a year before, the Bolsheviks, who had then just come into power in Moscow, had reigned for awhile in the neighbouring Estonia, and had only been driven away by the advance of the German troops. But even in that short time they had done much evil. Among other things, they had carried off a number of members of the bourgeoisie and nobility as hostages to Moscow and as far as Siberia. And now that the Tartar hosts, rolling forward slowly but irresistibly, had arrived before Riga and were threatening at every moment to pour in, a cry of despair passed from mouth to mouth: "Flee for your life!"

Many people actually did run for their lives on that fatal January day. Some of them dashed to the station and crowded into trains; others rushed down to the harbour, where a few cargo boats were still lying, and tried to escape to sea; and a few simply flung themselves on to horses and sleighs, galloped out of the town and fled on and on through the open, snow-covered country, towards the west. . . .

Whither they were going, none knew or cared; they desired but to get away, no matter how, only away, as far as possible away from that dreaded, oncoming monster.

.   .   .   .   .

Like other people then living in Riga, my family and I had already fled from Bolshevism once; we had come from Russia and had only been settled there a year.

Our family consisted of my two parents, who were advanced in years, my sister, who was still a child, and myself. My father, a retired Tsarist general, had held a high administrative post in a provincial town in the interior of Russia. We had lost our house and all our possessions there through the Revolution, and had finally reached Riga—which in earlier years had been our home—amid all kinds of difficulties and troubles with not much more than our bare lives.

The town, at the time of our arrival (early in 1918), had been occupied by the German troops, and a state of security and order prevailed which was comforting after the Russian chaos. We had taken a flat in a large block and furnished it after a fashion. We had gradually settled down peacefully, and now fondly imagined that we had escaped for ever from the persecutions of the wild men of Moscow.

It will therefore be understood that it was not a feeling of pure, unadulterated pleasure that came over us when we now became aware that our Bolshevist friends intended to arrive at any moment and visit us in our exile. After our experience in Russia we certainly entertained very little desire to renew their acquaintance. At the same time, however, owing to the fact that we had already once left house and home and set off into the unknown, the idea of a fresh flight appeared to us more terrible than to many others. We had already had a sufficient taste of the sad lot of the refugee. To strike our tents again, pack up and wander off almost penniless into a strange country was an impossible prospect. It would be better to stay where we were, to hold out until things perhaps changed for the better.

My parents therefore decided, after an exhaustive discussion of all the possibilities, to remain, in spite of all risks, in the menaced town. This meant that for me also there was no alternative but to stay by their side. They implored me not to desert them in this time of uncertainty. In this new emergency someone had to remain by their side to look after them and protect them. No one could tell what forms the Soviet regime would take in such a comparatively European country as Latvia. But, after what had happened in Russia, the worst was to be expected.

The morning of that day I had accordingly spent in making certain preparations at home to guard against the eventualities which I could foresee—thanks to my previous lesson in Russia—that our Bolshevist future would almost certainly bring. These preparations consisted chiefly in hiding away carefully, in the loft or in the cellar, all objects of value in our possession, laying in a substantial supply of victuals and collecting together as large a sum of money in cash as possible.

This done, I left my home and went to see two of my oldest friends, who were, I knew, in the same position as myself—Igor Somoff and Roy Carlyle. As it chanced, I met them both in the street—on the way to our flat. They were going to the harbour and invited me to accompany them, which I did without asking any questions.

Igor Somoff, a Russian, was a slender young man of middle height, rather more than twenty-five years old. He was fair and blue-eyed, with well-shaped features. There was something conspicuously dreamy and remote about the whole of his extremely Slav personality. The rough realities of our turbulent time seemed to repel and disgust him. He seemed out of place in our cold, cruel, highly unromantic century.

My acquaintance with him dated from the time of the war, when we had served in the same regiment of the Tsarist army. We had been together in Russia at the outbreak of the Revolution; and then, during the first days of rioting in Petrograd, I had often seen a look of horror on his face, as of one in physical pain, at the sight of the brutal acts of the rebel mob, and heard him murmur words of repulsion and disgust. And now this characteristic of his had developed into a timid reserve and shyness which at times took most pronounced forms. He belonged to a rich, aristocratic family closely connected with the old Tsarist court. Like myself, he had only recently escaped from Petrograd with his aged father, leaving, it need hardly be said, everything but his bare life in the hands of the new rulers. And now he and his father also had decided to remain and face the inevitable.

My other friend, Carlyle, I had known much longer than the Russian. We had been at school together in Riga. He belonged to one of those Baltic families of English origin which had been settled in Riga for many generations and now occupied an eminent position in the local business community. He was tall and dark, with a fresh, open, boyish face and merry brown eyes, an energetic fellow and man of action, Somoff's opposite in everything. His attitude in face of the revolutionary events of the last few days was anything but depressed and resigned. The idea of fighting the advancing Reds pleased and excited him, opened before him an agreeable prospect of warlike adventures. Moreover, in his way, he believed in the cause for which he and his friends were fighting, and was confident that the Bolsheviks would be driven out again. All that was happening now was, in his view, an inevitable transition period. We must get through this time somehow, hold out, pull ourselves together; then we should soon be going forward again. And if anyone showed signs of depression in Carlyle's presence, expressed doubts of ultimate victory, or was unduly loud in his complaints, he was intensely annoyed and gave vent to his feelings in unparliamentary language.

Carlyle's parents were at that time living abroad. He was, therefore, under no obligation to be here at this dangerous moment. But Carlyle regarded the country as his home, and when the news of the danger threatening our town had reached him, he, like so many others, had come in haste to protect it from the foreign invasion. In the recent fighting he had received a light wound which had kept him in the town a few days longer than his companions-in-arms, who had already retreated. Now there was no more time for him to lose. He had to hurry back to join his regiment at Libau, near the German frontier, which had been fixed as the rallying-point of the Volunteer army. There, and in some other places in West Courland, the White forces were to be reorganized, in order later to be able to resume the struggle against the advancing enemy. Carlyle had decided to try and reach Libau by the sea route. He intended to sail on the last refugee steamer, which was to leave the port of Riga that night.

All this Carlyle told me as we went along, in hurried, disconnected words. Then we walked on in silence. Only a little snow covered the streets. The mud mixed with snow was frozen as hard as stone. The biting wind which had risen blew the dust and snow painfully into our faces and almost took our breath away. On the way to the harbour we had to pass through several desolate streets flanked by fences and warehouses. Then we crossed some large open spaces, white with snow. Though dusk was barely falling, an uncanny darkness lay over everything. The gas-lamps were not burning.

All the people we saw were hurrying silently, with frightened and nervous faces, in the same direction, towards the harbour. Some of them were carrying with them all sorts of bundles and packages; a few, even, various pieces of domestic furniture. Once a young woman, distraught and hatless, her hair streaming in the wind, with a crying baby wrapped in a woollen rug in her arms, rushed across our path.

When we reached the harbour, night had already descended. To right and left along the quay—nothing but sheds and warehouses and stacks of timber. An unexpected turning brought us to the water. I looked round for the ship which was to take the fugitives, but could not see it.

"Where can the ship be?" I asked my friends. They gazed at me in surprise and said, "We are standing in front of her!"

I looked up and found that we were in fact close to the bow of the vessel. In the twilight I had taken its huge black bulk for the walls of a warehouse. The steamer, which in reality was not very large, made the impression, as it lay so close up against the wharf, of some giant of the ocean, and its bulk rising up so abruptly and threateningly high above us blotted out the stars.

We went along the quay towards the middle of the ship, where we could see human figures moving to and fro. A great crowd of refugees was collecting here, waiting to embark. The whole scene was like some strange, nightmarish dream. There were no arrangements which suggested that this colossus was a passenger boat. There was not even a proper gangway. Two ordinary ladders were leaning against the ship, and, by pushing and pulling, every person, old and young, together with all his bags and baggage, was somehow got on board by means of this primitive arrangement.

Everything was done in frantic haste, and yet almost in complete silence. The ship was to put to sea in a few hours, and everyone feared that the Reds might arrive sooner than they were expected, and prevent the departure of the fugitives by force, bombard the vessel, perhaps indulge in a massacre. . . .

Carlyle seized his chance and climbed on board by one of the ladders. Somoff and I followed him. When we got on deck a still more deplorable picture met our eyes.

The dirty cargo steamer, kept pitch-dark as a precaution, was crammed full with hundreds of refugees, chiefly belonging to the middle classes, and in every possible corner men, women and children were sitting, lying and standing about in closely packed groups in the midst of an incredible confusion of luggage, bedding and household goods of every description. There was only very little space available below and in the cabins, and the large majority had to camp on deck in the freezing open air.

Everyone was waiting with nervous anxiety for the ship's departure. No one thought of sleep. The whole time an uncanny silence prevailed amongst all these people, only broken now and then by the curse of a sailor hauling luggage on board or the whimpering of a child snatched from its warm nursery out into the bitter cold night.

"How horrible! how ghastly!" Somoff muttered in an undertone, looking at Carlyle and me with a frightened, helpless air. But Carlyle and I said nothing; we only stared at the terrified herd of people huddled together, all the women and children so suddenly plunged into misery and suffering.

None of the fugitives knew where this fateful ship would take them, whether to Sweden, Denmark, Germany or elsewhere. A portion of the harbour was already frozen and the open sea, on account of mines and thick pack-ice, barely navigable. Nor could anyone predict how long the journey would last under these awful conditions, or if they would ever reach a destination where they could begin a new existence. Many of the fugitives were convinced that they were going to certain death. Their loathing for the Reds, however, was so great that even the most faint-hearted amongst them preferred to entrust themselves to this ship of ill-omen rather than fall into the hands of the Muscovite hordes.

Somoff and I helped Carlyle as best we could to arrange his sleeping-quarters among tarred ropes and rusty anchor-chains. I asked him to try—when he reached the Volunteers' camp—to send us news of the situation, and above all of the chances of a new White offensive. He promised to do so.

Then Somoff and I shook his hand, and clambered down from the towering deck. On the quay we waved a last good-bye, and turned back towards the town.

· · · · ·

I parted from Somoff half-way home, as he lived in a different direction, and hired a sleigh, urging the driver to the greatest haste, as my family were expecting me.

We drove for awhile through the harbour quarter. Right and left—the grey, dark masses of warehouses and depots. Filled only recently with busy, bustling life, they now stood forlorn and deserted. Completely empty, too, as though sunk in death, were the streets and squares of this once so animated district. We did not encounter any more of those scattered fugitives whom my friends and I had seen a short while before hastening down to the ship. Not a human soul, not a living creature was to be seen. Everyone was already hiding from the approaching disaster.

Only when we had penetrated into the centre of the town did we meet with some sign of life. We had, on our way, to pass by the former headquarters of the Whites. In this house, which was actually a school building, a tiny remnant of the retreating German troops had still remained behind as a kind of rearguard. It maintained a neutral attitude toward the Reds, and its duty was to prevent the arms and ammunition which were stored in the building from falling into the hands of the mob.

To inspire them with courage or warm them up, the commanding officer had evidently doled out amongst his men a rather too liberal supply of brandy, for every one of the sentries posted in front of the building was dead drunk. (In those days of general chaos even the German troops, usually such a model of discipline, had fallen into the saddest state of demoralization.) Unfortunately the intoxication of these fellows had taken a dangerous form, inasmuch as they fired aimlessly at everyone who happened to pass anywhere near them.

As we unsuspectingly approached this unpleasant spot, we suddenly came upon the body of a man lying in the middle of the road. I could not think what had happened; I told the driver to stop, got out and had a closer look at the man, ready to lend assistance if he should only be wounded. But I saw at once that he was dead: he was lying face downwards right across the tram-lines, his hands pressed to his chest; fresh blood was oozing from a wound in his head and had trickled down between the rails, where it had clotted already.

The man was decently dressed, and I remember wondering, as I looked at him, who he could be, why he was there, and why he should have had to die just here in so senseless a fashion. I was brought to my senses by several shots striking the frozen ground to my right and left, and I began to grasp the situation.

The driver, an old Lettish peasant, was quicker. He seized me unceremoniously by the sleeve, pushed me into the sleigh and whipped up his horses like one possessed; and, while the drunken soldiery continued to fire at us wildly, the sleigh darted off like a streak of lightning.

In the excitement the old man at first nearly lost control over his vehicle, and we went zigzagging from the road on to the pavement and back. I remember that this crazy cross-galloping aroused in me—although I could distinctly hear the shots smashing into the walls of the houses on either side—an emotion that was curiously compounded of fright and amusement.

Finally, however, we reached a quieter street and

were out of danger. The driver swore profusely when we arrived at my house, but I gave him an extra tip to enable him to drown the shock he had received in a larger quantity of vodka than usual.

Then I entered my parents' home. What a strange contrast! Outside, only just before—the death-like aspect of the town, the strange, silent panic in the streets, the pitiful sight of the overcrowded refugee boat, the drunken, madly shooting soldiery, and the dead man lying in the snow. And here, between these four walls—a patriarchal peace, a comfortable warmth and cosiness; people I loved gathered round the dining-room table talking, drinking tea or reading by the dim light of the oil-lamp. There were my old mother and father, my little sister, and Dr. Edgar Mey, our family doctor. He was a kindly, talkative old fellow, with a healthy, red face which wore a perpetual optimistic smile, and tiny light-blue eyes that blinked and sparkled cheerily behind gold-rimmed spectacles. His favourite habit was to stroke continuously his well-groomed, snow-white professorial beard. As with most family doctors, this man's whole being, radiating geniality and good nature, seemed to be almost a constituent element in the comfortable and cosy atmosphere of the home.

When I had finished my somewhat alarming tale, the old doctor gazed at me benignly, and began to reassure me in a placidly serene voice, insisting that "there was nothing to be afraid of" and "that all would turn out for the very best."

My father, with an old soldier's interest in warfare and military strategy, was calmly reading aloud the last war *communiqué* of the White Volunteers in a daily paper.

"After severe fighting, the enemy has occupied Ryezhitza and Dvinsk. Our troops are retiring in good order." He paused, as if making a mental calculation. "That's bad," he said, "at that rate, they should be here to-morrow morning at the latest."

In the silence that followed we were suddenly overcome by the feeling that there was someone else in the room besides ourselves. And when, almost simultaneously, we all looked round, we found that this was actually the case: unnoticed by anybody, our cook, Martha—a red-haired, pock-marked creature who had only been in our service a bare month—had crept in from the kitchen and, standing by the door, had apparently been listening for quite a long time to our conversation.

When we turned round and discovered her she was leaning against the door in an attitude which seemed to me rather more negligent than usual. And then she suddenly startled everybody by saying in an impudent, confidential manner which I had never seen before:

"I bet they'll all be here this very night! Why, I saw two Reds in the street to-day!"

"Then a new time'll begin for all of us!" she added, and was apparently about to make further provocative remarks. But when she saw that nobody seemed inclined to enter into discussion with her, she uttered a hoarse, rude laugh and left the room, ostentatiously turning her broad back on us.

I sat down by my mother and told her what I had

seen and experienced that evening in the town, and how thousands had fled, seized with panic terror.

More than half of all our friends and acquaintances had left the town, had set off into an unknown world. Others, like ourselves, had remained, unable or unwilling to leave their homes. Perhaps it had been rash to stay behind? But our fate was decided. It was too late to repent. We would have to see it through now, come what might.

My mother heaved a deep sigh.

"We are in for a difficult time," she said in a voice full of anxiety. "A terribly difficult time. . . ."

CHAPTER II

A TOWN BY THE BALTIC

It was hard to sleep that night, on what we might assume to be our last night in a bourgeois Riga. A nervous unrest lay over the town and penetrated even to my bedroom, whither, like everyone else in the house, I had not withdrawn until a late hour.

From afar, from the direction of the sea, came the unspeakably melancholy hooting of the departing refugee ship, which by now must have reached the Gulf of Riga—a last sad farewell from those we might never see again.

Meanwhile, in the streets of Riga, just under our windows, a disreputable rabble of military deserters and escaped convicts bawled and rioted; drunken women laughed and squealed. Gaily coloured rockets fired by the crowd still engaged in celebrating the New Year flew hissing through the air. And the sporadic firing which had been audible at intervals during the afternoon developed after midnight into a continuous and quite alarming crackle.

The rockets, and the rising and falling flames of the burning theatre, lit up the white walls of my room every few minutes like summer lightning. This destroyed the last possibility of rest and sleep and led my thoughts ever and again to the same dominating question—what new experiences, what fresh horrors the morrow would bring to us and our town.

For Riga had always been to me my native town; my

childhood and early manhood had been inseparably bound up with the place.

My parents had brought me to Riga when I was ten and sent me to school there; and the history of the town was as familiar to me as a family chronicle. I knew that the town, founded in the twelfth century by Hanse merchants, had in past centuries often been hotly contested—by Swedes, Poles and Russians—till it had fallen into Russian hands under Peter the Great and remained a Russian city for two hundred years. Then it was that its real era of prosperity had begun. For Peter the Great saw in the Baltic seaport one of those "windows into Europe" which he desired to open in order to strengthen and develop more natural relations between the giant Russian Empire and Western Europe. And Riga became, under the Tsars, not only the most important commercial harbour, save one, of the modern Russian kingdom, but one of the busiest ports in all Europe.

In the period immediately before the war—that is, at the time when I first knew it—the commercial prosperity of Riga was increasing with extraordinary rapidity. It was the world's leading port for the export of flax, timber and hides. Over 3,000 ships entered it yearly; and the population, which in 1815 was only a little more than 35,000, was at the outbreak of war well over half a million.

The population of Riga and the province of Livonia which surrounded it consisted mainly of three nationalities—Letts, Balts and Russians. The Letts, the most numerous race, formed the mass of the population. The Balts, a native race of German origin, furnished the intellectual upper class and the land-owning nobility. And in those days, when Livonia was still a Russian province, the Russian element consisted of officials, military officers and so on. (My father had originally come to Riga as a Russian official and had there married my mother, who was a Balt.)

In old Riga there was a special caste in the shape of the Balt business families, many of whom were descended from Hanse merchants and greatly resembled in every way the merchants of Lübeck, Bremen and Hamburg. A number of former mayors had come from German, Swedish and Norwegian ports. And the last mayor of Riga to hold office before the outbreak of the war had been an Englishman, George Armitstead, who came of a distinguished Yorkshire family and had rendered conspicuous services towards the development of the town.

This close connection of Riga with European trade and culture gave the city a conspicuously Western stamp, in striking contrast to the outward appearance of other Russian towns. Riga had that delightful freshness, brightness and cleanliness so characteristic of most northern seaports.

A broad river, the Western Dvina, took its course right across the city, and flowed into the sea only a few miles beyond. The river divided the town—just as the Danube separates Buda and Pest—in two halves, differing completely one from the other: on the eastern bank lay Riga proper and on the western bank the so-called "Mitau Suburb," named after the main road which led to Mitau, the capital of the ancient Duchy of Courland.

The "Old Town," situated on the eastern bank of the river, was undoubtedly the most interesting part of Riga. The foreign merchants and travellers who visited Riga in great numbers every year felt at home there at once. For as soon as the stranger, coming from the river, plunged, after a few steps, into the narrow crooked streets of the Old Town, he immediately had the sensation of having entered a familiar world that he had seen somewhere before. Those dim, sleepy alleys winding in capricious curves, those ancient gabled houses reaching up to the invisible sky, those antique-framed, half-blind windows, those old doors richly decorated with cunningly carved woodwork, those gloomy portals furnished with heavy iron knockers —all that and much besides made a stranger feel, if he came by chance from Bremen, Antwerp or any other trading city of Europe, that he had not come so far east after all, but by some miracle had been transported back to the heart of his own home city, rich in ancient buildings. At the same time, there were several buildings possessing a peculiar character hardly to be found elsewhere; for example, the spacious and imposing fifteenth-century castle of the Knights of the Temple, the quaint "House of the Black Heads," founded in the fourteenth century, the Cathedral, dominating the whole panorama, and many other buildings.

The "Petersburg Suburb," where my parents lived, formed a half-circle round the Old Town. This district, full of blocks of flats, Government buildings and private villas, was of quite another and more modern character. The chief beauty of this quarter was its abundance of trees. The string of boulevards, parks and public gardens which ran through this quarter made Riga one of the greenest cities in Europe. The centre of the "Petersburg Suburb" was a broad square, surrounded in summer by beautiful walks and flower-beds, called the Esplanade. It had formerly been a parade-ground, and was so large that several regiments could be drawn up on it at the same time.

Quite a different aspect from the rather gloomy Old Town and the green suburbs was presented by the harbour quarter on the lower Dvina, in which I had so often wandered as a schoolboy, eager for adventure, and gazed admiringly and longingly at the many foreign steamers with their curious flags, gaily striped funnels and alien crews. I had never known this quarter, with its many sheds and warehouses, except noisy and busy. Here, where the big British, German and Scandinavian steamers were moored, where the great shipping companies had their offices, where the most varied merchandise lay around in towering piles and stacks, English, German, Dutch and Swedish words continually reached one's ears. And strolling here, no matter at what time of day, hardly an hour passed without some foreign ship berthing at the quay or leaving the port.

How changed all that was now! Where was the cheerful bustle of Riga harbour? All life had completely vanished from the scene. When, that evening, I had visited the river and its wharves for the first time after a considerable interval, I had found them utterly desolate and abandoned. The big cargo steamer in which so many citizens of Riga had fled from the advancing Reds was the only vessel lying in the harbour.

This vessel carried, with its 2,000 passengers, a large part of the history and the life-blood of our town. For these 2,000 men and women of Riga belonged without exception to the educated classes—the official world, the nobility, and above all the famous old native merchant community.

This caste, many of whose offspring had been at school with me, and which I had known well from my youth up, was distinguished by a mass of solid bourgeois virtues—the virtues that had made Riga what it was in pre-war days. The business men of Riga sat from early morning till late afternoon in their offices, furnished in somewhat old-fashioned style and imbued with patriarchal traditions and the probity of centuries, earning afresh "the wealth inherited from their fathers, that they might justly possess it." They always felt themselves to be a special, free community. The independent, democratic spirit of the merchants and seafarers of the Hansa dwelt within them; and many of them had more than once, with proud modesty, declined the titles of nobility and other distinctions offered them by the Crown.

Nor had wealth and prosperity brought with them intellectual torpor. On the contrary, Riga had always been an active centre of thought and education. Riga had its own university, and there, as in the neighbouring university of Dorpat, German art and culture had for centuries unfolded their blossoms. In the eighteenth century Johann Gottfried Herder lived in Riga, and thence first attracted the attention of the world; in the

Riga town theatre, in the late 'thirties of last century, no less a personage than Richard Wagner produced his first opera *Rienzi*; and from Riga and the Baltic Provinces, for centuries on end, the mighty Russian Empire had drawn many of its most conspicuous men of learning, jurists, generals and statesmen.

The peculiar charm of Riga lay in its intermediary position between Western Europe and Russia and the mingling of two cultures; along with a purely Western environment and civilization there prevailed a truly Russian spirit of sociability and hospitality. There had always been an abundance of supplies of every kind; and so the people of Riga, like their Russian neighbours, had always understood how to eat well and drink well and enjoy life in a careless, peculiarly "Baltic" manner. Their tables were richly supplied, and their hospitality had been renowned for centuries.

It was, indeed, an easy matter for them to set epicurean dishes upon their richly laden tables before their guests. The Dvina, the native stream, yielded an abundance of the tastiest salmon—in such quantities, indeed, that salmon was once reckoned the common food of the people. An estimable magistrate of former times was once obliged to forbid the citizens of Riga by decree "to give their servants salmon more often than three days in the week," and ordered them to provide other food in its place. The cookery books published in Riga knew only of recipes for six, twelve persons or more, and in one of these books was actually to be read the following advice, given in all seriousness to the young housewife, as to what she was to do when unexpected guests arrived and she "had nothing to eat in the house": "then," so it was explained in this delightful book, "go down to the cellar, from there take out some salmon, some cold game and something sweet, and lay this—in the absence of anything better—before your guests." The good people of Riga of those blessed days simply could not imagine that even when "there was nothing to eat in the house" one nevertheless did not possess a cellar to which one could descend and find on every side an abundance of "cold or salted things, preserves and sweets" at one's disposal.

The excellent folk of Riga knew, also, like all good livers, how to appreciate a good drop of wine. All those English, Dutch and German ships which year in, year out, sailed into Riga harbour, brought to those shores, in well-rounded, nut-brown wooden barrels, many noble wines, which had gently matured on the banks of the Rhine, in the land of Burgundy or on the isle of Madeira, and here were highly prized. But the people of Riga were themselves also assiduous distillers of delicate drinks, and many liqueurs originating in Riga and Livonia, like the spicy "kümmel" and the aromatic Stockmannshof bitters, have rightly become famed all the world over.

How delightful life used to be! Not half an hour's railway journey from the town lay the seashore, a beach of fine white sand twenty-five miles long, with its peaceful, murmuring waves and its picturesque, wooded dunes, worthy of comparison with the most renowned beaches of other countries. Our family used to move down to the sea every May and spend several months there. From all the neighbouring countries, though chiefly from Russia, hundreds of thousands of

GENERAL VIEW OF RIGA, SEEN FROM THE MITAU SUBURB ON THE LEFT BANK OF THE DVINA

On the left is the Old Castle; in the centre the Cathedral; on the right St. Peter's Church

visitors used to come to the "Riga Strand." Numerous hotels opened their doors every summer, and for the people of Riga there began every May a life of summer bathing, as joyful and unclouded as the blue and laughing sky above their then so care-free heads.

But the most delightful recollections of my childhood were of the Livonian winter. At that season there prevailed in these regions a real, hard, Russian cold. Rivers and lakes froze over. Deep snow lay on fields and meadows. Then the people of Riga abandoned themselves to the boisterous joys of winter: the schoolchildren, shouting and laughing, noisily pelted one another with snowballs, young and old indulged in skating and ski-ing, and everyone who could drove in the sleighs which, small, light, and swift, swarmed in hundreds in the streets of Riga. As far back as I could remember, I saw myself, in the company of cheery friends, driving through the streets piled high with snow, accompanied by the most delightful of all melodies, the clear silver tinkle of countless tiny sleigh-bells. . . .

CHAPTER III

THE ENTRY OF THE MUSCOVITES

The next morning I got up early and went at once to the window to see whether there was any sign in our street of any new events which might have taken place during the night. I fully expected to see that the Reds had already made their entry. My father had also risen early, and together we gazed curiously out of the window.

However, there was nothing to be seen—in the literal sense of the word, nothing: the street in which we lived, usually full of people and traffic even at this hour, was completely deserted.

This was significant, considering that we lived in one of the busiest streets of a very populous town, which even then still contained over 200,000 inhabitants. What did this mean? What had happened? There was no sign of the Reds, and yet not a sound or movement broke the stillness that hung over the street and over the whole town.

Had our Volunteers, contrary to all expectation, been able to recover themselves and push back the enemy at the last moment? I suggested this to my father, and he nodded silently.

As these optimistic thoughts occupied our minds, we suddenly saw something which extinguished our hopes in a twinkling.

At the east end of the street there appeared a troop of strange horsemen; they were very few in number,

THE ENTRY OF THE MUSCOVITES

only about six or seven; but their appearance left no doubt that they were the vanguard of the Reds. With their narrow eyes, their huge fur caps, their shabby uniforms, primitive saddles and small shaggy Kalmuck ponies, they came galloping along, glancing furtively to right and left, reconnoitring in all probability to obtain information about conditions in the town for the army behind them. They carried their rifles in their hands, and seemed determined to shoot at anyone who dared to look at them in an unfriendly manner or oppose them in any way whatever. They passed rapidly under our window, and then disappeared from our sight.

For a few minutes my father and I waited in silence, listening to the receding clatter of the horses' hoofs on the frozen ground.

Then, after a short while, the same horsemen returned by the same route, this time with their rifles slung over their shoulders, and dashed back at full speed in the direction whence they had come, out into the open country.

The meaning of this short visit was plain: the Reds were about to make their entry.

"Well," said my father, "they're here!"

It was about eight o'clock in the morning when this happened. Meanwhile, the news of the entry of the first hostile troops had spread rapidly to everyone in the house. Immediately there was a general commotion; doors banged, bells rang, women and other troubled beings rushed up and down the stairs in a half-dressed condition and burst without ceremony into every flat, announcing one after the other in awe-struck and excited tones:

"The Reds have come! Did you see them? The Reds have come!" On every side it was the same chorus.

The feminine elements in our house, however, soon proved that they had other uses besides the creation of unnecessary noise and fuss. In the hours that ensued, the women tenants in the flats above and below us revealed that mysterious gift, common to their sex, of obtaining knowledge of certain happenings with a rapidity which arouses admiration and often astonishes even the most wily journalists. In this way, for instance, one of the many female inhabitants of the house, an elderly lady called Frau Walter, who lived in the flat above us, was able at an early hour to announce to us with pride that the "official entry" of the Muscovites would take place at 11 a.m.

This was at least something definite, and I decided to walk to the main street of the town when the time arrived, in order to get a good view of this memorable event. My parents tried to dissuade me from exposing myself unnecessarily to our dangerous visitors; nobody knew, they said, whether the entry of the Red Army might not provoke further shooting. However, my curiosity proved stronger than my filial obedience, and with a few cheery words of reassurance I left them and sallied forth.

The broad main street of Riga, called Alexander Street, ran through the centre of the town from east to west. On the east it began as a continuation of the roads coming from the interior of Russia; on the west, after winding for a short distance through the Old Town, it reached the river, and then branched off on

THE ENTRY OF THE MUSCOVITES

the opposite bank into the high road to Mitau and other roads leading to Courland, to Germany and to Western Europe. Since the visitors, coming from the east, from the interior of Russia, were not arriving by train, but were making their entry into the city, as in the more picturesque days of old, on horseback and on foot, they could not choose any other route but this.

By eleven o'clock a large crowd of people had assembled, all talking excitedly about the event while waiting with impatience for the coming spectacle.

We had a long time to wait, and our feet soon began to freeze on the snow-covered ground. At last, shortly after midday, we saw the enemy's army approaching from the east end of the street.

First of all, a few of those disreputable-looking horsemen, whom I had recognized in the morning as the vanguard of the army, cantered past. Then came the main procession: first the banners, pieces of red cloth with unintelligible inscriptions; after that a military band, made up chiefly of dilapidated wind-instruments, drums and cymbals, which blared forth wild, discordant airs; immediately behind it rode a group of Red leaders with the commander-in-chief, only recently a common soldier, at the head of it; the bulk of the army followed, numbering about 10,000 men.

The soldiers, including the officers, were no better turned out than the men on horseback whom I had seen in the morning. They were all dirty and almost in rags, wearing brown soldiers' cloaks, black fur caps or peculiar pointed Mongolian bonnets over their greasy hair, rifles carelessly attached to their shoulders by thick pieces of string, and whips of black leather hanging down their sides. Many of the faces were rough and primitive, with slit eyes and prominent cheekbones.

The townspeople gazed in astonishment at this outlandish army of invaders from the Muscovite empire, and then looked questioningly at one another. They exchanged whispered surmises concerning the different regiments that passed. "Lettish rifles . . . Russian infantry . . . Caucasian Division . . . Cossacks——" they murmured dubiously.

But those of the onlookers who knew Russia, and had in some cases served in the Russian Army, could not help saying to themselves that these were not regular troops at all. The Russian Army had never looked so shabby and savage, not even in the last year of the war.

They were right. For these advancing hordes really belonged to no particular nation. There were a few dozen Lettish Communist leaders at their head, and several battalions consisting entirely of men from the Bolshevistic Lettish rifle regiments. These constituted the majority. At the same time one could not help being struck by the large number of Mongolian types —torn by their Muscovite masters from the remote steppes and forests of Siberia and Asiatic Russia; Tartars, Bashkirs, Kalmucks, Kirghiz, Yakuts, and similar obscure, semi-barbaric tribes, in a confused medley.

Alongside these were a number of former prisoners of war captured by the Russian Army—Germans, Austrians, Hungarians, Poles, Czechs, etc.—who at the outbreak of the Revolution had joined the Bolsheviks and were now taking part in the invasion

THE ENTRY OF THE MUSCOVITES

partly of their own free will, partly under compulsion. It was the misfortune of war that had driven them into the arms of the Muscovites. But now that they had been for some time in close association with the Reds, they had all become transformed into a special "Bolshevist" race, had all taken on that peculiar Oriental stamp, to such a degree that they could hardly be distinguished from the genuine Moscow Bolsheviks.

The colour of the Muscovites was red, and many of the advancing warriors had adorned their breasts with small red bows or large red rosettes, or even long fluttering ribbons. All these adornments looked slovenly enough, being made of a cheap material, and so dirty that the red of some of the ribbons was more like black.

Now that the Whites were gone and the Reds had arrived, a section of the populace, chiefly the mob of young hooligans loafing around, suddenly seemed to feel a kind of sympathy for their new masters kindling in their breasts, and manifested these tender feelings, not only by loud yelling and cheering, but also by immediately adopting the same red emblems as were worn by the invaders. Many of the onlookers produced from their pockets pieces of red cloth and ribbons, which they proceeded to wave enthusiastically in honour of the new arrivals.

But the Muscovite horsemen remained perfectly indifferent, sitting mute and motionless on their shaggy ponies, their yellow, expressionless faces staring glumly straight in front of them.

The march past lasted about half an hour. Finally the last soldier had gone by, and the column moved on in the direction of the town. At once the crowd overflowed onto the street and began to stream after them.

Hoping to be able to observe further interesting details of the change-over to the new regime, instead of returning home immediately I began to stroll casually through the streets.

Almost the first, and the most astonishing, thing that I noticed was that certain eminent and highly respected citizens of our town, personally known to me, had decked themselves with red badges and emblems just like those which were flaunted by the invading troops and their proletarian sympathizers. There was not the slightest doubt that the sympathies of these worthy gentlemen were anything but red. They apparently thought that by wearing these badges they could somehow protect themselves. Whether this ruse would be successful or not remained to be seen. But I remember well what a disagreeable impression it made to see those people parading their cowardice and hypocrisy in such a childish and ostentatious fashion.

They were, moreover, mostly just the sort of people who, but a short time before, when the Kaiser during the war, and only a few years earlier the Tsar, had visited Riga, had welcomed these monarchs each time decorated with entirely different emblems, and on all such occasions had always been particularly eager to display their "frenzied joy" and their "ardent enthusiasm" as conspicuously as possible. And now many of these worthy citizens, in their efforts to appear "Red," suddenly began to act like candidates for a madhouse.

It needs such a sad emergency as we were then experiencing to show what an astonishingly large number of people there are who are always ready at a moment's notice to hunt with the most impossible hounds.

. . . . .

As I walked about the town I saw that placards printed in Lettish, Russian and German—proclamations and orders of the new government—had already been pasted up at every street corner.

The most conspicuous of these was a document printed on red paper and opening with the familiar motto: "Proletarians of all countries, unite!"

Manifesto

In the name of the World Revolution uniting and liberating all proletarians, we declare that from to-day onwards the supreme power in Latvia lies *in the hands of the Soviet Government*.

We declare all the provisional governments and ministries which under the protecting wing of one imperialistic group or another have attempted to impose fresh bonds on the Lettish working-people to be dissolved and overthrown. We annul all laws, orders and institutions which the feudal German Junker nobility, the Tsarist despotism and the Russian bourgeoisie have placed as a yoke on the necks of the Lettish workers. The place of these old organs of power has been taken by *the Dictatorship of the Proletariat*—the armed authority of the workers' Soviets!

In the name of this Dictatorship we announce the freedom of Soviet rule in Latvia and the law of the proletarian revolution.

Hardly had the Soviet of Workers', Peasants' and Soldiers' Delegates worked out, in December 1917, in the still unoccupied part of Latvia, the plans for a Socialist State than the country, and Red Riga also, were overrun by the army of German robber-Imperialism, supported by bands of Baltic Junker noblemen and cliques of Lettish bourgeois, and the Lettish proletariat again slaughtered or thrown into chains. Nevertheless, the Lettish proletariat did not yield: debarred from public activity, it pursued an "illegal," underground, revolutionary activity—both in its own ranks and among its foreign comrades-in-arms. And it openly fought in the foremost ranks of the Communists of Russia, on the foreign as well as the home front, against the united counter-revolutionary bands of the entire world.

Now the mighty German Imperialism lies smashed to pieces on the ground and above its wreckage already the first Red Socialist banners wave. But the German revolution has not yet gained its final victory. Over Europe flows the stream of the victory-drunk English–French–American Imperialism; it longs to drown the world revolution in the blood of the proletariat, and therefore looks upon the Latvian working-people as one of its fiercest enemies.

But notwithstanding all the menaces of Imperialism the Latvian proletariat boldly rears its head and founds its Soviets over all Latvia, in the towns as well as in the open country!

This Workers', Peasants' and Soldiers' Government hereby declares:

(1) *All bourgeois government in Latvia is abolished* and all central and local power passes into the hands of the Soviet of Workers, Peasants and Soldiers.
(2) The armed workers abolish all existing government authorities and condemn to immediate extermination every member and supporter of these authorities who does not voluntarily give himself up and resign his post.
(3) *Private landed property in town and country* is abolished; accordingly, in the first place, all noble, Crown and Church estates are handed over to the administration of the Soviets without any compensation whatever.
(4) The right of private ownership of all other means of production, as also of business enterprises, means of communication, banks, etc., will gradually be suspended; for which purpose these will forthwith be subjected to a strict supervision by the workers.
(5) Any kind of disposal of property rights or other rights to buildings in the towns is prohibited.
(6) *All decrees of the Russian Socialist Federative Soviet Republic* for the safeguarding of the working-classes come into force at once.
(7) All available food supplies will be taken over by the Soviet administration for management and distribution.
(8) It is necessary to proceed at once with the organization of public works necessary for Communist Latvia.

We are clearly conscious that the change over to Socialism cannot be the work of one day. Still, we are treading the road which leads towards it unhesitatingly and resolutely. *We shall begin without delay to construct in Latvia a new Socialist working-class State.* With arms in our hands we will march against the social traitors of this country, as well as those of all other countries. In this stern struggle we are not alone and deserted. Behind us, in the first rank, stands the Russian Socialist Federative Soviet Government, with which we shall henceforth remain most intimately united—with bonds which are not only external. Behind us, too, stands the Communist Revolution, which will certainly change not only Germany, but very soon also the rest of Europe into a *Federation of European Socialist Soviet republics,* of which we will then be a constituent part.

From the Rhine to Vladivostock and from the Black Sea to Archangel on the White Sea the civil war rages. Soon it will break through the walls and ramparts raised by victorious Imperialism. In France, as in England and Italy, the first voices of the Proletarian Revolution are already heard. A swift victory of the Soviet power in the whole of Latvia and its firm establishment there will itself be the surest means of throwing another burning torch into the revolutionary powder magazine of our opponents.

> To arms!
> Long live the Soviet Government of Latvia!
> Long live the World Revolution!
>
> The Workers', Peasants' and Soldiers'
> Soviet Government of Latvia.

RIGA, *January* 3, 1919.

Besides this "Manifesto" I saw everywhere a whole series of other notices or "bulletins," as they were officially styled, all informing us more or less of the fact that from now onwards the country was under Soviet rule. The democratic republic of Latvia, founded only a few months before, in November 1918, as an independent State, had ceased to exist. Our country had now, as "Soviet Latvia," become a part of Soviet Russia!

At the foot of some of the "bulletins" appeared the name of the head of our new Soviet Republic. It was Peter Stutchka. This was an individual of whom we knew practically nothing; we had only heard his name mentioned now and again as one of the leaders of the extreme left wing of the Lettish Socialist Party. He was said to have been Commissary for Justice, or something of the kind, in Moscow in the earliest days of the Bolshevist domination. That was about all we knew of him. But now, it was clear, we had to regard this unknown personage with the curious, almost comical name as supreme lord of our lives and property, the president of our new Soviet State—in short, as our local Lenin—and blindly carry out all his orders and regulations.

In one of the notices, all of which were signed by Stutchka, we read: "The Government of Moscow must be regarded as the central authority of all Soviet Republics; its decisions must be taken as absolutely final and are to be strictly obeyed!" So the Latvian Lenin was unconditionally subordinated to his suzerain residing in Moscow.

The contents of all these placards made it perfectly clear to us that in future everything in this town and this country was to be organized on exactly the same lines as in Moscow and throughout Soviet Russia. All personal freedom was to be taken from the citizens; the right of private property was to be suspended; no one would be allowed any longer to own houses, factories, shops or any kind of private business; the total abolition of money was to be held in prospect; the entire population was to be State-fed; in short, we were ordered to alter our entire existence from top to bottom and from beginning to end.

The townsmen of Riga, now finding themselves treated as an immense flock of brainless sheep, flocked round these placards and gazed at them dumbly. They were too frightened to express any opinion openly, and soon they dispersed and went on their way pondering.

Later, when they thought that no stranger could overhear them, they shook their puzzled heads and began to comment on their fate among themselves. But no one would admit the possibility of serious steps being taken to enforce these fantastic decrees. . . .

When I returned home that day full of tumultuous impressions, I found that everyone there already knew about the drastic decrees of the new Government. They, too, were astonished at the new rulers proceeding so swiftly and precipitately with their reforms.

My mother threw up her arms in despair crying: "The world is upside down!" My father remained silent. But I could see by the expression on his face that he, too, found it very painful to contemplate the sudden collapse of the old order and accept the strange realities of the "new era."

Our pro-Bolshevik cook, however, seemed to have lost her balance completely. A gigantic red ribbon already adorned her ample bosom, and her unlovely pock-marked visage beamed from ear to ear.

"Aha! A new time has come! Everything's going to be different now," she cried again and again, "everything quite, quite different. . . ."

As to what this "difference" was going to be she did not seem to be clear. But from her dark allusions one could conclude that she pictured the coming "Red paradise" above all as a degradation of the "masters" and a corresponding exaltation of the "servants."

For my own part, I must say that on this first day of revolution I was amused rather than disconcerted by the new happenings. I was a young man, fresh from the experience of the war, and not, therefore, to be easily upset by eccentric happenings of any kind.

"One must take things with a certain sense of humour," I said to myself many times. "After all, it is a question of one's attitude towards life, which in older people is naturally different from what it is in younger people." The different way in which my parents and I reacted to the situation struck me only as a new confirmation of the old truth—how easily youth has always put up with the overthrow of the existing order and accepted the establishment of a new regime, however senseless, and finally somehow or other has assimilated itself to it; how incredibly difficult, on the other hand, it is for the old to accustom themselves to violent changes like those which have characterized our time, and to become reconciled to the inevitable.

CHAPTER IV

"THE BEGINNING OF A GLORIOUS NEW ERA"

More than a week had gone by since the arrival of the Muscovites. Having now recovered from our first shock we were beginning to take stock of our new masters, and of the new conditions which they had brought with them. The Reds made this quite easy for us; from the very first day they took pains to enlighten the population, through the spoken and written word, concerning themselves and the objects of their rule.

All the Riga newspapers, on account of their "bourgeois" opinions, had been ordered by the Muscovites to cease publication from the day of their entry. In their place there appeared three new Communist newspapers which, though published in three different languages—Lettish, Russian and German—were all edited in the same central office and displayed exactly the same contents. The German edition called itself the *Rote Fahne* (*Red Flag*), and my family and I now had to regard this journal as our "family newspaper."

The *Red Flag* was a tiny sheet, usually of only four pages. It was wretchedly printed on ordinary packing-paper, and made a positively unappetising impression. There was practically no foreign news at all.

At the top, above even the title, the sentence "Proletariats of all countries, unite!" was printed in conspicuous type. Then, below the title *The Red Flag*, came every day a political poem. These appeared as a rule in the top left-hand corner of the front page, and were generally Communistic doggerel by some self-constituted Bolshevist "court poet." Now and again, however, Heinrich Heine, Freiligrath, Herwegh, and other poets long dead and bourgeois enough according to modern ideas, were torn from their well-deserved rest and, helpless to defend themselves, quoted in support of Bolshevism.

Thus, in the very first number of the *Red Flag* which we ever saw, we were confronted with Heine's famous *Song of Freedom*, which had been given the place of honour and was printed in such prominent type that one could only suppose that the paper intended it as a kind of motto of the "glorious new era."

> Ein neues Lied, ein besseres Lied,
> O Freunde, will ich euch dichten:
> Wir wollen hier auf Erden schon
> Das Himmelreich errichten!

Through this poetical variation on the familiar Moscow theme, it seemed, our new masters wished to remind us once more that, after Russia, they now proposed to turn Latvia also into the "earthly paradise" of which the poem speaks.

Immediately below Heine's poem was a leading article from the pen of Peter Stutchka, who was now the highest power in the land. It was entitled "Our Programme," and explained most clearly how and when the Muscovites thought they were going to realize the "kingdom of heaven on earth" among us.

With regard to the personality of Comrade Stutchka, whom none of us had yet seen, we had now ascertained the following facts. He was a man already advanced

"THE BEGINNING OF A GLORIOUS NEW ERA" 57

in years, an experienced politician and one of the "Old Guard" of Bolshevism, the type of a convinced, fanatical Communist. Nevertheless, he was no savage terrorist or bloodthirsty tyrant, but rather a quiet thinker and deliberate theorist, a sort of Red professor. Moreover, in private life he was a pleasant and good-natured old fellow, by no means inaccessible to argument. Comrade Stutchka came of a prosperous Lettish peasant family in the Kreuzburg region; he had had a good school and university education, and had been for many years a lawyer in Petrograd, and at the same time a member of secret revolutionary organizations. He had made the acquaintance of Lenin, Trotsky, Zinoviev, and the other Bolshevist leaders at party meetings and for years had been on terms of intimate friendship with them, with the result that he had now been appointed president of this new Soviet Republic.

"Our programme," wrote this theorist in this his first article, "can be summed up in a few, short words: *we are going to march straight towards Socialism*! We know, of course, that between Capitalism and Socialism there will be a long period of transition, which will be filled with bitter struggles. For nobody can doubt that the wealthy classes will never voluntarily cede their power, and that now indeed the last battle will be fought. It will be a bloody battle, which cannot be fought out without a powerful executive. The class war will take the form of an armed civil war. In this civil war, however, which is now beginning, the dictatorship of the proletariat will have to fight to the death against the bourgeoisie. . . ."

Passing from theory to practice, and in wise preparation for the struggle between proletariat and bourgeoisie predicted by him, Comrade Stutchka issued that very day—it was published in the same portentous number of the *Red Flag*—an order concerning the fate of all weapons then in the possession of the inhabitants of Riga.

"Every person is obliged," it was stated in this first decree of the Soviet power, "to give notice of all weapons and all kinds of military stores and ammunition in his possession or in his care. Reports are to be made within two days at the Riga Town Commandant's office. . . . Anyone not reporting weapons and deliberately continuing to carry them will be most severely punished, possibly by shooting."

Everyone who appeared at the Town Commandant's office to hand over weapons was closely examined, and anyone stamped as a "bourgeois" was invariably deprived of his weapons; while those found to belong to the "ruling class" were given permits on the spot and allowed to retain their weapons. In consequence the greater part of the population of Riga, the "bourgeoisie," was soon entirely disarmed, while the other and considerably smaller part, the "ruling class," was armed to the teeth.

Thus the first copies of the *Red Flag* and the first days of Soviet rule furnished us with a very clear idea both of the aims of our new masters and of the methods by which they intended to achieve them. It was, indeed, all very simple: A. Ultimate object—the kingdom of heaven on earth; B. Transition period—a fight to the death between bourgeoisie and proletariat;

"THE BEGINNING OF A GLORIOUS NEW ERA" 59

C. Method—the disarming of the bourgeoisie and the arming of the proletariat, the "ruling class."

But who could regard himself as belonging to this "ruling class" which enjoyed such manifold privileges? This question too was decided in a simple and trenchant manner.

The Muscovites constituted a "party" which was strictly separated from the larger, bourgeois part of the population and purported to have been formed exclusively from the local "proletarian elements." This, however, was not the truth: Riga had always been a predominantly bourgeois town, and a numerically strong "proletariat" had never existed before. Before the Muscovite invasion there were not more than a few dozen Communists in Riga. A "Bolshevist revolution," a spontaneous rising of the people, had never taken place at all. So the Muscovites had provided the town and the whole country with a ready-made "Communist Party" brought *en bloc* straight from Russia.

In Riga this newly arrived "Communist Party of Latvia" was joined by various local elements, chiefly liberated convicts and all kinds of hooligans. But the foreigners still remained in the majority. The party numbered, as we learned with some surprise from official Soviet statistics, in the whole of Latvia (which still possessed over one million inhabitants) not more than 7,000 adult and 900 juvenile members. Of this total only 2,000 belonged to the local population. The bulk, that is nearly 6,000 members, had been imported from Moscow. And it was this clique, composed three-quarters of persons sent from Moscow and one-quarter of natives, supported by 10,000 soldiers of the Red Army, that we had from now onwards to regard as the "ruling class."

A special "Soviet" or "Council of People's Commissaries" represented the actual Government, which ruled without parliament or reference to the people. At its head stood, besides the already mentioned president, Peter Stutchka, several other individuals, till then completely unknown to us, of whom the most prominent were called Danishevsky, Simon Berg, Endrup, Peterson, Wahzeetis and Mangul. These gentlemen now played much the same role amongst us as Messrs. Trotsky, Zinoviev, Kamenev, Dzerzhinsky, Voroshilov, Bucharin and the other Soviet leaders were fulfilling in Moscow.

Theoretically, any ordinary mortal who so desired could join the "party." Children were even granted special facilities for entering the "Communist League of Youth" for—so it was declared in one of the first proclamations—"their minds had not yet been contaminated by the capitalistic outlook on life." But in practice adult candidates were only admitted very rarely and only after elaborate ceremonies. First of all they were obliged to pass through a special party school as "sympathizers." But, since very few were to be found anywhere who did "sympathize," the Muscovites had no difficulty in remaining—as, indeed, was their intention—restricted to their own little circle, the circle of the "ruling party."

The whole organization of the Soviet power strongly recalled an Asiatic despotism. The same Asiatic stamp which we had noted on the faces of the Muscovites on

"THE BEGINNING OF A GLORIOUS NEW ERA"

the day of their arrival was just as strongly evident in their methods of government and in their ordinary behaviour. There was about them something barbaric, Vandalic. Often, indeed, when we saw their regiments marching through our streets, yelling and whistling, we felt that we had been drawn into the whirlpool of a new migration of the peoples.

Yes, they were modern barbarians, modern Vandals. So, indeed, they designated themselves. One day their official Government organ the *Red Flag* (No. 7, January 12, 1919) even produced a "Song of the Modern Barbarians," composed by a Bolshevist rhymester. The following is a rough version of this masterpiece:

> We are the Modern Barbarians;
> We march forward man for man—
> In unconquerable hordes,
> In ever-swelling hordes!
>
> We are the Vandals of kindness—
> We are the Barbarians of Right—
> We carry Freedom on our shield—
> The Freedom of the Human Race!
>
> There is a trembling and groaning
> Through the wide spaces of empty, worn-out civilization;
> There is thunder and lightning where we step,
> And fertility rises like vapour from our tracks.
>
> We are the Modern Vandals,
> Wandering with heavy and ponderous tread,
> In iron-knobbed sandals,
> Along the Path of the Future.

.   .   .   .   .

As they had announced in their first proclamations, the new rulers had compelled a great number of privately owned shops and businesses and public institutions to close their doors; shops selling foodstuffs alone were excepted.

The immediate and inevitable result of this was that thousands of people of every class were thrown out of employment. These people were only allowed to obtain fresh work in the new State institutions which had been or were being organized. Moreover, the mysterious "Workers' Soviet" had first to testify that they were politically well disposed—an act of grace which as often as not was refused, particularly if the applicant was unlucky enough to belong to the "bourgeois" class.

One of the next steps was to decree that "from now onwards, under penalty of imprisonment or even death, every citizen, with the exception of men and women over the age of sixty, is compelled to have some kind of manual or intellectual work."

The following is the full text:

CONCERNING COMPULSORY WORK FOR THE BOURGEOISIE

Regulation of the Soviet of Workers' Deputies of RIGA

I. In order to root out the parasitical bourgeoisie, bring them into closer relation with proletarian circles and accustom them to socially useful work, the Soviet of Workers' Deputies of Riga hereby proclaims the obligation to work of the bourgeoisie.

NOTE.—By "bourgeoisie" are to be understood all inhabitants who perform no socially useful work and who can show no approved certificate relating to such work.

II. All inhabitants belonging to the above-stated category must register themselves within five days in their respective military districts.

III. After the registration is over any person who is without work or without an approved certificate relating to the performance of some socially useful work will be treated as an adversary of the Soviet State and punished administratively by the extreme penalty (shooting).

IV. All district officers of the Revolutionary Militia of Riga will have the duty of enforcing the registration of all persons living in their districts in connection with the performance of socially useful work.

The President of the Riga Soviet of Workers' Deputies:
SIMON BERG

This decree placed thousands of people in a most awkward situation: on the one hand they were put under an obligation to work, on the other no possibility of working was provided them. In the face of this dilemma most of the citizens could do nothing but sit in their homes waiting for the Red soldiers to come and arrest them.

There were, indeed, a few people, more fortunate than the rest, who managed somehow to be recognized as "politically trustworthy" and obtain some sort of apparent employment, performing some perfectly superfluous function in some Red Government office. They were counted as "workers" and thereby hoped to escape unpleasantness of any kind.

There was yet a third class of people—isolated renegades, who entered into relations with the Reds. These people not only "worked" with them and for them, but—in return for the payment of money and all kinds of special favours—shammed "identity of opinion" and "sincere loyalty."

Personally, I was saved from getting into serious trouble by the lucky circumstance that before the invasion, besides my professional work, I had also attended the old Riga University. This school had now become a "Red University," and its students were counted as "workers" and were left unmolested. I, therefore, could secure myself by simply remaining on the lists of the revolutionized institution. I registered myself as a "Red student" and received an identity card which enabled me to enjoy a certain immunity.

My parents were above the age-limit for compulsory work and were therefore, for the moment, left in peace. My sister was still at school. Compared with other people, our family had survived the first onslaught of the Reds without serious inconvenience.

The theoretical object of the Bolsheviks was the actual abolition of the bourgeoisie. The "complete physical destruction" of the whole "bourgeoisie" was the quickest means of realizing the "proletarian State." When the Reds were in humorous mood, they even referred to the middle-class population as the "cattle still to be slaughtered."

The bourgeoisie, on their part, not being over-anxious to accelerate the advent of this ideal state of affairs, decided that it was advisable to take some measures in self-defence. The most obvious and necessary of such measures was the habit, which everyone quickly acquired, of always taking care to dress in as "proletarian" a fashion as possible. Everybody, when going out into the street, put on his oldest and shabbiest clothes.

Some people went a little too far in this. I could now meet daily in the streets distinguished old gentlemen, once important persons in our town, venerable Councillors or "Excellencies," whom one was not accustomed

COMRADE PETER STUTCHKA
President of the Latvian Soviet Republic from 2nd January until 22nd May, 1919

"THE BEGINNING OF A GLORIOUS NEW ERA" 65

to see otherwise than correctly attired in respectable top-hat, black overcoat and white gloves, dressed all of a sudden like tramps, in the most incredible outfits. One surprised them furtively creeping along the walls of the houses, unshaven, with a rough cap pulled over their ears, ragged trousers and woollen mufflers, and their hands buried deep in their coat pockets.

Or else I saw old ladies, who had always been noted for their refined elegance, now wearing peasants' handkerchiefs tied round their heads and wrapped in the shabby sheepskin furs of their cooks. Young ladies of social position, once so smart and dainty, now ran around looking like scullery maids or uncouth peasant girls. In spite of the strained and precarious situation in which we all were, the spectacle of some of these good bourgeois trying to look like proletarians was so ludicrous that often, when I met them, I was hard put to it not to burst out laughing.

There were, however, a few people who took the matter much more seriously and who would not submit meekly to the newly imposed fashions in clothes, regarding the question as a point of honour. These Don Quixotes refused point blank to make concessions in this matter to the spirit of the times, and continued to parade the streets of the Red town in regular "bourgeois" dress. Many had to pay for this misplaced pride with their freedom. They were simply arrested in the street, entirely on account of their respectable clothes, thrown into prison, and confined there for an indefinite period.

It sometimes happened, however, that one or other of these people, favoured by some extraordinary luck, escaped harm altogether. Among these was a fellow-student of my own acquaintance, a member of a well-to-do Riga family and always a rather spoilt and wilful young gentleman. During all these months this original fellow persistently sauntered through the streets, just as in old times, dressed in the height of fashion, with kid gloves on his hands and a bowler hat cocked at a provoking angle on his head, jauntily swinging a cane, gaily whistling to himself—to the amazement of the shabby crowds of Reds, both real and sham.

Many times the myrmidons of the law would approach and be on the very point of grabbing him. But the sight of such a display of boundless bourgeois impertinence seemed to strike them dumb and powerless. By some miracle nothing ever happened to him. The good man is still alive; and this very day—now that all these events are over and past—he still continues to lead his unruffled and fashionable existence in the bosom of the same old town.

· · · · ·

As the days went by, the town began to experience more and more alarming results of Muscovite rule. The worst of these was the epidemic of "domiciliary visits."

One of the first acts of the Muscovites, on the very day of their entry, had been to throw open the gates of every prison in the town and to empty fifteen hundred common criminals into the streets. These, naturally, at once joined the ranks of their liberators and then, like a swarm of locusts, overran the town and began

"THE BEGINNING OF A GLORIOUS NEW ERA" 67

everywhere, on their own initiative and without any orders from their superiors, to carry out sporadic "political searches" in private houses, with the sole object of seizing anything they could lay their hands on.

As soon as these scoundrels had broken into a middle-class house or flat they "confiscated" all the valuables that could possibly be removed or that they declared to be "bourgeois luxuries" or "inadmissible possessions." In this connection they presumably regarded their own case as an exception to the general Communistic principle of the inadmissibility of private property. They not only seized money and valuables, but also clothes and foodstuffs—anything, in fact, that took their fancy.

A popular saying among the Muscovites was: "Steal what has been stolen from you." It is said to have originated with Lenin, who meant thereby that the working-classes should steal back the wealth stolen from them by Capitalism. Lenin's Riga disciples took this teaching in its most literal sense and made use of it in a most profitable fashion.

In order to protect themselves somehow from this plague, everybody began to think day and night how they could save their belongings from the clutches of these greedy brigands, where and how they could hide this sack of flour or that bundle of bank-notes, this suit of clothes or that piece of jewellery. They climbed down to the cellar or up to the loft and hid their valuables there. They went to friends and acquaintances living in houses of modest appearance and entrusted them with the care of some of their possessions. Or they constructed double partitions in chests and cupboards, pulled up floor-boards, tore open the upholstery of beds and furniture, and invented a thousand-and-one cunning hiding-places where they could conceal objects of value.

But the liberated convicts evidently had already a wide experience of the art of thieving behind them and had no difficulty in extracting what they were looking for from the most out-of-the-way places of concealment.

This spontaneous activity of the released burglars went so far that the Soviet authorities were soon forced to take steps against it. They issued (in the *Red Flag* of January 7) this draconic regulation whereby nobody would be entitled to carry out domiciliary visits without full and formal authorization by the local Soviet:

In view of the arbitrary domiciliary visits, requisitioning, etc., which are being carried out by dubious elements representing themselves to be Red Guards, the Commandant hereby announces that domiciliary visits, requisitioning, etc., in institutions, business establishments or in private dwellings can only be undertaken by persons who are able to show a written order to this effect issued by the local Soviet organization.

Should the written order appear to be doubtful I request an immediate report to the Commandant's office of the City of Riga, in order that the documents may be examined on the spot and the guilty persons arrested.

The Commandant of the City of Riga.
January 6, 1919.

This, however, by no manner of means put an end to the domiciliary visits. They were now merely "officially organized" and were taken over by other hands, no less rapacious. Indeed, the "authorities"

"THE BEGINNING OF A GLORIOUS NEW ERA" 69

showed themselves even more zealous in the performance of these profitable operations than the "dubious elements." The more they devoted themselves to this pursuit the better they came to like it.

Little troops of Bolshevist soldiers and armed women, fully provided with all the written orders that could be desired, began to patrol the town and break into any house of promising appearance.

And this was not all. We heard more and more often of people who, after their houses had been ransacked and hidden money or valuables discovered, were themselves carried off and thrown into prison by those who had robbed them.

It is not surprising, therefore, that all the comparatively well-to-do became more and more nervous, and that the words "domiciliary visit" summed up for them a regime of crushing tyranny; it was a sword of Damocles hanging constantly over their heads. Besides this, to increase the general uneasiness, rumours of impending massacres of Jews and Germans began to circulate in the town.

From time to time, it is true, the Soviet authorities tried to allay the anxiety of the population. Thus one day Comrade Peter Stutchka appeared in person at a meeting consisting chiefly of German Balts and Jews belonging to the intellectual professions and delivered a speech before them, the aim of which was to pacify the bourgeoisie.

I attended this meeting with some other students, professors and lecturers. It was the first time most of us had seen Comrade Stutchka, the Lenin of Latvia; and I must confess that he won all our hearts immediately

—indeed, he made an exceedingly agreeable impression. What a charming old fellow he seemed as he stood there on the platform, and how quiet, highly moral and "unrevolutionary" was all that he said! An extreme Socialist, of course; but not a trace of the savage tyrant, the rabid Bolshevik! He was more like a comfortable, good-natured shopkeeper, a professor or a clergyman. He made the impression of a man of fifty-five, or possibly more. He had greying but abundant hair, which he wore long and untidy in true professorial style. He had a snow-white Nietzsche moustache, which hung down over his mouth and gave him the appearance of an amiable walrus; he dried it from time to time with a clean handkerchief. He spoke in gentle, paternal tones, without any demagogic arts or a trace of oratorical ability.

And it was the disarming simplicity, modesty and frankness of his whole personality that at once held his bourgeois hearers and made them listen attentively to his words.

"Nobody," the Red President cried in genial, fatherly tones, "need have any fear. There is no danger of massacre! The Red movement, which no power on earth can now arrest on its triumphant march across Europe, makes no difference between nationalities. We want equal rights for all peoples. We do not even want to kill the capitalists. We only want to destroy their economic power. We want to relieve them of the burden of their fortunes. As soon as they have become workers, the distinction will be removed."

But not even reassuring statements like these could prevent us from hoping that perhaps one day the Red

THE "BEGINNING OF A GLORIOUS NEW ERA" 71

domination itself would vanish from our town like a nightmare. To the west of Riga fighting was still going on: at a distance of only a few kilometres, in the neighbouring town of Mitau, the Whites were still entrenched, and any day they might advance against the Reds. . . . The thunder of the guns, which before the entry of the Muscovites had reached our ears coming from the east, could now be heard in the west. This constant, dull booming seemed to tell us that our friends were near and that we were as yet not completely deserted.

But then something happened which finally dissipated all our remaining hopes. One day a terrific explosion in the distance shook the town like an earthquake, spreading a real panic for a few moments among the population. It sounded like the subterranean roaring of a volcano. At first no one knew what the mysterious rumbling meant. It was only on the evening of the same day that we learned the sad cause; the White munition store at Mitau had been blown up. This could only mean that our Volunteer Corps had abandoned this place and had retired farther westward.

Next day this ancient and beautiful town, once the seat of the proud dukes of Courland, was occupied by the Red Army. Thereafter the roar of battle, the boom of the guns, became with each successive day more and more distant, and finally died away altogether. The front now receded to a distance of more than 100 kilometres to the west of our town and approached the ports of Windau and Libau, not far from the German frontier.

CHAPTER V

THE ATTACK ON THE HOME

I have left you! You can be thankful that it has happened so peacefully. For I've joined the Reds!

This was the strange message, scribbled on a piece of cheap writing-paper, which I found on getting up one morning lying on our dining-room table. Under these words, in a rough peasant handwriting, but quite legible, was the name, "Martha." This name, it will be remembered, was that of none other than our worthy red-haired cook, who, although she had shown a certain recalcitrancy a few weeks earlier, had nevertheless remained with us till now.

At first I could hardly believe my eyes. I read the slip of paper several times, thinking it might be some joke. But I soon found out that the matter was serious: the servant's bedroom was empty. Martha had disappeared!

She had decamped during the night, taking with her not only all her belongings, but also—as it turned out later—sundry chattels of our own which she thought might come in useful.

Although I was prepared for almost anything since the arrival of the Reds, the dramatic disappearance of our servant worried me a great deal and set me thinking. The flight of this unsuspected spy was a warning that we must in future expect a denunciation, followed by a domiciliary visit.

There had been similar cases already in the town:

THE ATTACK ON THE HOME

we knew of other people whose servants had deserted them after the entry of the Reds, denounced them to the Soviet authorities and then arrived in their employers' homes accompanied by Red Army soldiers, to whom they pointed out the places where these people had hidden their valuables, what "forbidden articles" were in their possession, and which of the members of the family was without work and therefore liable to punishment.

The Soviet authorities encouraged the "proletarian" section of the population in every way to make intimations and denunciations of this kind. The *Red Flag* (No. 22, February 1, 1919) published under the heading "Local News" the following appeal:

> In order to aid in the successful combating of certain undesirable phenomena at present occurring amongst us, all workers (male and female) must give notice of secret food-stores, of illicit traders, and, in general, of all persons who are fighting against the Soviet Government and the working-people by means of sabotage. It is requested that information be given orally or in writing to the Revolutionary Tribunal, daily from 10 a.m. till 8 p.m. (workers' holidays excepted).

Grounds for denunciations existed, of course, in abundance, for in reality everything in the slightest degree resembling bourgeois ways of living and domestic organization was prohibited. The decrees which the Muscovites had issued already provided them with ample opportunity for interference in the minutest details of the private life of each individual. Nothing was more indifferent to them than the sanctity which all civilized people attach to the home. The inviolability of the domestic hearth and the freedom of the individual were ideas completely unknown to them.

Among the latest decrees published, the most important were those forbidding the owning of more than a certain fixed quantity of the necessaries of life, such as clothes, food, furniture, money, etc. The possession of all these things was strictly regulated in the decrees. Whatever remained in excess of the stated amount was to be delivered up to the authorities.

The decree relating to the compulsory tribute of suits, linen and footwear published in the *Red Flag* (No. 35) was worded as follows:

TAXATION OF THE BOURGEOISIE

At the front a severe shortage of warm clothing is being felt. Our Red warriors are fighting there badly clothed and badly shod. On the other hand, the well-to-do people in Riga are going about in warm fur coats and are hoarding up comparatively large supplies of warm linen and clothes. In order to do away with this wrong state of affairs and alleviate the lot of our heroic guards at the front, the Workers' Soviet of Riga has decided to impose a tax in clothing and footwear on the members of the entire property-owning class—the bourgeoisie—and to issue the following resolutions:

I. All members of the property-owning class, between the 19th and 22nd of February, are to bring and deliver up at the centres of collection enumerated below the following articles:
1. Men's linen (vests, pants, socks, etc.);
2. Men's suits, overcoats, furs, articles of military uniform, etc.;
3. Top-boots, lace and other boots, warm socks and gloves;
4. Bedclothes, warm blankets, sheets, quilts, white tablecloths (which can be used instead of sheets);
5. Towels, handkerchiefs;
6. Unsewn materials.

II. *All* supplies of the above-named articles are to be given up and not more than the following fixed minima are to be retained: 4 sheets, 3 handkerchiefs, 4 pillow cases, 3 tablecloths (per family), 1 warm blanket, 2 pairs warm socks, 1 pair gloves, 4 sets of underclothing, not more than 1 woollen vest, 1 winter and 1 summer suit, 1 winter and 1 summer overcoat, 2 pairs of boots.

III. All *better quality* articles of clothing are to be delivered up. Old or damaged articles will not be received. All servants must consider it their duty to see that these orders are carried out by the bourgeoisie. All concealment of clothes and footwear or purchase of these, in order to escape confiscation, will be punished with the greatest severity.

The Workers' Soviet of Riga is convinced that this is the smallest tax which can be laid on the bourgeoisie for the benefit of the Red Army. Should this tax not be voluntarily paid, then the entire possessions of the bourgeoisie will be confiscated and the guilty handed over to the Revolutionary Tribunal.

For President of the Soviet of Workers' Deputies:
ENDRUP

After the publication of this order numerous "Red tax officers," mostly unemployed workmen and dismissed servant-girls, began to penetrate into bourgeois residences and make lists of the clothes and washing they found there. Some behaved correctly and courteously. Others, especially the women, stole, abused and threatened. The things entered on the lists were to be delivered later at places indicated.

Most of the citizens of Riga set up an energetic, though passive resistance to this thieving ukase. They still supposed that the Soviets would not really carry out their threats of punishment by imprisonment and death; and so they responded to the decree ordering the delivery of their possessions merely by hiding everything which could possibly be hidden.

The decree met with this response in our own home.

As *émigrés* who had already been robbed once in Russia, we were far from possessing an over-abundance of clothing or any other material goods. Still, even our modest possessions exceeded the maximum allowed by the Soviets. This "superfluity"—now that a domiciliary visit was likely to take place—might have fatal consequences for us.

Without losing any time, therefore, my parents and I held a council of war; then we all got to work. The first essential task was to reduce the quantity of our household goods to the amount prescribed by the new laws. This we did by getting rid of all "superfluous" articles of clothing and all our reserves of food, either by hiding them away in the loft or the cellar, or by carrying them off to friends and acquaintances living outside the town in more unpretentious-looking houses, which the Reds were less likely to visit than ours.

So far all went well. But when it came to finding a place to conceal the money, the question was not nearly so simple. I had luckily been able to collect, just before the invasion, a considerable sum of money in Swedish bank-notes. It was on this money alone that we were supporting ourselves as best we could.

The possession of "considerable sums" was, however, a contravention of Red orders: although the value of money in Riga was at that time so low that 100 roubles had no longer the purchasing power of £1, the Red Government permitted only 100 roubles per person to be kept in the house. A special decree to this effect (in the *Red Flag*, No. 32) had settled the matter once and for all. It ran:

THE ATTACK ON THE HOME

In no family must more than 100 roubles in small change be kept to hand. All money in excess of this amount is to be deposited in the Soviet State Bank. If this is not done the money will be confiscated. The Commissariat of Finance recommends the Red Militia to take energetic steps to stamp out speculators, and to this end the severest penalties—shooting not excluded—will be applied.

This invitation too met with very little response: naturally nobody felt inclined to entrust his possessions to such people, who openly declared that they would make no effort to return them.

There was therefore no other way out of it but to conceal what money one possessed to the best of one's ability.

In such dilemmas the human brain develops extraordinary energy and inventiveness; and, just as a drug-fiend imagines all sorts of ruses to procure his favourite poison, I began to cudgel my brains, thinking out the most cunning and unlikely hiding-places for the concealment of those fateful bank-notes.

At last, after puzzling for hours, urged on by the thought that I must lose no time (for our Red friends might burst in at any moment and grab everything we possessed), I decided on the following method of disposing of the precious money which was to keep my family and myself from starvation during the weeks to come.

I divided the bundle of bank-notes into three packets and chose for each a different hiding-place. First of all I turned a large wardrobe completely upside down. I spread out the first packet of notes on the ceiling of this piece of furniture, nailed over them a thin wooden board which covered them exactly, and stood the wardrobe on its feet again.

Secondly, I took down from the upper part of my bookshelf a stout volume, Karl Marx's *Das Kapital*; I slipped the more important bank-notes of my second packet between its pages and carefully replaced the excellent volume in its accustomed position, where it made a most advantageous impression, without in any way betraying the somewhat paradoxical role it had been called upon to play.

Finally, I unhooked the bird-cage that was hanging up by the window, pulled out its sliding floor, spread the remaining bank-notes on it, covered them up with fresh white sand, and then put everything back in its place.

The canaries turned out to be the most artful of accomplices, and their charmingly feigned innocence was more convincing even than that of Comrade Marx: they continued to hop gaily about in their cage, chirping and twittering as usual, now and then pecking at a grain of seed or sipping a drop of water. Nor did their faintest chirrup betray the presence of the treasure which they were now guarding under their tiny claws. . . .

. . . . .

Sure enough, only a few days after we had, with so much care and ingenuity, put our home in a state of defence, the enemy delivered their attack.

At a very early hour there came a loud ringing and knocking at the front door, then a violent banging. I

THE ATTACK ON THE HOME

hurried to open, but at once had to leap back as our "visitors" burst in of themselves in a body, crashed into the hall and in one moment overran the whole flat without so much as a glance at me. One rushed into the dining-room, another attacked the kitchen, a third penetrated the bedrooms.

By the way in which most of them at once made straight for those very rooms and corners in which we had originally concealed all sorts of provisions and belongings, it was easy to guess that they had entered our flat following a denunciation and had been informed by someone about the general arrangement of the rooms.

Our uninvited guests—about ten in number—were all Lettish Communists belonging to the Red Army; amongst them were a number of armed females, dressed, like the men, in ragged coats and high muddy boots, with fur caps stuck on their verminous heads and loaded rifles in their hands.

With some difficulty I managed to accost the leader of the horde as he searched round the flat—a somewhat less disreputable-looking fellow whom the others addressed as "Comrade Bittner"—and demanded an explanation of the reason and object of the raid.

I was told that the Red militia suspected us (only, of course, in order to have an excuse to search our flat) of being "in sympathy with the Whites and of cherishing counter-revolutionary sentiments." I protested against these accusations with such well-feigned indignation that the Commissary, instead of returning at once to the search, started to interrogate me. This was a favourable sign, for, as a rule, these fellows were in the habit of going straight ahead with their job, without waiting for any explanations.

Comrade Bittner wanted to know above all if we belonged to the "native population" or if we were "immigrants." As I was able to declare and prove to him that we had come from Russia, had settled in the town only a short time ago, and were practically without means, he gradually became more amiable and remarked grumpily that I "might have said so at once."

It should be explained here that the fury of the Reds was at the beginning directed chiefly against the Lettish and Balt bourgeoisie, whereas outsiders, especially people who had come from Russia, were often left unmolested, or at least were treated less harshly than the rest. My parents and I had only been resident in the town a few months and our passports proved that we had lived in Russia for years. This circumstance and our Russian family name saved us for the time being from worse things.

Comrade Bittner made a sign to his auxiliaries who had set to work on the spot, opening all our cupboards, trunks and chests, and were already busily rummaging inside them. Not without some cursing, these hired looters reluctantly left off their ferreting and gathered round Bittner like a gang of brigands round their chief.

It appeared that one of them was absent from the muster, for Bittner was glancing impatiently round. Obeying, as it seemed, a sure instinct, the chief went through to the kitchen, followed by several of his companions and myself. There we were witnesses of the following scene.

One of the "gunwomen," a brawny, masculine-looking woman, was busily occupied at the dresser. She had discovered a bottle of methylated spirit—and was just about to pour this liquid down her throat, when Comrade Bittner leapt on her from behind like a tiger, snatched the bottle from her and dealt the thirsty Amazon a vigorous thump on her extensive hinder parts with the butt end of his rifle. This act of supervision he accompanied with the words: "Don't you know, Comrade, that our party discipline strictly prohibits the consumption of alcohol?"

And then, even while his reproachful eye seemed to pierce the female offender through and through, Comrade Bittner quietly but deliberately allowed the confiscated bottle to vanish into the capacious pocket of his own overcoat.

After this salutary moral lesson the leader prepared to leave. Followed by the same escort, he traversed several rooms, among others my study, so that each inquisitor in turn passed by my wardrobe with its precious deposit, then by the bird-cage—my improvised safe—but neither the impassive cupboard nor the cheery little canaries betrayed their precious charge.

After the Reds had gone we rejoiced that the first raid had ended so harmlessly. To be sure, a few trifles, besides the above-mentioned bottle of methylated spirit, were missing—a dozen silver spoons, a watch belonging to my father and various other small objects which we had been careless enough to leave lying about within reach. These the guardians of the law had abstracted so cleverly that none of us had noticed anything, although during the whole visit we had all kept our eyes constantly on their fingers.

However, we almost forgot all about these small losses when we discovered with joy that the raiders, in spite of all their fishing and delving, had overlooked two bottles of good Moselle wine which we had hidden in the same dresser where the gunwoman had found the methylated spirit. We had been saving them "for a special occasion." This occasion seemed now to have arrived.

And so, to celebrate our good fortune, the two bottles of good German wine were duly emptied between us at lunch that very day. We excused our extravagance by the sound argument that "in any case the Reds would certainly run away with them next time," and it would be better to drink up our last drop of wine ourselves—before it was too late.

. . . . .

Our feelings of relief were not to last long. Only two days after the first raid the invaders carried out a new attack—this time decisive—on our defenceless home.

The new Bolshevist Commissary of our district appeared at our flat early in the morning carrying a red document; and, addressing himself to the whole family, which had assembled in the entrance hall to meet him, he announced in a matter-of-fact voice the following agreeable tidings.

The Soviet Government, he said, had decided to move as many "bourgeois" as possible out of their own houses in order to make room for working-class families who would be moved in to take their place. The district Soviet had accordingly arranged for the family of the workman Balgal in future to occupy our premises, and for the present owners of the flat to be transferred to the one-roomed lodging of the said Balgal family, situated in a working-class quarter in the southern suburbs of the town. Nothing must be taken away except the most essential articles of clothing. Everything was to remain for the use and enjoyment of the new tenants.

And—in order to avoid useless arguments and save unnecessary delays—the new owners themselves had come along with the Commissary, ready to take possession.

"Here they are," added the Commissary with a rather dubious civility; and he indicated a little knot of human beings who were, in fact, huddled together on the landing behind him, just visible in the dim light, and apparently waiting for his sign to make their entry.

Not unnaturally my family and I, although by then we had become accustomed to the most extraordinary and unexpected happenings, were completely taken aback.

"Move? What do you mean? Where to? When?" we protested with one voice.

But this Commissary, a dark, gloomy-looking fellow, was far less amiably disposed than his colleague of two days before. Indeed, it was absolutely impossible to reason with him.

"I've no time to argue with you. You've got your

orders and you'd better obey," he said rudely, and turned to the waiting family on the landing.

At this critical moment salvation came to us from above, that is, from the flat above us, which was inhabited by a family named Walter, with whom we had made friends—people who had once been very well off but were now impoverished. When they heard the commotion that was going on down below these people had come downstairs, and on hearing that we were to be turned into the streets, the old lady of the house kindly volunteered to take us all in.

Her offer was at once gratefully accepted by us. This, however, was not sufficient. We had first of all to obtain the consent of the Commissary: would he allow us after all to remain at least in our own house, instead of moving into the workman Balgal's single room in the suburbs?

A general courting of the all-powerful man began. It was not easy to persuade the fellow, as his mission was precisely to give a "pack of bourgeois" a shaking-up which they would not readily forget.

Only by the greatest efforts on our part and after a discussion of a quarter of an hour, in the course of which the most varied arguments were brought to bear, as for instance the fact that I belonged to the Red University, and similar points in our favour, could he be persuaded to give his consent to the proposed compromise. Then he shoved the Balgals, the new occupants of our flat, into the hall, seized his cap and slammed the door impressively behind him.

The Balgal family consisted of father, mother and two young offspring between the ages of ten and twelve.

In face of this egregious situation they seemed to be suffering from a certain embarrassment: they had never sought promotion of this kind, and had no particular wish to change their abode—the Soviet authorities had forced them to do so. To the man—a quiet but pleasant-looking workman—the whole thing was obviously utterly distasteful. The children stared blankly in front of them and seemed unable to grasp what was happening.

But Madame Balgal, a squint-eyed woman with oily, untidy hair, showed herself less shy. She started at once on a round of inspection through the rooms, murmured a few words of general appreciation, and then announced straight away and conclusively, to prevent any misunderstanding, that "nothing, absolutely nothing" was to be removed from the flat.

Again the greatest arts of persuasion were required before she would let us take, as an exception, a few pieces of furniture and personal belongings—in particular one wardrobe, one bird-cage, and my favourite book, that excellent work by Comrade Karl Marx, *Das Kapital*.

The family whose flat, one floor higher up, we were now to share, consisted of an old lady, her son, and his young wife, who was almost stone deaf. Once wealthy land-owners, they were now completely impoverished. Old Frau Walter had formerly occupied a prominent social position in our town. Her son, a slightly consumptive man in late middle age, had been a land-owner and a judge in a small country place, and was now in hiding here. They were all extremely obliging, and immediately rearranged their flat, crowding themselves into one half of it and leaving us the remaining rooms.

We at once began to carry upstairs the few objects which Madame Balgal had kindly allowed us to take away. There was not much—only a few pieces of furniture and some clothing and books. When everything had been moved in, we sat down in our new and very overcrowded home, feeling somewhat bewildered by the suddenness of our forced evacuation, but trying hard to reconcile ourselves to our fate. There was only one thing which afforded us a certain consolation. This was that we were now seven persons occupying four rooms, which was well within the ratio fixed by the Government, and we therefore hoped that we should not be compelled to move again.

This cramming of several "bourgeois" families into one apartment, this destruction of the home, was called by the Reds "condensation," and they seemed to be very proud of this new method of social reform.

As for us, the "condensed" ones, there was nothing for us to do but to try to face the situation with a sense of humour and thank Providence for having at least provided us with this new "condensed" home, which we could regard as a haven of refuge.

CHAPTER VI

THE TERROR BEGINS

The first executions took place about a month after the Reds had entered the town. During the night, in a wood outside Riga, called Bickern Wood, thirteen well-known citizens were shot. If, up to then, it had been possible to have the least doubt as to how far they would carry their fanaticism, the fact had now become clear: the Reds were certainly not going to stop at murder.

It was my friend Somoff, of whom I had seen very little since the night on which we had both said good-bye to Carlyle, who one morning appeared in our new "condensed" home and brought us the details of the first massacre ordered by the authorities.

"Something terrible has happened, something horrible," he said, as he entered the room, with slightly quivering, painfully compressed lips. "A hideous murder...."

He had come to tell us that among the executed men was our old friend and family doctor, Dr. Edgar Mey, of whom we had all been so fond—the optimist, the enthusiast, who, only a few weeks before had been our guest the whole evening and had been so full of hope and confidence in the future.

The motive for Dr. Mey's arrest had been an absolutely trivial one: ten years before the war, he had occupied the post of physician to one of the prisons of the town, and in this capacity it was frequently his duty to declare fit certain convicts who, in order to escape forced labour, were in the habit of simulating illness. As fate would have it, some of these same convicts had now reappeared in the town in the shape of prominent officers of the Bolshevist administration. As soon as they heard that Dr. Mey was still in the town, their vindictive instincts were aroused against him; the fact that he had once refused to countenance their simulated infirmities was enough for them to accuse him of "torture"; they seized him, threw him into the Central Prison, the very prison to which he had once been attached as doctor, and avenged the alleged wrong of more than a decade earlier by brutally murdering him.

This case was characteristic of the insignificance of the motives which sufficed the Reds for the execution of the citizens they arrested. No counter-revolutionary acts on the part of the citizens of Riga had compelled them to take such a measure. The other victims who were shot at the same time with the doctor had been condemned without any real cause, similarly to gratify the Reds' hatred of the bourgeoisie.

While Somoff was telling us about poor Dr. Mey, our Bolshevist paper, the *Red Flag*, was brought up. I opened it with an eagerness that will be understood and found the announcements of the death-sentences on Dr. Mey and his companions among a number of official notices. This is what we read:

THE TERROR BEGINS

LOCAL NEWS

Riga Revolutionary Tribunal

At the session of the Revolutionary Tribunal on February 13th the following criminal cases were dealt with:

On account of counter-revolutionary activities:

1. Against the land-owner Friedrich *Lieven*, for organization of the White Guard;
2. Against Pastor Hedrich *Bosse*, for agitation against the Soviet Government;
3. Against the students Fritz and Alexander *Nugge*, for membership of the White Guard and open activity against the Red Army;
4. Against the forester Johann *Pihkan*, for service in the Police Force;
5. Against the farmer Ernst *Bergson*, for handing over Communists to the German army of occupation and for organization of the White Guard;
6. Against the physician Edgar *Mey*, for torturing political prisoners in the Central Prison of Riga, and
7. Against the citizen Robert *Radetzky*, for service in the White Guard.

The Revolutionary Tribunal judged the accusations to be proven against the prisoners Friedrich Lieven, Pastor Hedrich Bosse, Ernst Bergson and Dr. Edgar Mey and sentenced them *to be shot*; Robert Radetzky, for lack of evidence, is *to be acquitted*; the cases against Fritz and Alexander Nugge and Johann Pihkan are to be adjourned for closer investigation.

The President of the Revolutionary Tribunal.

The names of the nine other citizens, condemned to death by the Revolutionary Tribunal a few days before, appeared in separate "bulletins" printed lower down. Among them were the following persons: a Lutheran pastor (Xaver Marnitz, of Uexküll), a German officer (Lieutenant Walter Meier), a Russian officer (Lieutenant Alfons Krümmel), a land-owner, three former police officials and two members of the Baltic Volunteer force. All had been condemned for similar offences: for having served with the army or the police, for belonging to White organizations, for having fulfilled their professional duties in pre-Bolshevist times, or simply for having manifested "bourgeois" sentiments hostile to the Soviet regime.

It was remarkable that under each of these bulletins announcing the death-sentences stood only the grim phrase: "The President of the Revolutionary Tribunal." No name, no signature. Who was this anonymous, death-dealing individual? Amongst the population his identity was a mystery. But rumours went round that this Red Torquemada was a very prominent member of the Bolshevist ruling clique, a notorious officer of the Moscow Tcheka. It was further rumoured that he was a man of a sadistic nature, who had already become noted in Russia for a whole series of cruelties. People asserted that he was fond of boasting that he pronounced hardly any but death-sentences and was known in Moscow by the sinister nickname of the "Death Commissary." At that time we could not know whether all these reports were true or not. Still, it was evident that for some reason or other this dispenser of Red justice seemed to fear too much personal publicity, and for some good reason preferred to suppress his name.

One thing, at all events, was certain: the minions of the Revolutionary Tribunal, male and female soldiers of the Red Army, who were entrusted with carrying out the death-sentences of the President, boasted of their deeds with a cynical frankness. Their stories had gone from lip to lip and had already become public property. Thanks to the communicativeness of these butchers, Somoff had heard about the circumstances of the shootings in Bickern Wood and told us the details.

Dr. Mey and his condemned companions had been forced to dig their own common grave and to perform all sorts of humiliating tasks on the actual scene of the execution; then, in a calm and clear voice, the pastor who was one of their number had said a short prayer; standing on the edge of the open grave, the others had begun to repeat it after him; the crash of rifles suddenly drowned their voices; ten bodies collapsed, one on top of the other, into the freshly dug grave, writhing in their last agony.

The Walters, my three relatives and I listened to these gruesome details in awed silence. It was indeed difficult for us not to feel strongly affected by the news of this first bloody act of terror. It opened up for us all extremely disquieting prospects for the future. Somoff himself, though perfectly self-possessed, was obviously making an effort to hide his own uneasiness. For he had now every reason to fear for his own life, and for his father's also. Both had been connected in Russia with a "White" organization. This fact might one day reach the ears of the Red authorities, and the consequences might well be fatal.

Who, indeed, could now have any feeling of security? In our own little group of "condensed" bourgeois we three men at least had cause to regard our lives as in danger. My father's past position as an official of the Tsarist Government would be sufficient excuse for the Reds to seize him at any moment; I myself had once served in a Tsarist Guard regiment, which made me an equally suspicious character; and as for Walter, who had had to flee in haste from his estates in Livonia, there was little doubt, in view of his position as a Baltic land-owner, that the Reds would have thrown him into prison without any hesitation if they had discovered him.

. . . . .

The first executions were accompanied by a number of fresh arrests. Those who found themselves in a Bolshevist prison quickly discovered the difference between Red and bourgeois justice. The possibility of explaining one's case before a court of impartial judges, of justifying oneself against false accusations, did not exist under the Muscovite regime.

According to the teachings of Moscow, the "Proletarian Courts" and the "Revolutionary Tribunal" —as the People's Commissary, Danishevsky, informed the citizens of Riga in a special declaration (*Red Flag*, No. 14, January 22, 1919)—"were under no obligation to deliver their judgments in accordance with bourgeois ideas of justice; their task, on the contrary, consisted solely in dealing effectively with the enemies of the Soviet power, in depriving them of their inherited rights and in excluding them from the community of the working masses...."

Besides this speech laying down the official point of view concerning the Red methods of justice, the Soviet powers issued further and more specific statements regarding the organization of the Revolutionary Tribunal and the Proletarian Courts. These instructions were intended to give the "Red judges" fuller advice as to how they were best to carry out the task entrusted them—the stamping out of the heretically-minded bourgeoisie. Partly from them, and partly from the first Soviet trials, we obtained a picture of the new Red judicial system which had absolutely nothing in common with the juridical procedure in use in all civilized States.

The Revolutionary Tribunal and the Proletarian Courts sat in secret and made use of an entirely arbitrary procedure. They were not so much intent on proving a crime against the accused person as on establishing his "anti-Soviet attitude" and condemning him for that. For them, an ill sentiment counted exactly the same as an ill deed. The greater part of the case was conducted in the absence of the accused. Just as most arrests were carried out by surprise and solely on grounds of suspicion, so the accusations were based only on the testimony of "proletarian" informers or on the reports of Red investigation commissions. As witnesses testifying against accused bourgeois even children from the age of ten upwards were declared admissible. The names of the witnesses and informers who had denounced him were withheld from the prisoner, so that most of the accused people never knew who it was that had calumniated them. At the same time none of them were permitted to produce witnesses for their own defence. Neither was any written indictment laid before them.

The guilt of each accused person was assumed

a priori. The sole object of the whole so-called legal procedure was "to legalize"—evidently only as a matter of form—the preconceived decisions of the Red judges. As a rule only two demands were made of the accused persons—that they should "confess everything" and "expose their accomplices." The President of the Revolutionary Tribunal or of the Proletarian Court was judge and accuser in one. The spirit in which the Red judges were advised to make their decisions was explained in a specially characteristic sentence of the above-mentioned decree. "The members of the Revolutionary Tribunal," it was said there, "pass their sentences—including the death-sentence—entirely according to the circumstances of the case and according to their revolutionary conscience, for this is the best guarantee of the justice and leniency of their sentences."

The punishments consisted of heavy fines, confiscation of the accused person's entire property, rigid imprisonment, forced labour lasting between two months and twenty years, etc., but more usually—death by shooting. The sentences passed by the Revolutionary Tribunal and the Proletarian Courts were final, and there was no appeal from them. The public announcement of the decisions, above all in cases of the death penalty, followed only *after* the execution had been carried out.

After all this we were hardly surprised when we learned also that those accused before the Bolshevist Courts were not granted a defending counsel. For the benefit of accused Communists there were, nevertheless, special Communist barristers approved by the

President of the Tribunal. Bourgeois prisoners were not even accorded an advocate appointed by the State. In the circumstances prevailing this could only be called logical; for any advocate defending an accused bourgeois would himself obviously have to be regarded as a counter-revolutionary and be accused in his turn. It was therefore only natural that the Soviet power, very soon after its establishment, abolished the legal profession altogether. Solicitors and barristers were henceforward not allowed even to give advice in a private capacity to clients seeking their assistance. The actual decree relating to this, published in the *Red Flag* (No. 40, February 22, 1919), was as follows:

ENACTMENT OF THE COMMISSARIAT OF JUSTICE, No. 7

Regardless of the fact that according to the decrees of the Russian Socialist Soviet Republic, which are also effective in Soviet Latvia, the practice of advocacy is abolished, certain solicitors and barristers have as yet not suspended their activities. In order to put an end to this, the Commissariat of Justice announces:

1. All former solicitors and barristers are in future strictly forbidden to prepare petitions and documents, give advice, etc., in return for payment.
2. Within three days from the publication of this order all solicitors and barristers must take down their professional plates. (Newspapers will be forbidden to insert their advertisements.)
3. Offenders against these orders will be held responsible and delivered up to the Revolutionary Tribunal.

The Head of the Commissariat of Justice,
DANISHEVSKY

Once a person had been summoned before the Revolutionary Tribunal, he was completely at its mercy. His friends and relatives could do nothing for him. Almost invariably, if he escaped being shot at once, he disappeared into prison for an indefinite time. As likely as not neither his judges nor the prison authorities would take the trouble to find out or record his name, and nobody would know why he was in gaol. Petitions for his release or requesting a fairer trial were futile; dozens of them reached the Revolutionary Tribunal every day. They were never answered.

That this state of affairs was not unintentional was revealed in a striking manner by a further communication published in the *Red Flag* (No. 32), direct from the mysterious "Death Commissary" himself. The cold cynicism of this document had a particularly depressing effect on the Riga bourgeoisie to whom it was specially addressed.

General Notification

Whereas the Revolutionary Tribunal has recently received large numbers of petitions, in which are contained the usual complaints, "he is innocent," "he has been falsely denounced," etc., which deserve not the slightest attention and only hinder the work of the Revolutionary Tribunal, and whereas further petitions continue to flow in in such quantities that in order to inspect them and answer them a new chancery would have to be formed, for which purpose the Revolutionary Tribunal possesses no means, the Revolutionary Tribunal hereby informs the general public that, beginning from to-day, only petitions presented by institutions of the Soviet regime will be attended to, and that all other petitions will be left unanswered.

The President of the Revolutionary Tribunal.

To what previous domination in the history of the peoples could one compare this extraordinary system?

The example that comes to one's mind almost irresistibly is that of the Inquisition in the Middle Ages. Judging by externals alone, the comparison may seem scarcely fitting. Externally, the Bolshevist tyranny was as different as it could be from that of the Inquisition. The spirit of the Inquisition, the hateful spirit of intolerance and control of opinions, had nevertheless a certain kinship with the Bolshevist revolutionary judicial system. The mixture of brutal despotism in action and sanctimonious self-righteousness in speech, the fanatical persecution of entirely innocent people merely because they held different opinions, and much else that the Reds said and did, evoked in our minds visions and pictures which we had previously only associated with descriptions of conditions during the tyranny of the Spanish Inquisition.

The very phrases used during the examination of prisoners recalled formulae of Inquisition days. Had not that familiar assurance of the Muscovites that their "revolutionary conscience" was the best guarantee of the legality of their sentences, and that the Proletarian Courts would on principle exercise justice leniently, a striking resemblance to that unctuous formula used by the Spanish Inquisitors when handing over a condemned man to the torturer: "Be merciful with him, remembering the clemency in exercising justice of the Church which alone makes blessed"?

It is easy to understand that in these circumstances the idea of arrest filled the whole bourgeoisie of Riga with an icy terror. The complete lawlessness of this regime, the impossibility of a fair defence, the likelihood of being literally forgotten, like a piece of dead meat, in a dark, damp prison cell made every individual shudder at the prospect of falling into the hands of the Bolsheviks.

And now, to make everything far worse, it had become absolutely certain that these Red inquisitors, working in their secrecy and obscurity, did not shrink even from brutal murder—that it was nothing to them, in an outburst of "revolutionary enthusiasm," to shoot down a few dozen entirely innocent people in some remote wood outside the town.

That meant the public inauguration of the Red Terror, already so well known in Russia. It left no room for further doubt as to the direction in which things would develop; and even those among the citizens who had hitherto contemplated the doings of the Reds with a certain indulgence now began to look to the future with grave anxiety.

CHAPTER VII

WAR ON RELIGION

The immediate reaction to the first shootings was that all the bourgeoisie began to shut themselves up in their homes even more hermetically than before. From now onwards they only ventured out of doors in cases of the most urgent necessity and for as short a time as possible. The greater part of the day they remained comparatively safely hidden in their indoor retreats, occupying the long hours in talking, reading or sleeping.

Among all these people obliged to lead this mole-like existence together a strong feeling of unity soon sprang up. Just as in our own home, so in many other houses two, three or more families, either voluntarily or under compulsion, had joined forces and faced the adversity of the times with a united front.

The Reds were well aware of this defensive union of the bourgeoisie. They knew that the bourgeoisie, lacking more effective weapons, were shutting themselves up in their homes, as in fortresses. They had even found a special name for this phenomenon, which they used in their speeches and articles to jeer at the bourgeoisie. They called these assemblages of several families "gatherings of petty bourgeois cowering before the fresh gust of revolution."

Of late, since the news of the first executions, we had begun to feel this "fresh gust" of Bolshevism particularly keenly. It was not only the *Red Flag* which brought it every day into our home. One of us had only now and then to leave the house and prowl a little through the streets to be able to bring back accounts of things seen and experienced as strange and exotic as those of people who, in ordinary times, had just returned from some wild, distant country.

My family and I and the Walters had settled down as best we could to our new communal existence. Of the four rooms which Frau Walter's apartment contained we had had to convert three into bedrooms, and the fourth served as a general living- and dining-room for both families.

Into this living-room of ours not only had much furniture been moved from the other rooms, to make way for the beds, but also those articles which "Comradess" Balgal had allowed us to take away had been put. The space was therefore so encumbered that we could scarcely move with freedom. Nevertheless, this room formed our chief meeting-place, in which we were now obliged to spend practically the whole of our time.

Among all the monotonous days that we spent in this room one evening at the beginning of March has remained in my memory because of a dramatic incident which had taken place that day in our midst and abruptly broken up our circle.

The party in our flat that evening consisted of my parents, my sister and the three members of the Walter family, my friend Somoff and myself.

Somoff had, like myself, registered as a student at

the Red University and had visited us more frequently of late. I had not been to the university for over a month, but on that day I had attended with Somoff. When we returned to my home, we described to the others what we had seen there.

In this institution, as a result of only two months of Bolshevist management, the strangest transformations had taken place. Any person of either sex who had reached the age of sixteen was admitted without previous study, examination or payment. The result was that entire families of illiterates matriculated during the first weeks, with the sole object of being able, under cover of their students' cards, to carry on their ordinary occupations without being molested by the Red militia. For people who wished to study seriously there was nothing to be done there. The new Government had abolished most of the usual academic faculties, which it considered too impregnated with "bourgeois ideology"; in their place a new and unique science had been introduced which they called, literally, "Red Science." Red Science meant that all branches of learning, from mathematics, physics and chemistry to medicine, economics and philosophy, were, from now onwards, to be considered and taught only from a Communistic standpoint. Those of the professors who would not entertain the new methods of study and teaching were promptly dismissed, and, to fill their place, new "Red professors" were secured by notices in the newspapers or sent from Moscow.

When Somoff and I had appeared in the building that morning, we had found that no lectures were being delivered on account of some "anti-religious manifestation" or other which was apparently taking place that day. Everything was in an incredibly dilapidated and dirty condition. The once familiar halls and lecture-rooms were hardly recognizable. The greater part of the so-called students were sitting or standing about, bored and idle, smoking, talking or doing nothing at all. An unpleasant smell—indeed, it might have been called a most offensive stench—emanated from some of the "students," whose ranks had lately been joined by a multitude of illiterates, soldiers, Bolshevist women, and rabble of all kinds, and made the air of the large vestibule of the university stuffy and nauseating.

My friend and I, after standing about for some time, could see no use in remaining; and after this visit we determined to keep away from the Red University as far as possible.

Herr Walter, our hostess's son, who had fled from his country estate to take refuge in his mother's modest flat, had also been out that day. Although no longer young and of weak constitution he had taken a long walk to a suburb of the town, where he had called on an acquaintance and entrusted to him various objects of value which he felt would be safer there than in his own house.

On his way back, having safely fulfilled his mission, Walter had passed St. Gertrude's, the parish church of his own family, and, hearing an unusual noise coming from the interior, had peeped inside. Of the wild spectacle which met his eyes he now brought back the most amazing description.

WAR ON RELIGION

The Reds, whose doctrine was itself really a kind of religion, did not intend to recognize any other faith except that of orthodox Bolshevism. Every other belief must be stamped out as "anti-Communistic heresy."

The Soviet authorities had arranged an "anti-religious campaign" for that day throughout the town, and had organized Bolshevist meetings in no fewer than six well-known churches, at which violent and blasphemous attacks were being made on religion.

With the aim of gradually abolishing religion in our new Communistic State the Soviet leaders had already, in the course of the previous weeks, issued a series of anti-religious decrees.

In the first place, they had ordered that "the giving of religious instruction in schools is prohibited. No prayers must be held either at the beginning or at the end of the classes. All pictures of a religious nature and other attributes of religious worship are to be removed from the schoolrooms."

My sister, who was still at school, had been able to tell us something about the way this decree was being enforced. A Bolshevist school-inspector, she said, had appeared one day in her class and had delivered to the school-children a long lecture on the dictatorship of the proletariat and the coming world revolution; then he had urged the school-children to lose no time in forming a "Godless Club" and to take part zealously in all anti-religious demonstrations. Finally he had with his own hands removed from the class-rooms and corridors of the school "all pictures of a religious nature," and, satisfied with his achievement, had departed.

A further important decree of the Soviet power prohibited the free celebration of religious services in the churches. "The Administrative Department of the Riga Soviet," ran the decree, "informs all religious bodies that gatherings for the holding of religious services can in future only be permitted with the approval of the Riga Soviet. Offenders against this regulation will be handed over to the Revolutionary Tribunal."

Finally it was declared in a third order that all church buildings were to be henceforward "nationalized," but that churches could be "let out for Bolshevist meetings, proletarian concerts, games of Communist sports clubs, dances of the members of the Red Army and *also* for religious purposes."

As managers the Soviet authorities had installed special Red Commissaries, among them several "gunwomen"—one for each church. On these people it now depended whether religious services could be celebrated in the churches or whether they were to be given over to Bolshevist meetings.

The "people's meetings" which had taken place that afternoon in six of the best-known churches of Riga had been ordered by the Praesidium of the Latvian Communist Party. At these meetings leaders of the party of Latvia were to report on "the achievements of the Soviet power to date." Early in the morning placards announcing them had been displayed all over the town. Their text was also published in the *Red Flag* (No. 53, March 9, 1919):

WAR ON RELIGION

The People's Meetings

To-day, at 6 p.m., speeches will be delivered in the following churches:

1. *In St. Gertrude's Church:*
    on the activities of the Soviet in Latvia in general.
2. *In St. Paul's Church:*
    on the activity of the Red Army.
3. *In the Trinity Church:*
    on the activity of the Food Department.
4. *In the Magnushof Meeting-house:*
    on the war against counter-revolution.
5. *In St. Martin's Church:*
    on the activity of the Commissariat of Education.
6. *In the Luther Church:*
    on the activity of the Revolutionary Tribunal.

The speeches will be delivered by the following responsible members of the Soviet: Adamson, Berg, Danishevsky, Endrup, Kahrklin, Linde, Mangul, Stutchka, Wilks, Wezgailis and others.

The Riga Committee of the Latvian Communist Party.

It was at one of these meetings (the one in St. Gertrude's) that Walter had been present on his way back from the outer suburbs. The picture of this Bolshevist meeting in a Christian church which he described to us reminded one vividly of the things one had read of those "devils' masses" which used to take place in the Europe of the days of the Thirty Years' War.

The church, decorated with red cloths and glaring Bolshevist placards—related Walter—was packed with Bolsheviks, who did not observe the slightest restraint in their behaviour. All the men had kept their caps on their heads; many of the women dressed as soldiers and carrying rifles were conspicuously rouged and powdered and were easily recognizable as former harlots. The whole gathering was smoking, shouting and laughing as though in a tavern; many had even brought drinks with them and were swallowing them on the spot, lounging without embarrassment on the church chairs. Others strolled round the aisles of the church, crowded in front of the religious pictures and made foul jokes about them. The organ alternately played military marches and dance tunes. Then the speakers of the day mounted the pulpit and thence delivered their speeches on the achievements of the Soviet regime and the prospects of Bolshevism; they were followd by voluntary speakers from the Red audience who, with the impudence of the lowest music-hall comedians, jeered at all religious sentiment and mocked at the "superstitions" of the God-fearing; at the conclusion, the whole assembly yelled out the "Internationale," to the accompaniment of the organ, and then, many of them already drunk and visibly swaying, dispersed with loud shouts and cat-calls. . . .

. . . . .

"A small group of clergymen," said Walter, continuing his narrative, "made to-day an attempt to prevent these sacrilegious acts. They advanced courageously against the Red demonstrators as these approached the churches, and tried to stop them from entering the places of worship. But they were seized by the ring-leaders and all of them were at once thrown into prison. . . ."

"And besides that," Walter said, "from the ranks

of the clergy themselves there has arisen a champion of Communism who not only says 'yea' and 'amen' to everything that the Reds undertake, but also indulges every day in long sermons, speeches and written articles justifying and even glorifying the Bolshevist Revolution."

The clergyman to whom he alluded was already a well-known figure in Red Riga. His name was Edgar Model, and he was a pastor of the Evangelical Church. He was still a young man, and his peculiar appearance proclaimed him a visionary and enthusiast. An untidy mane of reddish hair, like an artist's, surrounded a thin, almost consumptive face, from which a pair of abnormally large light-blue eyes looked out with an unsteady flicker. He had a small but sharply curved nose like Don Quixote's, in contrast to a very receding chin concealed to some extent by a scanty reddish beard. Pastor Model was rather short, slender, almost delicate, in build, and very restless in his movements. He was inclined to dribble when speaking, and his beard and the exposed part of his shirt were often covered with saliva. At his first words, generally confused and disconnected, one felt that he was a man in whose brain intellect and folly, fanaticism and narrowness, clarity and obscurity had combined to form a peculiar world of the imagination, in which he lived and had his being.

None the less, Pastor Model was doubtless a man of some spiritual gifts and a straight, honourable man, who was ready to stand up boldly for his convictions, however they might diverge from those currently accepted. He had always occupied a special position among the Riga clergy on account of his eccentricity. Even before the war he had felt the symptoms of social dissolution more strongly than most of his fellow-citizens, and had always believed that the only redemption from the injustices of this world was to be found in Socialism.

On the arrival of the Reds he began to preach his own Communistic interpretation of Christ's teaching and on the basis of it attempted to justify Bolshevism, not from the Marxian, but from the "ethical standpoint," reminding everyone that Christ Himself had renounced all kinds of material goods; and he hailed the Soviet rule as "the pure, bright dawn of a great, new era for mankind. . . ."

Of the sincerity of his convictions and his complete moral integrity there could not be the slightest doubt. He was an idealist in the fullest sense of the word. But Pastor Model and all those who, like him, hoped for a "new salvation" from Communism looked only at the theory and not at the practice of Bolshevism. And the well-meant, enthusiastic appeals which they from time to time addressed to the enslaved and terrorized population of Riga could not, in these conditions, but make an incongruous impression.

Walter picked up a copy of the *Red Flag*, which lay on the table, and opened it. Model's Bolshevistic sermons were printed almost daily in the *Red Flag*. We knew their contents well. But on that day, when the Reds had just broken into and desecrated almost every church in the town and had just thrown a number of clergymen into prison, the apologetics of this misguided churchman afforded a particularly crude contrast to the events of the moment. Walter began to read out loud to those present an extract from this article, a reprint of a sermon which Pastor Model had preached in his church a few days before and which was called "The Turning-point in World History."

"The idea of Communism must triumph!" recited Walter with exaggerated emphasis. "It must triumph, because in reality property does not exist. Property is foreign to our earth, to our nature. Because men have erected their whole cultural edifice on this false foundation, it must now collapse irredeemably. It was no true life that we have been living up to now. The twilight of the present age precedes a sunlit day, heralded by a red dawn. . . . I long to greet it, this bright dawn of a new era!"

"All hail," Walter went on declaiming, but in a lower voice, "thou new Sunday of the world! Thy dazzling sunshine blinds our dim, light-starved eyes. We long to greet thee, thou resurrected humanity, where brothers and sisters will make the earth habitable for one another on the sunny side of life, where our old earth will let the daily bread of life grow up for all its children, where there will be only *one* right for all, the right to Life and Freedom, to none refused and to none restricted, where . . ."

Walter had now got well into his stride and had by no means come to an end of the Red clergyman's outpourings when he was interrupted by a loud ringing and banging at our front door. We all gave a sudden start.

Expecting the worst, I went and opened the door.

It was a raid, as we had feared; in the space of a few seconds our living-room, lately so peaceful, was filled with Red soldiers armed to the teeth. Their leader, a sinister-looking, slit-eyed fellow dressed in a black leather jacket and clutching a revolver in his right hand, advanced towards us.

"Which of you is Citizen Walter?" he shouted at us, without a word of explanation; and, when Walter at once stepped forward, he added sharply:

"You, is it? Walter, the former land-owner and judge? Get ready and come along with us. You are arrested!" And he approached Walter as though intending to drag him away by force if necessary.

But poor Walter, who suffered from consumption and was anything but of a violent nature, was the calmest of us all. He did not make the slightest attempt to remonstrate with the Commissary; without losing his composure for a moment he went into the hall, took his hat and coat and, perfectly impassive (though he was as white as a sheet), said, almost drily:

"I am ready."

The rest of us—my parents, my sister, the two ladies, Somoff and myself—stood by silent and as though petrified, not daring to interfere. Meanwhile the Commissary was glancing with wrinkled brow at our tea-table with its bourgeois set of cups, saucers and plates.

I looked round our circle. Were the Reds looking for someone else amongst us? Anxiously, my eye came to rest for a moment on Somoff; it was he, I knew, who was in the greatest danger.

Somoff, however, showed no signs of agitation;

there was a strange expression on his face, as of submission to the inevitable; and an inexplicable sensation of pain came over me—a presentiment, as it were, of some cruel, ghastly fate which lay before him. . . .

But to-day the minions had come only for Walter. They had in the meantime surrounded him and had already begun to march him off towards the hall. The Commissary followed. Still not one of us spoke a word.

Not till the Red Guards had already led the defenceless Walter out of the room did the eyes of his young, deaf wife open wide in horror. Up to then she had merely looked bewildered: she had understood nothing of the words which had been so rapidly exchanged. Only at the sight of the departing soldiery and her husband in coat and hat amongst them did she grasp what had happened. She understood that she might never see her husband alive again—and she threw herself, like a child in a fit of anger, with raised fists, in front of the Red officer.

"What are you doing? Brutes! Leave my husband alone! What right have you to kill him? Scoundrels! Murderers!"

Then, seized by uncontrollable despair, she burst into hysterical, heartrending sobs.

Contrary to all expectation the Commissary, instead of flying into a rage, stopped on his way, turned round slowly and said, addressing himself to the despairing Frau Walter, in measured and even courteous tones:

"Don't worry, Citizeness, your husband will be treated fairly and mercifully, according to our revolutionary conscience. Our just proletarian laws mete out justice leniently, and no one who has committed no crime has anything to fear."

With these words, which he uttered with a certain theatrical aplomb, he abruptly turned his back on us, pushed Walter before him, and disappeared with his companions, leading the prisoner to some unknown destination.

CHAPTER VIII

ABOLITION OF MONEY

Although several days had gone by since Walter's arrest, no one had yet been able to ascertain where he was or what had become of him. His old mother and his wife had gone from one Soviet official to another and from prison to prison. But nowhere could anybody give them any information about "Citizen Walter"; all the people they applied to were, or pretended to be, totally ignorant of such a person's existence.

"Walter? Former land-owner? Lawyer? Quite unknown to us. . . . Hasn't been registered anywhere . . ." was the usual answer supplied to the two relatives.

The officials were not necessarily lying; the Reds had arrested so many people already that they hardly knew the names of all those who now crowded the prisons. It was very possible that Walter had become one of this nameless horde of prisoners.

The two women returned home every evening weary and discouraged and abandoned themselves, in a heavy silence, to dreary speculations as to the fate of their lost relative.

This misfortune which had befallen the family of our hospitable hostess, and the execution of our family doctor a short time before, had a very depressing effect on our household. And the equally distressing things which continued to happen every day were not designed to relieve the atmosphere of gloom which reigned in our flat.

First of all, during these weeks—the end of February and the beginning of March—the last remnant of our feebly cherished hope of a speedy deliverance from the Red yoke vanished once and for all. In their irresistible westward march the Reds now captured one place after the other; towns and villages of Courland, familiar to us—Tuckum, Schlock, Goldingen and others—fell almost without a struggle into the hands of the Reds. Yielding to their pressure, the Baltic Volunteer force withdrew farther and farther into the interior of Courland; the Whites appeared to have been completely routed and in their retreat had already arrived before Libau, in the vicinity of the German frontier.

These evil tidings we learnt daily from the despatches of the Red General Staff from the front, published in the *Red Flag*. At first we regarded them with some scepticism, hoping all the time to receive better news from other quarters. But this hope did not endure for long. All doubts as to the exactitude of the Red despatches were soon destroyed by confirmation from other and more trustworthy sources: from the localities captured by the Reds there arrived from time to time in Riga fugitives who certified that the reports of the Red advance were unfortunately true. The frontier between Riga and the civilized world of the West had been pushed far back and left us behind, lost in the dark confines of the Muscovite empire.

From this time onwards the feeling of being totally

cut off from the world of civilization and freedom grew stronger and stronger amongst us. We knew practically nothing about anything that was happening at that time in the rest of Europe—in Germany, France or England. At Versailles, during those very weeks, the statesmen of the world were assembled to construct a new order in Europe. But we were supplied only with the most meagre reports, mostly completely distorted, of these momentous events. And the question which most interested us—whether the Governments of Germany and the Allied Powers took any interest in the fate of our country, swallowed up by a Bolshevist invasion—remained wrapped in complete darkness.

The same mystery surrounded the fate of those countrymen of ours who had fled abroad before the Reds in January. What had happened to my friend Carlyle, who had been so confident, who had promised us speedy deliverance, but from whom we had not yet received a sign of life of any kind? What had become of that ship crammed with hundreds of refugees which I myself had seen as it was about to leave our port? Had it safely reached a friendly harbour, or had it gone to the bottom with all on board in the ice-covered, mine-infested sea?

In short, we seemed to have been completely abandoned and forgotten by the whole world. We were living, to be sure, in a town from which in normal times such European centres as Berlin, Copenhagen and Stockholm could be reached in a day or two. But at that moment it seemed to us that these cities had literally been transplanted to another planet. And at times we felt that we were no longer living in a town lying within the bounds of civilized Europe, but in some tiny Kalmuck village in the depths of Siberia.

In these circumstances one could only regard it as a blessing that the Reds left us practically no time for grumbling and complaining. Our lives now consisted in a perpetual struggle for bare existence. This struggle absorbed all our interests and all our energies. Where could we get money to live? Whence could we obtain our daily bread? These were the main questions of the moment, and they drove all other worries entirely into the background.

In our family—since both my parents were old people—the cares of providing the necessaries of existence lay exclusively on my shoulders. I had been able, a short time before the entry of the Reds, to lay in a store of the most essential supplies. I had also, for the sake of security, taken a further precautionary measure: from our stock of cash and provisions I had put aside a certain quantity as an "iron reserve" and kept it aside for the time of direct want, part in our flat and part in the care of acquaintances. We had at first lived only on the ready money which I had in the house. But as under the new regime we could only spend money but not obtain it, I saw our supplies of money and provisions rapidly shrink and finally exhaust themselves altogether. One day I found that I had no more cash left in the house. Somehow or other I should have to produce some more money.

In normal times the simplest way to this end would

have been to go to the bank, provided that one possessed a banking-account. But under the Bolshevist regime this simple way was no longer simple: the banks no longer existed!

For part of the programme of our new government was "the gradual total abolition of money"! Money was not required in the paradise on earth. Comrade Stutchka had already several weeks before expounded, in a lengthy essay, the Communist programme of the abolition of money.

"Our chief goal in the fight against the domination of capital," he had written, "is the total abolition of money! When the necessaries of life are no longer taken by private merchants to market for buying and selling, as has happened up to now, but are simply distributed by the State, then money naturally loses all value and all importance, and nobody will need it any longer! As soon as money is taken out of circulation, moreover, all forms of swindling, thieving and murder for the sake of money will cease. What is money, in reality, and who uses it? Money has not existed at all times. In the earliest ages of humanity, in the age of primitive communism, when the tribe or the family had itself to produce everything essential for its own needs, money was unknown. The value of goods was originally work and not money. We are therefore making a clean sweep of all money and are beginning again—in the present period of transition—with the original barter of goods. Later it will be possible to deal with the money problem in an even more radical fashion. Then each person who works, as the equivalent of his work, will simply receive from the State the quantity of food and manufactured goods necessary for the maintenance of his capacity to work."

Comrade Stutchka explained his plan at the conclusion of the article by a practical example. "Let us look at it in practice," he said. "In the month we have approximately 150 working hours; for the worker each hour represents one unit of work-money; thus the month will bring him in 150 units of work-money or, more simply said, 150 work-roubles. As soon as we possess a sufficiently developed State apparatus, each worker will receive from the State all essentials in return for his total performance of work, in return for his work-money. This will be done in this way: we will open for each worker and each Soviet employee an account-sheet in a special Soviet Bank; on one side his working performance will be recorded and on the other will be entered all the products which he has to receive in exchange; here an account will be kept for each Soviet citizen —of his domicile, his bread, meat, of all his food, clothing, etc., and likewise of everything necessary for the satisfaction of his spiritual needs; he will receive everything from the State and entirely without the intermediary of money. . . . We do not overlook the practical difficulties in the way of the fulfilment of this programme. Nevertheless this commerce without money is no Utopian idea. Money is living now the last days of its domination. The path to the realization of Communism can be cleared only thus. Be this our slogan: Away with money! . . ."

In harmony with the voice of Comrade Stutchka,

all the lesser Soviet leaders also spoke up and expressed themselves in much the same way as their chief. Not once or twice, but daily and hourly they spoke and wrote on this theme—in pamphlets, in newspaper articles, in speeches, in lectures. A sea, an ocean of spoken and written words—all directed towards one idea for the salvation of the Red State of the future: Away with money!

Pastor Model, the pro-Communist clergyman, took the field also for the abolition of money, again not from a Marxist, but from an ethical standpoint; and he published an article in the *Red Flag*, entitled "An Awakening Call," in which he expressed the following opinions, deviating somewhat from those of Comrade Stutchka, about the money question:

"Brother! Sister!" wrote the Red minister, "when you give money, then you give money out; when you give love, then you take love in. With money you can buy and have everything—except only love, the content of life. I cannot believe in the power of money! Brother! Sister! Neither can you do it! You must not believe in the power of money—not even in this world which lies worshipping at the feet of Mammon. Brother! Sister! Do not believe in the power of money! Believe in the power of love! Turn your face away from Mammon and turn it to the true God! Change your values! Change your ideas! Not money, but love!"

. . . . .

What resulted from all these fine theories as soon as the Soviet reformers began actually to put them into practice?

In practice, the idealistic war-cry "Away with money!" merely meant the same thing as "Give us your money!" This was very soon made perfectly clear: before very many days had passed the citizens of Riga received, through the medium of the *Red Flag*, a formal invitation from the Government itself to be present at the confiscation of their deposits of money lying in the safes of the various banks of the town.

The invitation appeared in No. 17 of the *Red Flag*, and its wording left no room for doubt as to its authors' intentions. It ran:

THE COMMISSARIAT OF FINANCE OF LATVIA

hereby announces that the contents of all safes containing valuable deposits lying in the banking-houses of Riga are to undergo a revision by a commission specially appointed for this purpose. All owners of such safes and deposits are accordingly requested to appear with their keys and identity papers, on the days and at the hours specified below, for the purpose of exhibiting their deposits. Those who cannot come themselves may send a representative. If nobody should appear, the deposits will be opened without the owner being present.

The talk about "revision" in this decree turned out only to be a delicate circumlocution for the simple word "confiscation": every owner of a deposit who presented himself with his keys on the specified days was informed, immediately after the safe had been opened, that his property was "to be regarded as confiscated until further notice"; the only thing which was handed over to him was a "receipt" signed by an official of the Commissariat of Finance "for the safe keeping of valuable papers, jewellery, etc., received." This receipt proved later to be completely worthless:

not a single one of the owners of deposits ever saw the smallest part of his property again.

The announcement of the intention entirely to abolish money sooner or later, and the simultaneous decision to confiscate all private money deposits, did not by a long way exhaust the "financial reforms" of the Soviet Government. One could reproach the Reds with many things, but one could not accuse them of leaving any work half-done once they had begun it. And they issued, hardly three weeks after their order concerning the opening of the safes, two further decrees "for the reform of the banking system in Soviet Latvia." Both appeared in the *Red Flag* (No. 35, Feb. 16, 1919). The first ordered the "nationalization of the banks," following the already well-known example of Soviet Russia.

DECREE
Concerning the Nationalization of the Banks

In order to attain a better-regulated organization of the economic life of the country, and at the same time to do away with the speculation of the banks and definitely free the workers in town and country from exploitation through the banks' capital and to organize one single People's Bank of Soviet Latvia, which should really serve the interests of the classes with small means, the Soviet Government of Latvia has made the following resolutions:

1. The operations of all banks and other credit institutions are declared to be a monopoly of the State.
2. All private banks at present existing with their branches will be incorporated in the newly founded (Soviet) People's Bank.
3. All the assets of the enterprises to be liquidated will be transferred to the (Soviet) People's Bank.
4. With regard to the liabilities of the different banks further special arrangements will be issued later on.

The President of the Latvian Soviet Government:
P. STUTCHKA

The second decree concerned "smaller banking-accounts." Among the possessors of money deposits in banks were to be found many workmen, peasants and all kinds of people of small means whose economic situation, owing to the Bolshevist experiments, had already been severely injured. The Government wished in some way to encourage these more naïve people to pay their cash savings into the new Soviet bank. It therefore announced that:

For the protection of the interests of the owners of smaller banking-accounts and of the working and poorer classes in general, the following is resolved, until further notice:

1. Persons whose banking-accounts do not exceed the total sum of 10,000 roubles will receive from their accounts a subsistence minimum of 400 roubles a month.
2. All banking-accounts which exceed 10,000 roubles will be confiscated.
3. Persons guilty of fraud will be handed over to the Revolutionary Tribunal.
4. Accounts opened after January 9, 1919 [i.e. after the foundation of the Soviet rule] are not subject to any kind of restriction.

The "roubles" mentioned in this decree referred of course to the already much depreciated Russian currency which was in circulation in Soviet Russia at the time. The currency question was extremely confused. There existed Tsarist, Kerensky and Soviet roubles, which were all differently valued among the population, but whose rate of exchange fell continuously. The Soviet roubles, of course, had the lowest value, as the only fund by which they were guaranteed was Karl Marx's *Capital*. On an average 100 roubles were worth scarcely £1.

ABOLITION OF MONEY

The 10,000 roubles fixed as the highest permissible limit of each man's fortune thus represented the lowly sum of £100, while £4 (400 roubles) was the maximum one was allowed to spend per month on the bare necessities of existence.

In the third month of Soviet rule the absurdly small monthly income permitted by the Government was quite insufficient to buy everything necessary for the maintenance of even the most modest household. For this purpose alone hundreds of roubles more were absolutely necessary; and thus the paradoxical situation arose, that at the moment when for the first time in history the idealistic cry "Away with money!" was resounding among men, only those who were able to spend large sums in cash to obtain the essentials of bare existence could be assured of not dying of starvation.

But how were these large sums in cash to be secured? The authorities, besides prohibiting the banks from paying out more than 400 roubles a month, forbade people to keep supplies of money in their houses. It was an evil predicament: if one did possess enough money to subsist on in one's house one had to live in constant fear of discovery; if, however, one conformed to the regulations and only kept the lawful amount at home there was no alternative but to go hungry.

Most people could see only one way of escape from this strained situation—to sell some article of their belongings from time to time. They sold all sorts of objects of value which had not yet been taken away from them—jewellery, pictures, clothes and the like—for whatever they could get. With the money thus obtained they procured themselves provisions. As soon as these were exhausted, a further object was sacrificed, and so on.

For this purpose numerous citizens of Riga now betook themselves daily to Sand Street, a street in the "Old Town," the Riga "City," which was formerly devoted to banking and now served exclusively as the centre for illicit trading, the "Black Exchange"; secondhand dealers and money-changers stood about there in large numbers and bought the things which the citizens brought them.

This unavoidable commerce was not without danger to the citizens who engaged in it. Buyers and sellers always ran the risk of encountering some Red patrol in the streets, having all their precious belongings or their money filched from them, and being thrust into gaol.

This was just the reason why the Soviet authorities tolerated the "Black Exchange"; it was said that every raid on Sand Street brought the Soviet Treasury in several hundred thousand roubles.

At the beginning of March there arose in my family also the necessity—for the sake of our daily bread—of selling some part of our possessions. Among the few objects of value which we had brought out of Russia and still possessed were one or two jewels belonging to my mother; these we would now have to sell, one after the other.

It was this that led to my making the acquaintance of the "Black Exchange" and discovering by personal experience that trading and money-changing now actually meant risking one's life.

When I reached the "Black Exchange" about noon on a bleak March day a brisk trade was in progress. The crowd consisted chiefly of two kinds of people: on the one hand there were the impoverished and already half-starved citizens of the town, who had come to sell their last belongings for the sake of their daily bread, and on the other hand there were the visibly better-fed but unscrupulous dealers, eager to seize the opportunity of grabbing something of value for nothing.

It was not difficult to distinguish these people from those who had come there driven by necessity. They were habitués of the "Black Exchange." Of slightly Oriental appearance, dressed in shabby but warm overcoats with turned-up collars, their heads sunk anxiously between their hunched-up shoulders, their hands buried deep in their pockets, these people strolled ceaselessly up and down as though they were simply harmless loiterers. From time to time, however, they would suddenly rub up against passers-by who they thought might have something valuable to sell, and murmur casually in their ear, as they passed, in low, yet sharp and businesslike tones, such short phrases as the following: "Anything to sell?" "I buy gold and silver things!" "I give good prices!"

Some of the dealers confined themselves entirely to the buying of foreign money and gold coins, which some citizens had stored up "for a rainy day" and were now obliged to relinquish in exchange for Soviet currency; or else they sold foreign money to people who had the intention of fleeing from the town to Western Europe. These traders of a rather superior type bore themselves with a somewhat prouder mien than their colleagues, the secondhand dealers, and called out straight in front of them, without addressing anyone in particular: "I take dollars" . . . "Buying gold roubles" . . . "Giving English pounds," and so on. (In Russian, "Beru dollary" . . . "Pokupayu zoloto" . . . "Dayu funty.") These subdued exclamations were the only sounds to be heard on the "Black Exchange." But in spite of the business activity, the atmosphere of the place was charged with a strong undercurrent of nervous tension. On the faces of all present there was the same look of uneasiness and anxiety.

I quickly found a dealer who was ready to buy my ring for a few thousand Soviet roubles, and driven by the desire to escape as soon as possible from this unrefreshing place, I carried the transaction through as quickly as I could. I counted the money and found it correct, pocketed it and turned to go. But I had taken only a few steps and was nowhere near the end of the street, when loud yells arose from the whole "Black Exchange" and everybody scattered in a wild panic.

I made an effort to get away with the others, who were running frantically in all directions. But there was no escape: Red troops blocked both ends of the narrow street to cut off our retreat. We were all ordered into an empty building which had formerly been a popular coffee-house.

The crowd obeyed like a herd of helpless sheep. In the coffee-house everyone was carefully searched. All money and valuables were confiscated; then, if one was lucky, one was allowed to go. People on whom too large sums of money had been found were at once put under arrest and taken off to prison; death would doubtless be their ultimate fate if they did not succeed in finding means of purchasing their release.

They found on me only the proceeds of the sale of my ring. In spite of my protests, a Red Army soldier took it away from me and handed me in exchange, with the words, "Here—your receipt!" a piece of dirty paper with something scribbled hastily on it, which was stamped conspicuously with the hammer and sickle—the Soviet arms—but was otherwise of no particular value.

Still unreconciled to the loss of my precious money, I stood looking questioningly at the soldier, expecting him to give me some further explanation. But instead he merely said in a dry and indifferent tone of voice: "That's all—you can go!"

I was in some doubt as to what I should do next. Even according to the Soviet laws I had been treated illegally: the confiscated sum, divided up among the members of my family, did not exceed the authorized amount. When I pointed this out to the Red soldier he replied in a casual voice and, it seemed to me, with a slightly ironical smile:

"If you like you can go and complain to the Commissary. . . . Perhaps he'll give you back your money. . . ."

"Which Commissary?" I asked. "Which authority?"

"Here, round the corner," the soldier informed me readily, but still in the same indifferent, slightly jeering tone. "Quite near, in Wall Street. At the Finance Department . . . the Finance Department of the Revolutionary Tribunal."

The meaning of the fellow's ambiguous advice and the curious smile was now clear to me: the "Finance Department," which organized the periodical round-ups of the "Black Exchange," was in reality nothing else than a branch of the Revolutionary Tribunal, and the man who stood at the head of this department was none other than the redoubtable President of the Tribunal, the Torquemada of our Red Inquisition State, the man who "on principle signed only death-sentences."

This was certainly not encouraging. Yet, I thought, my membership of the Red University, and the fact that I had been treated with such obvious injustice, should enable me to visit this man without particular cause for alarm; I knew also that he had, in certain cases, corrected his over-zealous henchmen's abuses of power with dictatorial orders; and as, moreover, I was curious to see the all-powerful man face to face, I decided in the end to risk the interview and attempt to recover my money, the possession of which meant so much to my family and me at this time.

. . . . .

The offices of the "Finance Department" were installed in an enormous, incredibly shabby block of flats. At the entrance Red sentries were posted, and only persons who could prove themselves to be reliable, that is, could show a passport or a "special pass" (*propusk*), were admitted. There was a good deal of coming and going. Thanks to my student's card I had no difficulty in securing entrance.

The "Death Commissary" received in a large whitewashed hall. When I entered there were in the hall only a few frightened-looking petitioners, the Commissary and his clerks.

The "Death Commissary" was a man of towering height, with pitch-black, unkempt hair falling over his face. He had the yellowish complexion of the Mongolian race, a small black moustache and an unspeakably dour and malevolent look in his narrow, greenish-yellow eyes. His whole frame—shoulders, chest, hands and feet—was peculiarly coarse. He was dressed from head to foot in black leather; short black leather jacket, black leather trousers and high, black Russian boots. He carried a Mauser pistol at each hip, and two Colt revolvers lay before him on the desk, within easy reach. A telephone which also stood on the table made an almost incongruously bureaucratic impression.

It was soon my turn to face this individual of not very encouraging aspect. I explained my case to the Commissary, who for some unascertainable reason gave all his interviews standing. He listened to me attentively, scrutinizing me suspiciously with his narrow eyes and frowning gloomily. From time to time, turning away from me, he gave his underlings, who approached him with cringing mien, various orders in a curiously high-pitched, thin voice, and in a Russian which, though fluent and faultless, betrayed a slight foreign accent. Then, when I had finished my story, he turned to me again and said (without asking me for such details as my name, address or any other particular) in rather a different tone, but in the same shrill voice:

"Wait in the next room. I shall give the necessary orders." And he turned to the next petitioner.

That sounded very vague. But it was no use arguing with the "Death Commissary": I had no choice but to obey. I went into the waiting-room next door—not particularly reassured by the Commissary's oracular pronouncement, but still, nevertheless, faintly hoping for a favourable settlement of my affair.

From this room, which was scantily furnished, like a doctor's waiting-room, and was only separated from the reception hall by a thin wooden partition, every word which was spoken next door could be distinctly heard. I had hardly entered it when, to my horror, I heard the voice of the "Death Commissary" uttering, in a calm and frigid tone, apparently over the telephone, these significant words:

"Is that the guard-room? Please send up an escort of three men at once to remove a bourgeois, a speculator."

I naturally understood this order to refer to me, for I had seen no other "bourgeois" in the waiting-room. For a few seconds I felt a kind of paralysis creeping over my limbs. Arrest, prison, execution—these three stages of my immediate destiny passed in logical sequence before my mind. . . . Driven by the instinct of self-preservation, my brain began to sum up with feverish haste all the possible chances of escape.

I looked round the waiting-room. Opposite the door by which I had entered was another exit; I did not know where it led, but there was no time to lose. Without hesitating for a moment, though I had not the vaguest idea of what might lie beyond, I opened this door—the only possible way of escape—and crossed the threshold. There was only one thought in my mind—to get away from the Commissary's unpleasant proximity.

The room I entered was a hall, as large as the Commissary's reception room on the other side. This hall appeared to be the chancery of the "Finance Department." There were rows of desks along the walls and down the middle of the room, which was full of people. Luck was on my side; just before I had opened that fateful door a bell, audible throughout the whole house, had sounded for the midday meal; and instantly all the clerks who had been working in the room had got up from their seats, and, laughing and talking noisily and jostling one another in their haste, were surging out in the direction of the dining-hall.

This proved my salvation. Nobody paid any attention to me. Along with the others I got out into the passage; from there I took the main staircase and so gained the entrance. I did not draw breath till I was in the street again, and in safety. . . .

CHAPTER IX

SOVIET SOUP FOR ALL

Money was not the only "capitalist institution" which was to be gradually abolished in our Soviet State. Private trading in foodstuffs, as in all other articles, was declared by the new rulers to be abolished: all the foodshops had been forced to close their doors!

But how was the population now to feed itself? From where were we to obtain "our daily bread," now that we could no longer walk into a shop and buy it for ourselves? Who was going to give us food and drink? There was only one answer to these questions: the State!

Immediately after their accession to power the Soviet leaders had decreed, first—that all trading in the most important foodstuffs should be a monopoly of the State; secondly—that in the Communist State every citizen was entitled to be provided by the State with food, which would be delivered free of charge from communal kitchens; and thirdly—all owners of estates or farms of any size were to be driven from their lands, as the Government itself intended to manage them.

The decision to nationalize all estates, farms and all land in general was contained in the very first "Manifesto" of the Soviet power. Clause 3 of this Communist charter had run: "The private ownership of all land, buildings and industrial and agricultural equipment is abolished. Accordingly, all estates owned by the nobility, the Crown and the Church will at once, without any compensation, pass under the control of the Soviet."

Simultaneously, detailed instructions were given to the agents and emissaries of the Soviet power as to the best way of carrying out these "land reforms" in practice. These were published in the first number of the *Red Flag* as follows:

> The Soviet Government is despatching special emissaries to all parts of Latvia with the task of supporting and strengthening the power of the local Workers' and Peasants' Soviets. The emissary is the intermediary between the local Soviet and the central Soviet Government. In every parish a Peasants' Soviet is to be formed. All resistance to this or attempt at resistance will be broken by force. All estates and industrial plant on them are to be placed under the supervision of the local Soviet. Stores of grain which can be dispensed with, or considerable sums of money found on the estates, must be placed at the disposal of the central Soviet Government.

The carrying out of these instructions meant that on each estate and on each farm, henceforward, the Soviet emissary who had been sent there began to lord it as an uncurbed despot.

Most of the Baltic land-owners and larger Lettish farmers had already fled before the Red invasion. The smaller farmers who had remained behind, however, felt no particular sympathy for their new masters. The Soviet emissaries, indeed, regarded those peasants who possessed two or three cows and employed one or two farm servants as "exploiters," and treated them accordingly. They only courted the favours of the "village poor," and "landless." From the others, as far as was practicable, all their property, their grain, their livestock and all their stocks of food were to be taken away.

The consequence was that very soon the whole country population, consisting chiefly of Lettish peasants, who in these parts had always been accustomed to a very high standard of living, began to show open hostility towards the Reds. The first thing the peasants did was to hide all the supplies they possessed, and—in comprehensible uncertainty as to the future—they were by no means inclined to give up any of their provisions either to the emissaries who scoured the countryside, "requisitioning" right and left everything they could grab, or to the townsmen who came into the country in search of food.

They no longer brought food supplies to the town markets. Meat, vegetables, flour, butter, milk, eggs and such essential products had almost completely disappeared. Finally, the peasants considerably reduced their cultivation; they only cultivated the amount of land which was necessary for their own upkeep; and the countryside, once so rich and flourishing, began slowly but visibly to go to waste.

Some of the Red leaders clearly saw the folly of such measures. For instance, at a meeting of the Riga Soviet, Comrade Rozin, an old Communist and personal friend of President Stutchka, got up and delivered himself of some blunt truths.

"You have, comrades, very strange ideas of Communism," he said. "I would call this Communism a hunger communism, or a burglar's communism, trying, pistol in hand, to rob others of what they have produced. Communism of the proletariat has other aims; it tries to increase production. Pistols are only needed for the protection of our produce. The Russian experiment proves that not even one half of what could be produced is produced. If there is bread just now it is only because people live by robbery, but in future this will become impossible. We Letts must, therefore, regard the Russian agrarian policy with terror. We have not a sufficient number of agronomists, and our Communists do not know very much about agriculture either. Agriculture is a very complicated and profound science, but the peasants know their fields through experience, so that we need not take their land away. We are in need of every loaf of bread and of every pint of milk, and it is of no use to nationalize land unless we can increase production. We have abolished all the privileges of the land-owners, but it would be madness to take land away from the peasants if we cannot hope to increase production by that means...."

But the extremist members of the Soviet, who were in the majority, paid no attention to rational arguments of this kind. Despite this and similar warnings from the more moderate Communists, and despite the unsatisfactory results of the first Red agrarian experiments, the Soviet leaders persisted in their fixed idea of feeding the whole population on a Communistic basis. And at the end of February came the following decree, published in the *Red Flag* (No. 37), relating to the free distribution of food to the population:

Order

Concerning the Introduction of Food-rationing for the Inhabitants of Towns and Villages

At all District Food Supply Departments:
1. Every inhabitant of large towns, small towns and villages is to receive half a pound of bread free per day.
2. Every inhabitant of large towns, small towns and villages is to receive half a pound of salt free per month.
3. Every child up to the age of three years is to receive one pound of jam or sugar free per month.
4. Every Food Office in towns and villages will receive free for the use of the inhabitants of its district 1 *pood* of carbide for lighting purposes.
5. Every smoker will receive 10 cigarettes per month.

The People's Commissary for Supply.

The existing bourgeois restaurants were everywhere taken over by the State, and in them public "feeding kitchens" were opened, with the aid of which the Soviet authorities began to feed the entire population free of charge. In Riga alone there were over 180,000 people to be fed. Nevertheless it would be a mistake to suppose that each Soviet citizen had a square meal set before him in these "communal kitchens." The State kitchens served nothing but a standard "Soviet soup," and every citizen who presented himself received a plate of soup and nothing else.

This "Soviet soup for all" was, moreover, of very doubtful quality. It was thin and watery and made out of half-decayed vegetables. Also, its distribution was exceedingly badly organized. Usually many more people appeared than could possibly be fed; they had to form up in long queues and wait for hours together.

A partial, though far from adequate, picture of what

went on in the communal kitchens of Red Riga is given by the following description of the conditions, published by the Communist Food Department itself in the *Red Flag* (No. 18):

> In the feeding kitchens of the Food Supply Department of Riga the number of portions demanded is continually increasing. Soup is now distributed daily to 168,000 persons. With the increase in the number of portions to be provided grievances and complaints on the part of consumers are becoming more numerous. . . . With the opening of new kitchens the queues will be diminished, though they will not disappear altogether. The mistaken attitude of the public is responsible for these queues. Petitions have been sent in by some people, both workers and non-workers, requesting the right to receive their rations without waiting their turn. Persons with doctors' certificates also demand preferential treatment. If all these petitioners were to be satisfied the only achievement would be that besides the existing queues other new queues would be formed. In so great an organization it is unavoidable that a certain number of people should remain unsatisfied.

. . . . .

At the end of the second month of Muscovite rule an acute shortage of food—the consequence of all the Bolshevist reforms I have described—began to make itself felt. The situation grew worse every day. The State supplies were dwindling noticeably and already were not sufficient to go round. So our rulers hit on a new idea.

Hitherto, all citizens, without distinction of class, calling or age, had received the same food rations and the same bread ration of one loaf per day. Now all that was to be changed. The Government evolved a scheme by which the entire population would be divided into groups, with the object of allowing one group to receive a larger food ration than another. Accordingly the whole population of Latvia was—by a laconic announcement of the militia authorities—divided up into three groups, or "categories," on the following lines:

1st Category.—Members of the Soviet Government, of the Communist Party, and of the Red Army, peasants and manual workers registered in the Red trades unions;

2nd Category.—Employees of Soviet institutions (not members of the Communist Party), students, professors, teachers, schoolboys, doctors, artists and all "intellectual workers" registered in professional organizations;

3rd Category.—All bourgeois sentenced to forced labour, old people over 65, and in general all members of the "bourgeoisie doing no socially useful work."

This division conveniently enabled the Soviets to show favouritism towards the desirable classes of the population at the expense of those less desirable: the members of the 1st Category were well treated, those of the second less well and those of the third really badly. The revised system of bread-rationing, for instance, showed this very clearly. It was arranged thus: 1st Category—One-and-a-half loaves per day; 2nd Category—One loaf per day; 3rd Category—half a loaf per day.

The bread distributed was an extremely bad rye bread of blackish appearance. It was strongly mixed with all kinds of inferior substitutes, with potatoes and turnips, and one would often come across large quantities of straw in it, or little pieces of wood.

The State distribution of bread and other foods according to the above categories was worked through a system of cards. Each citizen had to be in possession of a special food-card (with coupons), corresponding to his category.

It depended entirely on the caprice of the Soviet militia in which category each citizen was ranked. He had nothing to say in the matter himself. "The employees of the militia," the *Red Flag* hastened to inform us, "are not authorized to consider complaints concerning the ranking of an inhabitant in this or that category. All questions relating to this matter will be dealt with and decided later. ..."

By means of the food-cards one received, from time to time, besides the daily bread ration, other products such as sugar, jam, cigarettes, etc. These things the Soviet authorities obtained from the stores which they had found in various foodshops, provision-stores, etc., when they captured the town. But nothing at all came from Russia; nothing was produced in the country, and the "other products" were therefore only distributed very rarely, at the most once a month and then not always to all the categories.

One day, for instance, the Food Supply administration surprised the citizens with the announcement that on that day free "jam, butter, tobacco and cigarettes" would be distributed. But when one looked at the announcement a little more closely, one found there the following limiting conditions: "The distribution will only be to citizens of the 1st Category; citizens of the 2nd and 3rd Categories will receive nothing!" Such involuntary or, perhaps, deliberate mockery of the bourgeoisie took place quite often. Another time, for instance, we could read in the *Red Flag* the following tantalizing announcement:

On the 22nd of this month the Food Supply administration will proceed (by virtue of the third coupon of the 1st Category food-cards) with the distribution of one cigar and one egg per person. . . .

The introduction of the system of categories naturally divided the inhabitants of our home—as it divided the whole population—into more and less privileged groups. My two parents and the old Frau Walter, as "bourgeois performing no socially useful work," and who besides that had passed the age-limit, were put into the 3rd or lowest Category. The same fate befell the young Frau Walter, on account of her incapacity for work. My sister and I—she as a schoolgirl, I as a student—were admitted to the 2nd Category. The other tenants in our house were relegated to the 3rd or at best the 2nd Category.

Only one family were found worthy of a place in the 1st Category. These were the Balgals, the proletarian family living in our former flat a floor lower down. Henceforward these people represented creatures of a higher order. And Madame Balgal, whenever she passed anybody from our circle on the stairs or in the street, now looked down upon us with an expression of infinite contempt. . . .

The provisions which I had stored up in the house were sufficiently abundant to have lasted us, in an extremity, for three or four months. The outlook for the moment was therefore not desperate. The situation, however, changed suddenly and completely when one day the Government ordained that nobody had the right to keep more than certain fixed and limited quantities of food in his house, and threatened offenders against this law with the death penalty! The quantities permitted were: 10 lb. of bread or 7 lb. of flour, 3 lb. of butter or dripping, 5 lb. of meat, one lb. of sugar, half a pound of tea or cocoa. We were, therefore, again forced to think out ways and means of safely disposing of the "excess." A part of it we succeeded in concealing in our own house (in the cellar, loft and other hiding-places). But the things which remained in the flat were still far above the fixed level.

In this predicament some elderly ladies of our acquaintance, living in more remote and less threatened districts of the town, offered to keep some of our provisions for us. Therefore, in spite of risks and difficulties, we carried all kinds of supplies out of the house, with the secrecy of conspirators, to these friends, who were rewarded for their trouble by receiving for their own use half of the goods entrusted to their keeping.

We regarded these provisions as an "iron ration." In the meantime we subsisted partly on the State rations and partly on provisions procured by secret trading. Following the closure of all foodshops by the Government a flourishing secret and illicit food trade had grown up. It was obviously impossible to exist on the half-pounds of straw bread and the platefuls of Soviet soup distributed by the Government. Neither could one maintain life on one egg or one pound of war jam a month. And the carbide which was delivered from time to time could hardly be regarded as a suitable form of nourishment. Everyone, therefore —if he did not want to perish miserably—was literally compelled to procure for himself food supplies from other sources. Thus a busy illicit traffic in food sprang up on all sides.

The illicit traders grew up, after the introduction of the "reforms," like mushrooms after the rain. Most of them were extremely doubtful characters, and they asked inordinately high prices for their wares. But we could not do without them; they were never refused entrance, and so they crept from house to house, hawking their goods carefully hidden under their overcoats and anxiously whispering about "heavy penalties," "risking our lives," "last chance of getting supplies," and so on.

One of these fellows, Zazkin by name, who normally exercised the profession of a barber, had been calling at our house once or twice a week for some time. Peering round furtively with tearful, dog-like eyes, sniffing like an animal in the air with a long, reddish nose, his head sunk deep in his shoulders—he would produce from the capacious folds of a by no means clean overcoat now a smoked ham, now a calf's liver, now a pound of butter and, not without a certain ceremony, hand them over to us. In exchange for these dainties, which in those times were literally worth their weight in gold, he would receive small fortunes. In spite of that he was looked upon by all as a benefactor, welcomed as a rescuing angel, praised, and entreated not to delay his next visit.

Zazkin was obliging. He came regularly several times a week, and for some time he was actually our main source of supply. But as my reserves of cash melted away, and I could only buy more sparingly, his visits became rarer; and when at last the day came

SOVIET SOUP FOR ALL

when I had no longer money enough to pay for Zazkin's wares, he did not come at all, and our last source of supplies had dried up.

. . . . .

We were now threatened with starvation; we had had practically nothing to eat for over a week but bad rye bread and thin Soviet soup. All we had left was the "iron ration," those provisions which we had entrusted to the keeping of friends for a "rainy day." That day had come, and these last reserves would now have to be sacrificed.

We had deposited these reserves with four or five friends of ours, mostly elderly ladies. Living in the outskirts of the town, in houses of modest appearance, they had never occupied a conspicuous position among the bourgeoisie, and had to a large extent been spared the attentions of the Reds. The first of these confidantes whom I decided to visit lived in the other part of the town lying across the river, the so-called "Mitau Suburb." Thither I had to direct my footsteps. From our house to the other side of the river was a good distance, so that the expedition I had to undertake was quite an exhausting one, especially on a hungry stomach.

The expedition began with a little interlude even before I had got out of the house. When I had climbed down one flight of stairs and had arrived before the door of our former home, this door opened and Comradess Balgal suddenly stood, unkempt and squinting, in all her proletarian magnificence, before me. In a confused cascade of words she gave me to understand that, having heard footsteps on the landing and thinking it might be me, she had opened the door, as she wanted to ask me a small favour. Would I come in and explain to her some point connected with the gas oven? She had not had a gas oven in her former flat and had not come to understand this one properly.

I followed her babbling with some impatience. But I had long felt a desire to take a peep into our old home and see what it looked like now. I therefore readily accepted her invitation.

The moment I crossed the threshold I perceived that everything had been completely "proletarianized." To be sure, the furniture stood more or less in the same arrangement as we had left it. But the whole flat had got into an unspeakably filthy state, and every room was more or less untidy. Comradess Balgal's two offspring, filthy as little beggars, were squatting in the middle of the floor of our former drawing-room playing with dolls and toys of all kinds which had once belonged to my sister. They looked perfectly happy and seemed to feel quite at home; in fact, the whole family appeared to be in excellent fettle. Balgal was a factory worker, and the Soviet power treated him, like all other workers, with special favour. Besides being presented with the homes of ejected bourgeois, the workers received increased wages and were assured of a plentiful supply of food by being placed in the privileged "1st Category." The Soviet leaders and the workers who supported them—while the rest of the population was already suffering from acute hunger—had everything in abundance for their own use. The

Balgals, therefore, had at their disposal every kind of food and drink, almost to excess.

Comradess Balgal led me into the kitchen, not without a certain air of pride. Here there greeted me a sight so alluring and one to which my eyes were so completely unaccustomed that I involuntarily stopped short for a moment. On the broad expanse of the kitchen-table, made of a clean, light-coloured wood, there reposed a large, juicy joint of beef weighing certainly not less than ten pounds. Around it lay, in picturesque confusion, a variegated heap of vegetables; the potatoes, in a finely graded colour-harmony of brown and rose, beamed at me invitingly; the sharp-nosed carrots shone a cheerful red; close by was a bunch of juicy green parsley. It was a still-life picture of such luxuriance that it would have served as a worthy model for a painter of the Dutch school.

Although it was quite early in the day, a lot of cooking was going on. In a pan on the stove onions, cut into fine slices, were spluttering in brown butter and making, it seemed to my hungry senses, an infernal din; they squeaked and chattered like impudent boys making fun of an elderly gentleman. A stupefying fragrance rose out of the frying-pan, filled the room and stole soothingly into my nostrils. . . .

Comradess Balgal seemed to have noticed the impression which the Dutch interior of her kitchen had made on me. But she was not pleased by it. She pressed me to explain the detail in the mechanism of the oven which had been troubling her. I did as I was asked, and almost fled from the place which afforded so crude a contrast to our empty, hungry home.

I was still strongly impressed by my experience as I covered the distance of several miles to the other side of the river, to the Mitau Suburb. After about an hour's walk I arrived before the house of the lady with whom our miserable supplies had been left.

I knocked at the door. A voice sounded in the interior. The door, however, was not immediately opened. The voice of our confidential friend called out from within asking who I was and what I wanted. I gave my name and said (still through the closed door) that I had come to ask for part of our supplies.

But to my great astonishment the old lady was still unwilling to let me enter the house. Then, when the door was at last opened and I stepped into the hall, the lady gave signs of the greatest embarrassment. She began to utter all kinds of curious excuses, from which it was only evident that she no longer possessed the deposited goods. And then her embarrassment suddenly turned to rage; she suddenly flung at me a torrent of hysterical abuse, reproached us bitterly with "doing ourselves well," and accused me of intending to "leave her to starve."

It had, of course, been madness to entrust such tempting things to the keeping of people who were themselves suffering great privations. The spectre of starvation simply tore the mask of convention from them.

I had known this woman as a refined, old-fashioned lady who would be shocked at the slightest liberty in conversation. And now she was showing quite a different face. The impression was so disagreeable that I turned and began to walk away. But the old woman, with dishevelled hair and flaming eyes, her unwashed hands, formerly so carefully tended, raised in the air, screamed the grossest insults after me.

"You want to know where your food is, do you? Eaten up, I tell you! Because I don't want to die of starvation! You blood-sucker! Go to hell, or I'll denounce you to the Revolutionary Tribunal!"

After this fiasco I at once went on—without promising myself very much from it—to make a round of all the other acquaintances who had also taken over some of our stores to keep for us. The result was everywhere the same. Not so bitterly as the old lady, but with sufficient candour, they all declared that they themselves had consumed the provisions entrusted to them. Many expressed their regret at the occurrence, promised to replace the misappropriated goods later, excused themselves and so on. But all that was of very little help to us just then. . . .

It was late in the afternoon when I returned home from my fruitless expedition, weary and empty-handed, and recited my tale of failure to my discouraged family. The outlook for the future was now worse than it had ever been hitherto.

I looked at my old father and mother. The weeks of Soviet domination had not failed to leave their mark on them. Both of them had become visibly thinner. It even seemed to me that the constant privation had caused their bodies to grow actually smaller, that they were gradually shrivelling up like starved plants. . . . But in spite of everything, they still retained their cheerfulness and composure.

Old Frau Walter, on the other hand, who had once

been rich and happy and had had everything life could offer, now seemed completely broken down. The uncertainty as to the fate of her son depressed her deeply. She hardly spoke a word now. Painful consequences of perpetual under-nourishment and mental suffering began to show themselves in her. Symptoms of serious disease appeared: her hands and feet began to swell noticeably, and it became harder and harder for the old lady to move about at all.

CHAPTER X

THE CITY OF THE RED PLAGUE

Thus, in the year 1919, the Red plague, with its inseparable attendants—terror, hunger, sickness and death—ravaged, tormented and devastated the city of Riga.

In no other town of Eastern Europe lying near the Russian frontier, which the Bolshevists overran in the years 1918 and 1919, had they indulged in such an orgy of terror as they now did in Riga. In the third month of Soviet rule—spring was then just beginning—the terror took on forms more extravagant than had so far been experienced even in Russia.

The suppression of the bourgeois population and the Bolshevization of the entire public life were driven forward with fanatical persistence. Want and misery grew worse and worse from day to day. And after a Red rule lasting hardly more than ten weeks Riga literally presented the picture of a place which had been visited by some all-destroying natural catastrophe or malignant epidemic.

The domiciliary visits and arrests now degenerated into a mass persecution of the bourgeoisie. On some days the number of people seized and thrown into prison was several hundred. The Red myrmidons no longer troubled to give reasons for arrests. The faintest suspicion, an anonymous accusation were sufficient. In houses where "bourgeois" and adherents of the Soviet lived under the same roof, the latter were given instructions to pry into the most intimate affairs of the bourgeois, to ascertain whether the new laws were being observed and in suspicious cases to denounce the guilty ones to the Revolutionary Tribunal. Mean creatures devoid of honour, of whom there were now plenty about, and vindictive people, who saw in this an opportunity to avenge themselves, made all too good use of this repulsive weapon.

Servants who deemed themselves to have once been badly treated by their masters, or workmen who harboured some kind of grudge against their employers, now wreaked cruel vengeance upon their former superiors. Daily there poured into the Tribunal dozens of written and oral, open and secret denunciations against once prominent citizens. On the basis of these notifications the Soviet authorities drew up long lists of "suspicious bourgeois" and carried out their arrests by reference to this guide, composed without proof of any kind.

The prisons of the town, which had been emptied by the Reds on the day of their entry, were rapidly filled again to the last cell. Indeed, the number of prisoners was so great that there was not room enough for them in the town prisons. And it became necessary hurriedly to restore ancient towers and dungeons which had stood empty for centuries and had only possessed an historical interest, such as the "Central Prison" and the old "Citadel," disused since the war, and make them fit to receive fresh victims.

Not much happier were those people who—like my family and myself—were as yet not languishing behind prison walls, but who nevertheless were free only in name. At first the domestic hearth had been the last place of refuge where the bourgeois of Riga could still hope to find peace and quiet. They had regarded their homes as fortresses in which they were barricaded against the iniquity of the outside world; there they hoped to be safe for a little while from the clutches of the Red plague. But the grim reality had no respect for the sanctity of these lonely retreats, and each one of these little fortresses erected by persecuted human beings was in constant danger of brutal assault: at the first commanding knock of the inquisitor, the inmates would be forced to surrender without dreaming of resistance.

The arrests generally took place by night. The silence of the grave lay over the suffering town. From time to time, breaking the stillness, came only the rumbling of a motor-car driving along the street. That was the first sign of the approach of the Red executioners, the black motor-cars of the Revolutionary Tribunal. Needless to say, the Bolsheviks were the only persons in the possession of automobiles.

The noise of these motor-cars rattling through the night struck fear into the hearts of thousands of people lying awake in their homes. Each time that familiar rumbling resounded, they held their breath and listened: is it for us? Will they stop before our house, or will they pass on and spare us this time? The torturing seconds succeeded one another. The rumbling of the sinister vehicle came nearer and nearer, grew louder and louder, had already stopped? No, hastened on, receded, died in the stillness of the night, was past. . . . Thank Heaven! Saved from the worst for to-day. . . .

But if they halted before a house, then at once they poured like a pack of savage murderers over all the stairs and rooms. Doors were violently burst open. Coarse, drunken brutes broke into the rooms, penetrating without shame or hesitation even into the women's bedrooms and dragging their victims, often in their night-clothes, into the streets. Almost every house was visited at least once a week by the emissaries of the Revolutionary Tribunal. Sometimes they carried off whole families, including little children, into captivity. Everywhere people were lying awake in their beds, fully dressed, starting up anxiously at the slightest noise and imploring Heaven with childish simplicity to save their homes from the dreadful fate which threatened them.

Especially painful was the situation of those citizens for whom individual search was being made by the Red power. Many distinguished citizens of our town, whom the Revolutionary Tribunal had sentenced to death by default, had been unable to flee in time and were therefore compelled to hide themselves at all costs. It was the resurrection of the dark life of the Middle Ages, of the extravagant conditions of the Inquisition, in the days of electricity and wireless telegraphy. These hunted creatures had themselves walled up by their families in niches and hollows in the walls, leaving only a small, hidden opening for passing food. Or, where it was practicable, a double partition was constructed between two adjacent rooms, and in the space thus formed the fugitive was concealed. In this fashion a friend of my father, a former public prosecutor whom the Reds were particularly eager to

THE CITY OF THE RED PLAGUE

catch, hid himself for weeks. He existed there like Kaspar Hauser, Bonivard or some other legendary prisoner; he gradually lost his human appearance, vegetating in perpetual anxiety and tormented by uncertainty, until at last he fell into a state of semi-lunacy.

Those who were still "free" only left their homes in extreme cases, when obliged to hunt for the means of existence, to go to the public kitchens, or, once a week, to enter a church. The churches were always packed on the days when the Soviet administration released them for purposes of worship. Old and young, men and women, pious people and those who long ago had forgotten how to pray, all crowded now into the churches. Here, at least, they could feel safe for a short time from the raging of the horsemen of the Apocalypse who had been let loose against them; here, at least, they could feel the comforting fellowship of common suffering, and the spirit received a little of the feeble hope and consolation for which it had been thirsting during long sleepless nights. But as soon as they emerged from the calm precincts of the church, the awakening to the reality of their existence was the more frightful.

Riga, the fair and flourishing city of former days, now presented the appearance of a dying town. Most of the streets, squares and parks were empty of people; the windows of hotels and office buildings were nailed up; the markets, once teeming with life, and the places of amusement, once filled with music and cheerful voices, were now wrapped in silence; vanished were the nimble sleighs and bustling droshkis. The houses, the pavements, the many gardens for which Riga had once been renowned, even the lamp-posts were falling into decay. Snow and mud lay thick on the streets and pavements, once kept so neat and tidy, and no one troubled to sweep it away. Tattered, unclean red rags and cloths fluttered in the wind from the lamp-posts and railings. Here and there telegraph poles leaned over at a crazy angle and long wires hung from them down to the earth.

In the Old Town, where formerly had reigned such a busy and lively animation, the shops and offices, almost all the restaurants and coffee-houses were closed. The broad show-windows of once wealthy stores, which were now ruled by "Red Co-operatives," displayed pitifully wretched wares: a few thin cardboard boxes which contained doubtful substitutes for commonplace articles, some small bowls of dusty grain and inferior flour, one or two tiny pieces of grey war soap and two or three packets of the cheapest writing-paper. Nothing else.

The same picture of misery and deterioration offered itself throughout the whole of Riga. Everywhere one looked, whether in the Old Town or in the harbour quarter and the suburbs, everywhere the town gave the impression that a malignant, all-destroying plague had swept over it.

In the quarters where the well-to-do bourgeoisie had lived, the windows and doors of many houses stood wide open. The houses had been abandoned by their owners and stood empty. Anyone could enter them and do what he pleased there.

These were the houses which till lately had been the

scene of so much life and gaiety, the homes of that century-old culture of which the Riga bourgeoisie had been so proud. In some of them I myself had frequently been a guest.

The interiors of all these patrician houses, some in the pretty German rococo, some in a rather heavier, peculiarly Baltic style of the early nineteenth century, had always been distinguished by a refined taste and a peculiar Hanseatic dignity. All their beauty had been destroyed by the Bolsheviks, who penetrated everywhere and seized everything they could carry away. They had stolen and scattered the furniture of hundreds of flats and houses, and had used it to equip their own establishments and their "proletarian culture clubs." In not a few cases they had thrust some priceless piece of furniture into their stoves as fuel or smashed it up from mere savage love of destruction.

Now the wind whistled through these deserted houses; the paper hung in rags from the bare walls. Here and there a patch was still visible to mark the spot where an old family portrait had hung. The rooms, which had lately resounded with the gay careless voices of people now exiled or murdered, were abandoned to hideous desolation. . . .

Even the animals had deserted the streets. The sight of a horse was now rare. As for the cats and dogs, the faithful companions of every human community, they seemed to have all run away or crept into hiding, for none was to be seen. Not a bird fluttered in the air, not a cock crew. Only about dinner-time was any life to be seen. Then here and there one might observe a crouching, miserably clad human figure slinking hurriedly along the silent walls of the houses, a mug of the wretched Soviet soup in its hand, stopping at times to peer anxiously round and then diving through a half-open doorway or into a protecting side street, just like some rat or other creature that lives in underground holes and shrinks from the light of day. Thus men and beasts and even inanimate objects seemed to deny their existence and freeze themselves into a uniform and ghastly semblance of death.

Only the henchmen of death still cared about the living! At nearly every street crossing, in narrow side streets or hidden in doorways, the minions of the Soviet power lay in ambush for their prey. Human prey! Fearing that they might not succeed in laying hands on all the "suspects" by means of the house-to-house searches, they had resorted to the devilish method of catching their victims in the open. There were days when literally every passer-by was stopped, and if he could not prove by his papers that he was a worker or belonged to a "privileged class," he was arrested on the spot, and immediately carried off to perform some objectionable forced labour. People who usually stayed at home six days of the week, and on the seventh anxiously ventured to church, were often seized by the Reds within a few steps of their homes, and dragged off to hard labour.

One often saw prominent members of Riga society escorted, like dangerous criminals, in the middle of the streets between horsemen with cocked rifles. Men and women of all classes were forced to clean the streets, wash clothes and scrub floors in houses belonging to the Reds and Soviet offices, pull dung-carts, dig graves, and discharge many other degrading tasks specially invented for their humiliation. Thus, one day, a relative of mine, a poor old silver-haired lady of nearly seventy, frail and ailing, was forced with blows and kicks, and amidst the derisive jeers of the mob, to go down on her knees and clean out, with her trembling old hands, the unspeakably filthy lavatories of a Red barracks.

The town was starving. The inhabitants of Riga, which could once have been called "the city of abundance," were knowing the bitterness and hardship of a real famine. Was it really the same town whose cellars had been perpetually filled to overflowing with the good things of the table? Most of the citizens of Riga had now nothing whatever but the State ration. Even this meagre bounty was now bestowed with less and less generosity and regularity. In the third month of Red rule the Soviet soup consisted only of an eighth of a litre a head and was yet so watery and disgusting that it might more properly have been called dishwater than soup. The bread was now hardly more than a mixture of straw and earth; it was distributed to citizens of the 3rd Category in tiny pieces, an eighth of a pound in weight, and this not daily by any means.

Horse-flesh was now the only dainty which people who could still call some money their own were able to set upon their tables. The authorities had formally approved it as an admissible "article of consumption," notwithstanding the fact that, following the consumption of bad horse-flesh, cases of severe poisoning had occurred among the population. The starving population's instinct of self-preservation was so acute that but little attention was paid to the risk of illness. In many country districts, especially near the front, people endangered their lives more directly in the endeavour to obtain food. On March 27, for example, the Red Army Staff announced in its *communiqué* that, after a fight in which ten dead horses had been left on the battlefield by the Whites, villagers had hurried out and endeavoured to remove the carcases under fire.

It was no longer rare to meet people here and there in the streets, evidently belonging to the upper classes, crying out in a shrill voice to every passer-by: "I'm hungry! I'm starving!" If by chance one happened to have anything eatable on one, and gave it to these unfortunates, they devoured it ravenously on the spot, with an expression as if they were convinced that death, evaded to-day, would surely overtake them to-morrow. One day I saw an old man lying prostrate on the pavement, so feeble that he could not hold the pieces of food which he was offered; he was carried into the nearest doorway, where he succumbed, released at last from his tortures.

Starvation, combined with the bitterly cold weather which was prevailing that winter, gave birth to various strange, malignant diseases such as scurvy, hunger-typhus and many others. Many of these diseases seemed to be of Asiatic origin. Most people who contracted them had no power of resistance on account of their starvation diet, and almost every case ended in swift but painful death.

Succumbing to these scourges, the population of the martyred town began to die off at an alarming rate. People died everywhere like flies—from starvation,

THE CITY OF THE RED PLAGUE

from disease, from exhaustion. Never since the devastating plagues of centuries before had death reaped such a rich harvest amongst this population. Many, driven to a state of desperation by hunger and general hopelessness, put an end to their own lives. In one case an unhappy mother, unable to bear the sufferings of hunger any longer, buried first her children and then herself in the snow. Such tragedies were of daily occurrence, and passed almost unnoticed.

In many houses one inhabitant after another died until at last only one person remained alive, and these survivors were left to die in misery without anyone troubling about them, or even, in many cases, seeing to the burial of the corpse. As these cases increased, the "Commissariat of Public Health" issued this regulation:

In view of the fact that the corpses of deceased persons possessing no relatives have of late often not been interred and have sometimes remained lying for fourteen days or more in their dwellings, it is hereby ordered that all caretakers and domestic servants shall see that all deaths occurring in the house are immediately reported to the Burial Section of the Commissariat for Public Health.

But this ukase helped very little. In numbers of houses, especially in the remoter parts of the town, corpses still lay unburied for days and weeks, and only when the odour of decomposition became so strong that it infected the whole neighbourhood did the Soviet authorities take steps to have the poor wretch's body removed and, with other victims, thrown into communal graves specially dug outside the town.

But even the relatives of others who had died in more humane circumstances could hardly find means to bury their dead decently and according to custom. The Red Army having requisitioned every horse that had not been slaughtered and eaten, the coffins even of prominent citizens could no longer be transported in hearses, but had to be drawn in carts by members of the family or by paid cemetery attendants. These funerals, which were followed, on account of the general fear of going into the streets, only by one or two mourners, and at which the minister could only hastily read the burial service, were amongst the most gruesome spectacles of those days so rich in horrors.

While the town was thus groaning under the Red Terror and the population seemed to be on the way to complete extinction, those who had brought this plague upon us seemed in no way concerned at the indescribable havoc they had wrought; indeed, they often expressed satisfaction with their handiwork, and their only thought seemed to be the provision of a maximum of pleasure, enjoyment and indulgence for themselves.

The Reds and their followers had installed themselves in the finest houses in the town. They took up their abode in the ancient castle, in the noble Ritterhaus, the headquarters of the Livonian nobility, in the historic club of the Black Heads, and in the best hotels. The immeasurable wealth they had stolen from the bourgeoisie they collected in numerous empty houses, which were turned into stores for the accumulated booty. In one of these places could be seen great piles of costly furs; in another, heaps of silver, jewellery and valuables of every kind; in a third, real mountains of furniture of every style and period.

"GUNWOMEN"

But what the Bolsheviks valued above all was clothing and linen. To secure it they plundered even the dead; they broke open one day the coffins temporarily deposited in one of the oldest churches in the town—St. Peter's—and stripped the corpses of their few ornaments and miserable garments.

While the town was starving, the Reds ate and drank gluttonously. The larders of innumerable private houses, the depots of the German Army administration, the foodshops, the provision-stores of every hotel, the wine cellars of all the nationalized restaurants and cafés—all had been plundered by these insatiable rascals. They had carried off endless sacks and cases of food and barrels of wine to their dwellings and stacked them up with the other stolen goods.

The houses of the Reds were filled with a variegated collection of furniture stolen from bourgeois houses and noblemen's country seats. They even took from castles and museums pieces of furniture which had been kept there simply as historical exhibits. Sitting on silk- and velvet-covered chairs, they dined off antique porcelain dishes taken down from the walls, and drank the oldest and noblest wines together with their coarse, self-brewed spirits out of silver goblets and golden chalices snatched from altars in the churches.

It was especially the official and unofficial wives of the Reds, the so-called "gunwomen," who were nothing but common soldiers' harlots, who plunged into the most shameless excesses and debaucheries. After these perverted man-women, with Russian fur caps on their heads and smart patent-leather shoes on their feet, had spent a busy day rushing from one house to another, spreading terror around them, in the evening they sought pleasure and amusement in their own crude and bawdy way. Decked out in stolen dance-frocks and expensive furs, with grotesque-looking ostrich-feather hats on their heads and pistols hanging at their hips, these red Furies ate and drank and amused themselves till they were sated and weary. But as soon as night came, they rose, worked up into a drunken frenzy, and staggered off, grinning inanely before them and uttering inarticulate noises, to the work of execution; they dragged the trembling captives from the prisons, and hurried them to the place of execution outside the town.

For as if the death of the bourgeois population in masses from hunger and disease were not enough for them, the Reds continued to shoot from time to time a few dozen people arbitrarily chosen from among the prisoners. The Red Terror became more and more severe. In the third month of Soviet rule hardly a week passed without the *Red Flag* publishing long lists of people shot. Among these one could often find the name of some friend or acquaintance. Especially when it happened that unfavourable news came from the front, the Revolutionary Tribunal always retaliated by executing a number of citizens.

The announcements by the Tribunal of these executions became constantly shorter and more cynical. They no longer even included a brief statement of the reasons for the condemnation of this or that citizen. They consisted merely of the phrase: "The Revolutionary Tribunal had decided at its last meeting to execute the following citizens," followed simply by a list, usually very long, of persons executed.

Most of the shootings took place in Bickern Wood, the same spot outside the town where the first citizens of Riga had been murdered. But there were days when the Red executioners could not be bothered to transport the condemned men so far outside the town, and preferred to shoot their victims in the courtyard of the same prison in which they had been confined until the hour of their death. And on these days people who lived in the neighbourhood of these prisons could plainly hear the shots and the dreadful cries of the people being murdered.

There grew up about this time, in those of us who survived, a feeling of revolt and indignation against the merciless cruelty of Providence. A passionate desire for life and freedom sprang to life in everyone. Appalled by the rapid dying out of the population, by the starvation, the spread of diseases and the ravages of the Red Terror, all abandoned hope. Panic-stricken, they recoiled from the plague-infested atmosphere which lay over the town and countryside, and caught hold of but one idea, one plan, the only remedy against pollution—the possibility of flight.

Flight! But it was strictly forbidden to leave the area of the town. The Red front stretched far into the west. One day a few daring fellows of my acquaintance had vaguely marched off towards the west in an attempt to get away; but as they were crossing the fighting-lines they had fallen into the hands of the Red troops. They had been found the following morning hanging from a tree.

This news finally extinguished the last spark of hope in the bravest hearts. "Caught! buried alive! doomed!" we all said to ourselves. We could say nothing else. And with a gloomy fatalism the citizens of Riga awaited events to come, abandoning once for all all thought of escape and salvation.

CHAPTER XI

THE FEAST DURING THE PLAGUE

We younger people had taken the collapse of the existing order of things more lightly than the old. We had not the same difficulty in reconciling ourselves to material losses and adapting ourselves to the new conditions. What we found hardest was the terrible dullness of existence and the lack of any kind of amusement or entertainment. We found ourselves suddenly deprived of everything that up to then had filled a large part of our existence: dancing, drinking, amusement,—in short, all the enjoyments of youth.

It was only natural that, seeing no possibility of escape from the plague-ridden town, the younger members of our community should be seized by a desire for distraction, for some means of shaking off, at least for awhile, the consciousness of the troubles and misery around them.

Some may think it far from admirable that at such a time young people's thoughts should centre round such frivolities as drinking, dancing and the latest jazz tune; that even when a modern deluge threatened to engulf the world around, a number of them should say: "What do we care for politics? Why should we worry about all this misery? We've had enough of moping about, we want to enjoy life!"

But it has always been so. It was so in the Middle Ages when the plague was raging in towns and villages; it was so in all the countries that were in the grip of the world war; and it was just the same in the days when the barbarian hordes held our town in their clutches....

Among those few friends of mine who had remained in the town and were still alive there was one in whose company I had often been in more care-free times, but whom I had not seen at all since the invasion. His name was Herbert Lang, and he had been at school with Roy Carlyle and myself.

Herbert Lang was one of those cheerful fellows who always have some kind of amusement up their sleeve. He was very popular among his numerous circle of friends, and was the leading spirit where any kind of entertainment was concerned. His skill and enterprise in arranging all sorts of parties were renowned amongst us. He was gifted with an agreeable musical talent; whenever he sat down at the piano during one of his parties he would always be the centre of attraction, and his snappy and humorous songs were invariably loudly applauded.

But all this belonged to bygone days. I could hardly conceive of this cheerful fellow existing in the midst of the present desolation of our town. I was therefore quite astonished when one day he suddenly gave a new sign of life.

Somoff brought me the announcement, early one morning, that Herbert was planning a party at his house and had invited Somoff and me to take part in it!

Lang, it appeared, took the view that one should not allow one's spirits to be completely crushed by the Red domination, shut oneself up permanently indoors and renounce all pleasures. The best way to face the evil was precisely to try to have a good time, to enjoy life while one still had life to enjoy.

All this seemed to me very extraordinary. Dance, drink, give parties! How on earth could it be done in this town of misery? Everybody had long ago given up inviting people to their homes. Besides, there was a strict regulation that no one might be in the streets after 8 p.m., and nobody in these times would ever have dared to spend a whole night away from home.

But the ingenious musician had hit on an excellent idea: to have his party in the daytime, but behind drawn blinds and by artificial light!

Moreover, he had got everything carefully planned out. The guests, in order not to attract attention on their way to his house, were to put on the shabbiest and most "proletarian"-looking overcoats they could find. But underneath they were requested to wear "the smartest clothes they still possessed." Everyone was to bring some contribution to the party in the way of food or drink, and to appear at his flat as early as possible, before eleven o'clock in the morning.

The guests numbered about a dozen young men and women who belonged to what remained of the so-called *jeunesse dorée* of the town. Somoff told me who they were to be—all people I had hardly seen since the day the Reds arrived.

When Somoff and I arrived at Lang's flat, the others were already assembled.

"Are you really alive?" said Herbert, opening the door, and obviously in the highest spirits, as of old.

In the hall Lyda, our host's wife, came forward to welcome us. She was a Russian, with rather exuberant manners and an abundance of rich, dark-red hair. Her face was elaborately made-up. Impulsively she embraced Somoff and me and exhibited every sign of delight at our coming.

"How glad I am," she said in a loud voice and with a strong Russian accent, "that we are going to have a little fun again after all these dreadfully dull weeks!"

Then she took us by the arm and led us into the next room, the so-called "salon" of her little artist's home.

Here everything looked extraordinarily gay and festive. Our host, as an artist, was treated by the Reds with rather more consideration than mere "bourgeois"; and he took the view that one could get on quite well with the Muscovites if one only set about it the right way. Their home was as yet untouched by marauders and had therefore retained its comfortable bourgeois appearance.

In preparation for this party, the apartment had undergone some peculiar transformations. Not only had the curtains been drawn, but thick felt had been nailed across the windows so that not a ray of daylight could penetrate. A number of candles diffused a quietly flickering light in the room, casting a strange glamour over the whole scene. To enter this unreal nocturnal atmosphere at such an early hour was a weird sensation, but it gave one at the same time the pleasant feeling of being suddenly shut off from the harrowing facts of day. One had a strong impression of having been suddenly and magically transported to another world and being present at some peace-time evening party.

Somoff and I stood for a moment in the doorway,

THE FEAST DURING THE PLAGUE 169

full of admiration. But our hostess led us on to the other guests. We saw before us a group of young ladies, all— a new surprise—in gay frocks, evening-dresses, which no one now dared to wear. These gaily dressed, pretty young girls made at first glance a quite unnatural impression; we had been accustomed for so long to look on nothing but misery and poverty that the very sight of ordinary bright-coloured evening-dresses suggested a masked ball. The girls seemed to feel the same, for they appeared at first quite awkward and self-conscious in their dainty costumes.

Among the girls I noticed a former friend of my own; a fair-haired young thing, a Baltic baroness who belonged to a Livonian family ruined by Bolshevism. She had once belonged to our gay circle. Once! For now all her relatives and most of her friends had fled or been shot or died in some other way, and she was left alone in this stricken city to struggle for herself.

"I think you know each other," said the hostess, after we had greeted all the other guests, and had finally come up to an exceedingly smartly dressed man standing a little to one side. He squinted slightly and did not look one straight in the face, and there was a certain oiliness about his personality that made a disagreeable impression at once.

Yes, we had met him, though in quite different circumstances. He was a man named Yermoloff, a former Russian officer whom we had known in Petrograd; he was really a Kalmuck and came from Orenburg, but the war had brought him to Riga, and here he lived without any definite occupation. Since the entry of the Reds he had been suspected, along with a few other unprincipled young men, of maintaining relations of a dubious character with them in return for material advantages.

It was a most disagreeable surprise to most of us to see him there, and it was due to his unexpected presence, it seemed to me, that the atmosphere at the beginning of the party was somewhat restrained, and the guests were rather slow in working up the gaiety demanded by the occasion.

But soon Lyda, who had grown impatient, opened another door and we all went into the dining-room.

A murmur of surprise and admiration broke out: we were standing before a table laid for a peace-time banquet! Bread in plenty, dishes with all sorts of hors d'œuvres on them, numerous bottles of wine, and in the middle—a real joint of meat. The table was covered with snow-white linen. The wine-glasses sparkled. The hostess had even produced flowers and green foliage from somewhere and had decorated the table and the whole room with them. Involuntarily I thought—how had the Langs managed it?

Of course, everybody had undertaken to bring some contribution—something to eat or drink—to the communal feast, and everyone had brought what he could: one a tin of sardines he had held in reserve for weeks; another a pound of butter obtained with difficulty in exchange for an article of clothing; a third a bottle of pure spirit from the medicine-chest. But there was very much more than that.

It soon appeared that most of it had been provided by our host himself, and a large part of it by the mysterious Yermoloff: both possessed a friend among the Soviet authorities who had control of "requisitioned" food supplies. From this source they had obtained the bread, various preserves, some sausages and the wine.

In one corner of the dining-room, not far from the table, was an open piano. But the guests' attention was concentrated for the moment on the food on the table.

We gazed upon this amazing feast as if we could devour it with our looks alone.

"Supposing the Reds could see that!" one or two of us could not help exclaiming at the sight of the table furnished with such "bourgeois" exuberance.

But our host at once broke in. "Ladies and gentlemen," he cried, raising his hands to command attention, "no politics to-day! Not a word about Bolshevik rule and all the rest of it. That is a condition to-day." He added smiling: "If anyone talks politics he'll get nothing to eat."

Then, as we were getting ourselves seated, Herbert sat down at the piano and began to play.

The words and tunes of the pieces he played to us that day have long since gone out of my mind. I can remember clearly only one song. It had the somewhat banal but alluring refrain: "Friends, life is smiling. . . . Friends, love is calling. . . ." The music of it was a waltz tune which began dreamily and languorously, but soon went into a rhythmical, passionate swing and really had something infectiously intoxicating about it.

We sat round the table looking at the food and listening to Herbert's songs. At first everybody hesitated to begin eating. It seemed that no one wanted to show the others how ravenous he was. Yermoloff was the first to attack the food, perhaps because he was the only one who was not actually half-starving. Then we all followed his example and began to eat with ill-concealed greed. No one said a word.

"Exactly like peace-time!" Herbert's wife broke the silence at last, and she gave a loud shrill laugh.

"Just like Europe!" echoed the Baltic baroness from the other end of the table; she had found a seat next to Yermoloff and was a little tipsy after her first glass.

The conversation now became livelier, and soon came round to the favourite topic of the times: how things were going on in Western Europe. There people could eat and drink as much as they liked; there were theatres, cafés; anyone who wanted to could go to a hall and dance.

In Europe, in Germany, in France. . . . We had almost forgotten what life was like in those blessed regions. We ourselves were beginning to feel like wild Asiatics buried in the depths of Tartary. A Wall of China seemed to separate us from the Occident, and the world beyond that wall appeared in our imagination like some remote Paradise.

The women among the guests expressed their curiosity with particular energy and insistence. They bombarded their table companions with a flood of questions which nobody could possibly answer, mostly of this kind: "I wonder what the popular songs are now in Berlin!" . . . "What kind of dances are being danced in London?" . . . "What's the fashionable colour in Paris?" and so on.

Lyda kept on asking the same question, in a loud voice: "Are they wearing long or short skirts abroad? Long or short? Long or short?"

Words like "jazz," "cocktail," "Montmartre," etc., were bandied from one end of the table to the other; but all the questions remained hanging in the air unanswered. A sorrowful voice gave expression to the general feeling, "We are cut off from the whole world!"

Yermoloff pricked up his ears. He had not said a word the whole time. Only his squinting eyes had kept wandering stealthily from one person to another.

But Herbert was determined that his party was not going to be spoilt by gloomy reflections or by any kind of unpleasant incidents. . . . "If you please," he interrupted vehemently, "I said we weren't going to talk politics." And, as though to distract his guests from their gloomy thoughts, he went back to the piano and began to play again, loudly, with full chords, so as to drown the unpleasant conversation.

It quickly became evident that most of the young people present, having been underfed for weeks, could not stand much alcohol; they soon became noticeably merry, talking and laughing loudly all at once, without caring whether anyone was listening and what others were saying.

An hour passed like this, and the party was in full swing, when one of the guests suddenly cried out in alarm:

"Be quiet! Somebody knocked! There's someone knocking at the front door!"

The guests held their breath. . . . Yes, from the landing really came the sound of sharp, angry blows with fists against a door. . . . But it was not our door. It was that of a neighbouring flat.

Now we could clearly hear another sound: the

mechanical throbbing of a motor-car waiting outside in the street. For whom could it be? Names of other people living in the house were uttered. Theories were exchanged in hushed tones. Then everyone strained his ears again in silence. On the landing all was now quiet.

Then, as we listened, we heard the slamming of doors, the low sobbing of a woman, the heavy tramp of soldiers' boots on the stairs, and at last the sound of the car outside driving away.... The tension was relaxed.

"It was next door," said Yermoloff indifferently. He alone had remained calm and detached during this scene, coolly smoking and drinking, as if to show that in any case he knew that nothing could happen to *him*.

The others looked at him in surprise. Then they too breathed more freely, and soon the conversation, singing and laughter were as loud and unrestrained as before.

An hour later most of the party were drunk.

The table looked like a battlefield after the slaughter. Plates covered with the remains of food, overturned bottles, half-filled glasses with cigarette-ends floating in them were jumbled together in an unappetising mess. The chairs had been pushed far back from the table. Most of the people were sprawling about in them mindless of decorum; several guests of both sexes, indeed, had disappeared.

One of the guests was gently dozing with his head sunk on his chest. Another, with a fixed expression, was noisily singing out incoherent words. A third had got up and was cutting queer, erratic capers on the floor in an attempt, apparently, to demonstrate some dance step.

Lyda, the pleasure-loving mistress of the house, had let down her rich, dark-red hair, and, full of sweet wine, had thrown herself upon the breast of her neighbour; large tears rolled down her cheeks, leaving distinct tracks on her rouged and powdered skin. Yermoloff's blonde neighbour, the Baltic baroness, was leaning right back in her chair, singing loudly to herself; her blouse had come undone and one of her slender, girlish shoulders was uncovered.

Our host himself, oblivious of the clamour around him, was still playing the piano and singing his own popular song, "Friends, life is smiling. . . . Friends, love is calling. . . ." But the song no longer had the same rhythm and swing as before, and was only audible in spasmodic snatches.

Somoff, Yermoloff and I seemed to be the only sober members of the party. Yermoloff had drunk a good deal, but he could stand a lot, and was not even exhilarated. He had only lost his sneaking shyness and behaved more confidently and boldly than at the beginning of the party.

He had now laid his right arm round his neighbour's bare shoulder and was attempting to draw her to him. The blonde baroness laughed and rapped Yermoloff's greedily clutching fingers with a fork she was holding. But the Kalmuck became more and more persistent; he drew the girl to him by force and covered her heated face with kisses. As he leant over to do this he knocked over several glasses, which fell jingling to the floor and were smashed to pieces.

Somoff and I looked at each other. Each understood what the other was thinking. We knew by what means Yermoloff was accustomed to achieve his ends, the kind of blackmail he employed, the nature of the price to be paid. We had known that sort in Russia.

Somoff muttered something between clenched teeth, but I could only catch a word here and there on account of the noise. But I understood; his opinion of Yermoloff was the same as mine, as everybody's.

Yermoloff pretended to have heard nothing. He did not release his neighbour. He had risen, and was pulling the girl away from the table. But I saw a swift look of malignant hatred shot at my friend from his narrow, treacherous eyes. . . .

The man at once terrified and disgusted me. I felt that I could no longer remain in the room. The air, too, was stuffy and full of smoke. I got up and went into the next room, the sitting-room. Here it was quieter and more agreeable. I turned round and looked through the open door into the room which I had just left. Seen from here, through the smoke, the gesticulating crowd of revellers appeared to me like an assembly of phantoms in a far-away mist.

An irresistible craving for fresh air and daylight came over me. I went to the window, violently pulled aside a corner of the felt curtains and looked cautiously into the street to see if it was for the moment free from Red soldiers, and whether it might be possible to open a window at least for a second or two.

Brilliant daylight burst upon me. Outside—the glorious sunshine of a lovely spring day was pouring down. The light was so strong that for the first second my eyes, accustomed to the candle-light of the artificially darkened room, were painfully blinded and I could see hardly anything at all.

But that only lasted for a fraction of a minute. The moment my eyes could see again clearly and just as my hand had already caught hold of the handle to open the window, a spectacle so horrifying met my gaze that my hand dropped and I was held as though glued to the spot, staring through the closed window, breathlessly into the street.

In the middle of the otherwise deserted and lifeless street there was slowly passing a procession more grotesque and *macabre* than anything I have seen in my life.

In front of a large four-wheeled dung-cart, such as the Reds now used for compulsory labour of the bourgeoisie, were harnessed about twenty citizens of Riga, slowly and painfully dragging the cart along the street!

The old men were clothed in miserable rags. Some were barefooted, others were shod with rough wooden clogs. Most of them had long, shaggy beards. Nevertheless I thought I could recognize among them well-known personalities—a former Mayor of Riga, a bank director, a retired general, a lawyer, a big business man, a Livonian country gentleman, an old clergyman and one or two others. They had all been once well-to-do, respected citizens, now they looked like beggars. They were all so terribly emaciated that, with their hollow cheeks, greenish-yellow faces and sunken, dark-ringed eyes, they now looked like beings risen from the grave.

About ten of them were attached by long traces to the vehicle, like horses; three others pulled the cart on either side, while the rest pushed feebly from behind. In spite of their combined efforts, the cart, although it was almost empty, moved forward only extremely slowly as the men painfully put one foot before the other, with long pauses between each step.

The grim and ghostly procession suggested to me a throng of spirits of the underworld, condemned to perform some never-ending labour of Sisyphus.

Their torture was further increased by a horde of "gunwomen" who, armed to the teeth, escorted the prisoners, driving them on with rifle-butts and vile abuse. The wretched men could not dream of resisting; completely apathetic and resigned to their fate, with heads sunk on their chests and eyes fixed on the ground, they dragged themselves wearily forward without uttering a single word of complaint. The only sound that came from them was the clapping of their wooden clogs on the paving-stones, echoing uncanny and sinister in the midst of the churchyard silence which hung over the town.

I gazed in silence at the procession as it came slowly nearer and nearer. It was now quite close, and began to pass right under the window at which I was standing. I could see each of the figures more clearly; and as I looked, I saw one of the victims slowly raise his pallid face towards me. His face seemed more familiar to me than the others. Could it be poor Walter? He made a motion of his head as if to look up to the window, with unnaturally wide-open eyes staring into vacancy, and an expression of unspeakable despair. I let the curtain fall, and, completely shaken, retired into the lighted room.

With my head in a whirl, I wandered back to the party of revellers in the inner room. The scene which I found there now seemed to me insipid and idiotic. I wanted to rush out into the street, interfere somehow, help. . . . These thoughts kept hammering at my brain; but—was it cowardice? was it common sense?—something held my feet back, paralysed my will.

I gazed blankly at the revellers. Not one of them had any suspicion of the passing of that mournful procession. They went on drinking and shouting.

I did nothing. The din of the revelry rang in my ears. In the midst of the crazy strumming of the piano and the wild clamour of that drunken orgy, the same absurd refrain kept on recurring:

"Friends, life is smiling. . . . Friends, love is calling. . . ."

CHAPTER XII

A SIGN IN THE SKY

After long weeks of blank, unrelieved desolation there happened, one day in March, an unexpected event: up in the blue spring sky, high above the silent town, appeared an aeroplane.

When this event occurred I happened by chance to be out of doors. Together with the two ladies of our house, the old and the young Frau Walter, I had gone out in order to renew the search for our lost friend. We had just arrived on the chief square of the town—the Esplanade. As the drone of the aeroplane became audible, we halted and looked up into the sky.

The appearance of this aerial visitor caused something of a sensation. It was the first aeroplane that had flown above Riga since the German troops had evacuated the town just before the Reds arrived. We had not yet seen any Soviet aeroplanes. Everyone imagined the Baltic Volunteers to have been pushed back so far that this could scarcely be a White airman. It was therefore with rather puzzled curiosity that everyone gazed upwards at the new-comer.

He was flying at first in wide, leisurely circles very high up. But presently he began to descend lower and lower—so boldly that he must surely be a Red airman. But now we could see the marks on the wings—not the five-pointed Red star that a Bolshevist aeroplane might be expected to carry, but a symmetrical black cross—the sign of the Volunteer force, our friends and liberators! Could it be possible?

Now the airman was skimming just above our heads, so low that he seemed almost within reach. Several times he cruised over the town, which had swiftly sprung to life at his coming. Men and women poured into the streets. But the people of Riga had to restrain themselves from manifesting their joy too openly, from spontaneously waving their greetings to the airman. Their faces bore only an expression of blank astonishment, which could hardly be distinguished from painfully repressed joy.

Upon the Red soldiers and "gunwomen" who were lounging about the streets the effect produced by the White airman was quite different. Some unslung their rifles and fired at random. Others, who were unarmed, rushed, as though bitten by scorpions, into various buildings and hastily brought out arms; others fumbled in their holsters with trembling fingers and then began to shoot at the aeroplane with their revolvers.

For about a quarter of an hour they banged away, making a noise like a rifle-range. With half-frightened, half-angry faces the Reds shot unceasingly into the sky, swearing frantically all the while. But all in vain.

The White airman in the firmament seemed to pay not the slightest attention to the shooting and yelling of the excited hordes below him. He continued serenely to describe his graceful circles. In wide curves he flew once more round the whole town. And only when he had apparently seen everything that he wished to see, he flew away, calm and majestic, in the direction of the west, whence he had so unexpectedly come with his message of good cheer.

The angry curses of the Reds followed him. But no less warm were the blessings with which the citizens of Riga sent him on his way. . . .

When the airman had at last vanished from our sight, the two ladies and I set off again on our way. It led us towards a spot outside the town where we hoped we should see the arrested Walter again.

His mother's unwearying investigations had at last established the fact that he was still alive and was, as I felt certain, one of the poor wretches who had to draw the dung-carts escorted by "gunwomen."

Walter—they had managed to find out—was being kept in strict confinement in one of the worst prisons of the town, the Central Prison; to speak to him there or even to catch a fleeting glimpse of him was entirely out of the question; this might be possible, however—so the relatives of other prisoners had told them—outside the prison, during the daily procession. Several of these dung-cart processions went from one end of the town to the other twice a day. The citizens harnessed to the carts were obliged to transport dung and refuse from various prisons and Soviet offices during the morning to a refuse dump lying outside the town; and in the afternoon they had to return with the empty carts.

Numerous relatives of other prisoners, mostly women, had already tried to approach their fathers, husbands or sons during the waits at the refuse dump. For hours they had waited at a little distance. But all their troubles had as yet led to nothing. The "gunwomen" guarded the prisoners too strictly; they were not amenable to any kind of bribe and invariably drove off the poor mothers and wives with curses and threats.

Providence had, however, suddenly been kind to these poor people. By a lucky chance it happened that, only two days after my discovery, the prisoners' carts were escorted not by "gunwomen" but by ordinary Red soldiers. The women, by combining all their resources, had managed to bribe the new guards to allow them to see their relatives and bring them help.

As soon as Frau Walter and her daughter-in-law had heard of this they had immediately packed up a few eatables and clothes which they had kept ready and set out for the municipal refuse dump. They had asked me to accompany them; and, thinking that my Red student's card might possibly be of some help to them, I had willingly agreed to go.

The municipal refuse dump was situated a good way from the town, and we hurried in order not to be late. When we at last reached it we saw that we had arrived in time: the men undergoing forced labour had just been unharnessed from the carts and many were already talking to their relations.

The scene at the refuse dump was extraordinary. In the middle stood several carts full of manure and all kinds of evil-smelling refuse. Some of the prisoners—former land-owners, business men, lawyers, doctors and other well-known local personalities—had mounted the carts and were throwing their repulsive contents on to the ground with shovels. Other gentlemen were standing below and spreading the filth over the field with forks and spades. A number of ladies of Riga society were moving about amongst the prisoners, carrying baskets and bottles and offering the men food and drink. The prisoners eagerly accepted the proffered gifts, with timid glances at the guards. People who had once been accustomed to eat with silver forks and spoons could be seen hastily snatching pieces of black bread with grimy hands, stuffing it blindly into their mouths and greedily swallowing it.

Some of the women had brought their children with them, many of them almost babies. They chattered loudly and merrily, not understanding why their fathers were engaged on this wearisome task and why tears were running down their mothers' cheeks.

A little to one side we observed the following picture. On a pile of wooden boards sat one of the prisoners; he had a pale, refined-looking face in which his eyes shone with an almost supernatural brilliance; he had thrown his shovel aside and was resting for a moment. In his arms he held a small boy of hardly four, his child; the little one sat grave and silent, its curly head pressed against its father's chest. The prisoner's wife and elder son stood by them. The wife, young and fair with big blue eyes, had a faint smile on her lips: but the lad—hardly more than a child—looked down at his father with an expression of profound sorrow which it was terrible to see on so young a face. A book lay open on the knees of the prisoner and he was reading aloud from it in a low voice. It was the New Testament. The others listened in silence.

Some of the Red soldiers of the guard prowled round the prisoners like wolves, with their rifles slung; but they did not interfere; the prisoners' wives had given them not only money, but food and cigarettes as well. They therefore allowed the men to talk to their relations and rest somewhat longer than usual.

Some of the prisoners had lain down to rest in the field among the manure. We went from group to group and, after some enquiry, found Walter sitting with two companions on a little mound of earth. All three were gnawing at a small chunk of the earthy bread which the Soviet rulers supplied gratis to the citizens, whether free or imprisoned.

The two women turned pale when, instead of the man they knew, they saw a clothed skeleton. He himself could hardly utter a word for astonishment. His mother embraced him without saying a word. His deaf wife, on the contrary, immediately began to cry, and, amidst tears and sobs, to enquire about her husband's welfare: "Would he soon be free? "Was he comfortable in prison?" "How long would it all last?" she wanted to know. Walter hardly heard her. He hastily seized the few food supplies which we had brought—bread, cheese and a little meat—gave part to his fellow-prisoners and began to eat with obvious satisfaction. We watched him a little while in silence.

Then we spoke of the aeroplane which had so suddenly appeared over the town that very morning and had aroused such excitement everywhere. Yes, the prisoners had seen it too, though they were even more at a loss than ourselves as to the significance of the visit. It had nevertheless awakened fresh hope among them also, and they were in much better spirits to-day, Walter said, than usual. Then he returned to the food question, which obviously interested him more than anything else. "Come again soon, and bring something more to eat!" he said.

The visit had come to an end. A Red soldier, apparently the leader of the guard, walked through the rows of prisoners and their relatives and shouted right and left in a rough voice: "Enough! You've been talking long enough! Disperse! To work! Get on, get on!"

We hastily said good-bye to Walter, promising to return as soon as possible, and set off homeward together with the other visitors. At the edge of the refuse dump, before turning into the street which flanked it, we looked back once more. The women tried to wave a last good-bye to their men, to snatch a last farewell look.

But the prisoners could no longer look in our direction: the guards were busy harnessing them to the dung-carts again, exactly like beasts of burden, and were beginning to drive them away, with shouts and oaths, in the opposite direction, back to the prisons.

·   ·   ·   ·   ·

We made our way home. About two hours had passed since we had stood on the Esplanade and watched the aeroplane flying over the town. The appearance of the White airman seemed in the meantime to have set the whole town humming. The townspeople had forgotten their usual timidity and were showing themselves without fear in the streets. Everywhere we met people, acquaintances and strangers, excitedly discussing the event.

Very soon we found out something more: the airman, we were told, had not departed without leaving tangible souvenirs of his visit. Here and there he had dropped small leaflets bearing a message "to the population of Riga," exhorting them "not to lose heart, but to continue to hold out and be confident that deliverance is at hand."

At last! Here at any rate was something definite, a promise, a sign to which one could pin one's faith.

But the Reds at once took "rigorous measures" to suppress the "seditious propaganda." These little pieces of white paper provoked them to fury. Anyone found with one of the leaflets was at once pounced upon and put safely under lock and key.

In spite of this, the message of the leaflets spread with amazing swiftness through the whole town. When we got home we found that even my parents and my sister, who had been at home all day, knew every detail of what had happened.

For the next few days the people of the town talked of nothing else but the appearance of the White aeroplane and the comforting message which it had brought. Rumours sprang up, took definite shape: the Red Army, it was whispered, before Libau, had met with resistance from the Volunteer Corps; the Balts had received reinforcements from the side of the Germans; great things were impending....

Some of the more sanguine persons even went so far as to declare with the utmost assurance that "now the recapture of the town could only be a question of days, at the very most of a week or two," and that "all our troubles would now soon be over." But there were others, more cautious, who had always been pessimistic hitherto, and now repeatedly warned their friends against exaggerated hopes, dwelling on the inevitability of reverses and, above all, the possibility of Red reprisals.

A few days went by, and, indeed, nothing happened. The sceptics seemed to be right. The enthusiasm of the optimists began to fade away. The population found itself gradually forgetting the appearance of the aeroplane and the rumours which had followed it. Life in the city became just as it had been before the White airman's appearance. In fact, it was rather worse.

The Reds, as if to show that they still held power firmly in their hands in spite of all disquieting rumours from the front, took advantage of this pause to inflict on the town a whole series of new and draconic regulations. During these days a regular hail of decrees beat down upon the long-suffering heads of the people of Riga. The intention was that the State should take over the few institutions of public life which, for want of time or by oversight, the Reds had so far neglected to Bolshevize. Baths, photographic studios, family vaults, barbers' shops, and other hotbeds of capitalism were now to be nationalized.

No conceivable form of activity was to remain unadapted to the "Red" ideas, or allowed to continue without being reorganized on a Communistic basis: sowing and reaping, language and spelling, marriage and the education of children, art and amusement, sickness and death. In short, we were surrounded and hedged in by a perfect forest of regulations and laws, in the labyrinth of which the confused citizen could do no more than flounder in helpless bewilderment.

At this time the Commissary for Food Supply issued a decree forbidding anyone to keep in his home supplies

A SIGN IN THE SKY

for more than one day. The Commissary for Home Affairs fixed the amount of furniture a bourgeois family might possess at "one wardrobe, two chests of drawers, two tables, six stools, etc." And to prevent people from handing over their "superfluous" furniture to others, a decree was issued by the head of the Red militia forbidding anyone to appear in the street with any article of furniture, trunk, box, bag or even a parcel of any kind without special permission.

The President of the Soviet of Workers' Deputies, Simon Berg, showed especial zeal at this time. This was the same man who about one month earlier had solicited from the Riga bourgeoisie the "voluntary delivery" of a part of their clothes and linen. Now, presumably irritated by the rumours from the front, he came to the conclusion that "the first deliveries had not been sufficient." And, in order to make good this deficiency, he published (in the *Red Flag*, No. 51) the following ukase:

FOR THE INFORMATION OF THE BOURGEOISIE OF RIGA

In view of the very perceptible shortage of clothes, linen and footwear for the equipment of our heroic fighters and the recently enrolled volunteers, the Council of Workmen's Deputies of Riga on the 15th of February imposed a tax in kind in clothes, linen and footwear upon the bourgeoisie of Riga, and invited them to give back to the people of their own free will a small part of the wealth which in the course of centuries they have wrongfully appropriated. In spite of this categorical order and the threat of the Revolutionary Tribunal, most of the bourgeoisie has nevertheless preferred to ignore the invitation. Only a few of its members have considered it necessary to fulfil this injunction.

Do they think, perhaps, that they can deceive the institutions of the proletarian power by secreting and hiding away their superfluous reserves of clothing? You need not trouble yourselves! We will find them even if you have concealed them who knows where! We will force you to fetch them out of their nooks, corners and hiding-places and to carry them on your backs to the places indicated by us. The dictatorship of the proletariat is no empty word! The heavy hand of the proletariat will crush mercilessly every person who may seek to obstruct or to disobey its commands. Maybe you do not like the Revolutionary Tribunal? Very well, we know of a quicker way for you: we can settle matters with you on the spot! Every person who does not carry out the directions of the institutions of the proletarian power or violates them is a deliberate counter-revolutionary and as such will receive the deserved punishment.

In view of the above statements the Council of Workmen's Deputies of Riga announces that, as a measure of punishment for the non-fulfilment of the above-mentioned order, the bourgeoisie will not be left even the minimum amount of clothes which has been fixed for them, but *all their clothes, with the exception of those they are wearing on their bodies*, will be taken from them. Every bourgeois must convey them within 24 hours to a place indicated by our representatives. In case of resistance to our representatives, concealment of clothing, deception, or failure to deliver the clothing at the time and place fixed, those guilty will be punished by the extreme penalty, without trial before the Revolutionary Tribunal. To this Tribunal only those counter-revolutionaries whose case needs investigation will be referred. When, however, the disobedience is open and premeditated, it will not be necessary to wait long for the punishment. We do not permit our orders to be violated or ignored. Whoever violates them, on him the sun will smile no more!

The President of the Soviet of Riga:
SIMON BERG

As a result of this regulation, hundreds of men and women, mostly old, were to be seen the next day carrying their remaining clothes, boots and linen on their own backs to the "receiving office." There they were rudely questioned, abused and jeered at. Basing their demands on deliberately fictitious calculations and figures, the Red militia men demanded of them more than they actually possessed, and many of them, frightened by the threats, actually went to secret dealers, obtained from them, in exchange for their last penny, the "missing articles" and then laid these at the feet of their insatiable rulers.

The Soviet rulers dealt with the goods taken from the Riga bourgeois in a way which was certainly rather original. The entire confiscated merchandise was placed for the time being under the control of a Red "economic council." This body distributed part of the booty to the soldiers of the Red Army, to members of the Communist Party and to other people belonging to the Soviet following. The remainder, however, it disposed of in a more ingenious manner.

Comrade Stutchka had, at the beginning of March, concluded treaties with the sister republics of the Ukraine and Turkestan. These two Soviet Republics had plundered their own bourgeoisies, consisting mostly of land-owners and manufacturers, with equal thoroughness. Their booty, however, had been of a different nature from that in Riga, the town of merchants and business men. It had consisted principally of corn, rice, wool, cotton, soap, fish, dried fruit, etc. This difference in the results here and there naturally suggested an exchange. And this was the purpose of the treaties concluded according to all the rules of international statecraft and duly sealed with various Soviet seals: Soviet Ukraine and Soviet Turkestan were to deliver to starving Riga the "raw materials" stolen from the Ukrainian and Turkestan land-owners, while Soviet Latvia would send to the towns of Kieff and Tashkent a few goods trains loaded with clothes, linen, boots, clocks, furniture and other useful "manufactured articles" extracted from the bourgeois of Riga. The Soviets called this a "national economic exchange of merchandise" and were, as always, not a little proud of this contribution to economic science.

With the Soviet leaders displaying this redoubled eagerness to hurry the work of Bolshevization to its conclusion, Pastor Model naturally could not keep silent. Rejected by his community, he became more and more fanatical, as though in defiance. He saw everywhere "signs and portents" which, in his opinion, made the present moment particularly favourable for the renewal of mankind on a Communistic basis.

"Never," he wrote in the *Red Flag*—in the number containing Comrade Simon Berg's bloodthirsty threats and the news of the "exchange of goods" treaties—"has the time been so favourable for an awakening as now!" He called Jesus Christ "the first Communist in the world's history" and urged the people of Riga not to worry so much about "the unpleasantnesses of everyday life," which were after all quite trifling, but rather to reflect more carefully on the real significance of the parable of the vineyard.

Referring to St. Matthew xxi. 33–46; St. Mark xii. 1–12, and St. Luke xx. 9–19, Pastor Model declared that "this world around us is not given us as a possession or as property! There exists only one true attitude, based on justice, towards the goods of this world: the right of ownership of the vineyard belongs to One only—to the Lord alone! We are all only His tenants, we are all only His workers, we are obliged to render the fruits of the vineyard to the Lord. Anyone who does not construct his life on this basis, on this foundation, must strike himself against this granite block and be irreparably crushed by it."

Then, turning from the general to the particular, the Red Pastor referred directly to Russian Bolshevism: "Does not the literal fulfilment of that which Jesus described in His parable of the vineyard stand clearly before the eyes of all of us?" he wrote. "Russia! How great, how rich was once the blessed vineyard of the Lord in this land! And how foolishly did the wicked husbandmen there make use of their priceless wealth! How just was the revolt of the Russian proletariat, because the husbandmen of the vineyard kept back the fruits from the real owner, and took them for themselves! They forgot that we can only lay the fruits of the vineyard before God if we give them to our brothers and sisters. The husbandmen of the vineyard in Russia did not understand that. And a fearful judgment fell upon them: everything that they considered their own property, that they thought to be sacred and inviolable, everything, literally everything, was taken away from them and given to those who up to then had had no portion of the fruits of the Russian vineyard."

And in conclusion: "So it will happen to everybody! Woe to all those in other lands who retain the fruits of the vineyard as their own property and possession —at the expense of those standing without, who also desire to dwell within the vineyard! From them also will the vineyard be taken away. The same punishment awaits them!"

CHAPTER XIII

THE FIRST RESISTANCE

About a fortnight after the appearance of the White aeroplane we learnt that, as if by a miracle, the hitherto unchecked advance of the Muscovites had at last been arrested!

We now had reliable information on the subject. The Bolshevist forces had met with resistance from the White Army for the first time a few weeks before; but not only that—at the beginning of March the Whites had opened a counter-offensive; in West Courland, in the neighbourhood of Libau and the sea, the Baltic Volunteers had recaptured several places from the Reds, among them the port of Windau. The Red troops in that sector were slowly falling back. The Red General Staff itself announced these facts. Everything was set down in black and white in the *Red Flag*. There could thus be no doubt about the truth of the reports.

It was the 11th of March when the news of this decisive turn of events reached us. That morning, perusing the Soviet paper and turning, as usual, with all haste to the war news, I saw the first official admission of a definite retirement of the Red Army. The Red Staff, which hitherto had provided nothing but bulletins of victory, now issued the following report in a minor key:

In the direction of Libau we abandoned the Kursiten estate under heavy pressure from the enemy. In the sector near the small town of Ringen the enemy attacked with heavy forces and compelled our troops to retire. In the direction of Windau there has been an engagement with detachments of White troops. The result is still unknown.

Most of the occupants of our house were surprised and highly delighted at the good news. My father, as usual, was a trifle sceptical. As an old soldier, he was always more sober in his judgments than most people. He pointed out that the two ports of Libau and Windau lay on the extreme western coast of Latvia and were more than 100 miles from Riga. The small changes taking place on that distant front could hardly have a great effect on the situation in our town.

Nevertheless, a few days after this we learnt that this time matters were not going to end there. As early as the 15th of March the Staff of the Red Army was obliged to admit a further and this time much more considerable retreat of the Bolshevist troops. The Staff now named two localities—Tuckum and Schlock—situated much closer to Riga; their mention proved that the Reds had in the past few days been pushed back an astonishing distance.

What did it all mean? Between the places mentioned in the Staff report of the 11th and those in that of the 15th of March lay a distance of nearly 60 miles. The small towns of Tuckum and Schlock were both only a short way from Mitau, which itself lay barely 25 miles to the west of Riga. Consequently the Whites, within four days of the beginning of their advance, had put behind them more than half of the distance which had originally separated them from us. It was obvious, therefore, that this was a case of a regular

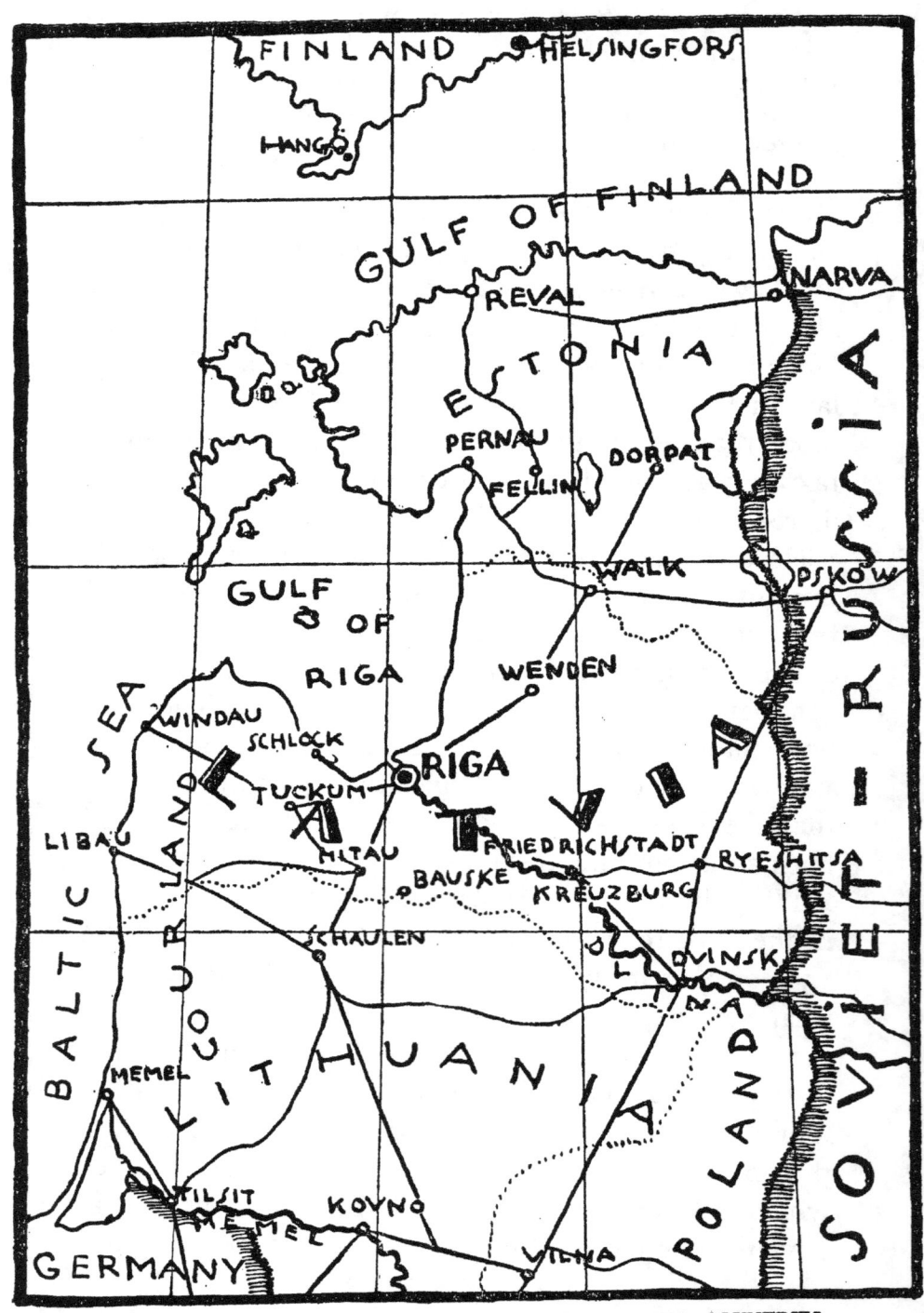

ROUGH MAP OF LATVIA AND THE NEIGHBOURING COUNTRIES

THE FIRST RESISTANCE

offensive undertaken with powerful forces after elaborate preparation.

Great news, if it was really so! Movement seemed at last to have come into the situation. The Muscovite phalanx had shown itself to be less unshakeable than we had at first supposed. The party of the optimists now gained strength visibly.

But when would deliverance come—when, when?

Next day we learned some details about what had been going on at the front during the last 48 hours. All kinds of people had fled from the battle area and had reached Riga. Their stories passed from mouth to mouth.

The reports of these refugees, however, were not all of an encouraging nature. Certainly, they told us, the Whites were strong enough to wrest one town after another from the Reds; but some places—Tuckum, for instance—which they had captured on one day, they had been forced to relinquish on the next. That the Whites had won a victory there could be no doubt; but whether they would be strong enough to hold the fruits of their victories, to push on farther, to win Riga, to rescue *us* from the domination of the Reds—nobody could yet foretell with certainty.

But while we were all puzzling our heads over this question, the Reds had become very uneasy. The unexpectedly rapid forward movement of the Volunteer Corps had spread bewilderment amongst them also. With the greatest haste they carried out all kinds of measures, the intention of which it was not difficult to guess.

On the roofs of some of the corner houses dominating the streets leading to the river they set up machine-gun posts. To the workers with Communistic sympathies they distributed arms, ammunition and extra money, double food rations and quantities of gifts in the form of valuable articles confiscated from the bourgeois. The Red soldiers received in addition a considerable rise in their wages.

In the banks a number of safes and money-chests which had not as yet been properly plundered were now burst open in a great hurry with the aid of explosives and crowbars. Passers-by heard loud reports and the sound of smashing coming from the strong-rooms of the banks. A few hours later Red soldiers were seen carrying off the contents of the safes crammed into large sacks and cases. A portion of it was used to pay wages to the "gallant defenders of Red Riga," the bulk of it was despatched that very day by train to Moscow under a military guard.

The Red leaders, indeed, from all appearances, were actually planning a gradual evacuation of the town. They seemed to be already reckoning with the possibility of being forced to give it up. At any rate, a series of exceedingly noteworthy happenings pointed definitely to this.

Numerous officials of the Soviet administration packed up their belongings; heavily laden transport wagons rattled through the streets; telephone and telegraph wires were hastily dismantled, often forcibly torn down; trunks and boxes were brought out from different Soviet administrative buildings; and lorry after lorry, heavily loaded, rolled off towards the station, towards that station whence the railway track led eastward into the Muscovite Empire.

This departure of a part of the Red hordes could be observed particularly clearly at night. The citizens were forbidden to walk in the streets after 8 p.m. The Reds who were making off, therefore, generally chose the night hours for their departure. They did this partly to avoid the impression of a panic, partly in order to carry off unseen, as far as possible, all the booty which they had stolen from the inhabitants.

But they were seen in spite of this. In nearly all the houses of Riga, during this week of panic, the inhabitants stayed awake at night and peeped out of the windows at the many little bands of departing Reds. In darkened rooms, so that they should not be seen themselves, the people of Riga sat by their windows through several nights and watched with secret rejoicing the fully laden wagons hurrying towards the station.

Certainly it was *their* property which the Reds were carrying off into the safety of their Muscovite Empire; endless rows of wagons, hour after hour, night after night, rolling away, loaded full with goods and valuables stolen from *them*. . . .

But the people rejoiced all the same: "Liberation is coming," they said to themselves, "let all that go! Let them take everything we possess! If only liberation really comes!"

But supposing liberation did not come? Was not this rejoicing perhaps premature, ill-considered, even dangerous?

Immediately after the first news of the White advance had been made known, the "Supreme Revolutionary War Council," which had been formed specially for the defence of the town, had placards posted on all street corners, addressed to the bourgeois portion of the population and intended as a "serious warning."

"The bourgeoisie," these placards declared, "are earnestly warned not to abandon themselves to a delusive joy. Through false and sensational rumours they have purposely sown panic among the population, in order to be able to assemble their forces secretly under cover of this confusion. The sharpest repressive measures will be taken against such agitators. The Revolutionary War Council hereby empowers every member of the Communist Party to arrest any citizen who appears to him suspicious, to disperse any kind of street-gathering, and to shoot on the spot any person offering resistance to the Soviet authorities."

To enforce these threats, reinforced patrols of Red soldiers and "gunwomen" made their appearance in every quarter of the town and began their usual work. They now sought with particular zeal for the mothers, wives and sisters of the members of the Volunteer Corps who were fighting against the Red Army at the front.

With the aid of special lists containing the names and addresses of female relatives of White soldiers living in Riga, parties of Bolsheviks burst at night into the homes of these women deprived of male protection, seized them and dragged them to the military posts for examination or threw them straight into the prisons, which were already filled to overflowing.

Here drunken fellows subjected elderly ladies to offensive bodily search, vulgar bullies amused themselves by completely undressing young girls and tor-

THE FIRST RESISTANCE

menting them with all kinds of ribaldries. By way of a joke, they used to place them, half dead with fright, against the wall and inform them, laughing, that they were all to be "shot immediately." If one of the women was ill-advised enough to offer the least resistance, then these inhuman creatures redoubled their insults and often inflicted on their defenceless victims the very coarsest of outrages. . . .

   •   •   •   •   •

A few days later the Reds suffered a third serious reverse; the Volunteer Corps captured Mitau from them as well!

This town, Riga's nearest neighbour and the capital of the former Duchy of Courland, had been stormed by the Whites on the afternoon of the 18th of March and after hot fighting the Bolshevists had been driven out. This joyful news, however, only reached the population of Riga two days later. For two whole days the Red Army Staff had kept silence about this new blow.

That some kind of catastrophe must have happened to the Reds at the front we noticed, however, already a few hours after the fall of Mitau. On the evening of the same day, and still more on the following morning, the 19th of March, all Riga was full of nervous activity and excitement. For fully twenty-four hours a dull cannonade from the front reached our ears, the first we had heard for a long time. Three White aeroplanes showed themselves simultaneously over the town. Military wagons loaded with wounded came rattling from the direction of the river. Soviet officials fleeing from Mitau arrived in crowds. And outside the great

Soviet warehouses by the port the populace was already gathering sacks and baskets—in expectation of the moment when it could begin to plunder the food-stores....

As for the bourgeois population, warned by the fatal reaction caused by the first White push forward, the predominant feeling among them, when the first rumours of the fall of Mitau trickled in, was not so much joy as fear of Red excesses.

A dull feeling of apprehension lay heavy upon the whole city. Everyone was waiting uneasily for the things which were to come. At first wild rumours flew round everywhere: the advance of the Whites was proceeding impetuously; they were already marching on Riga; on the Mitau high road White cavalrymen had already been seen.... But then, as none of this turned out to be true, fear gained the upper hand in all, an aching presentiment of new horrors to come. Somewhere in the town isolated shots were heard; railway engines about to start whistled in the distance; from different quarters the dismal, long-drawn-out howl of factory sirens floated on the air charged with uneasy foreboding.

At last the crushing news gradually filtered through that the progress of the Whites had not been so rapid as it had seemed at first. After the capture of Mitau they had again called a halt; for the third time there was a stoppage.

At the same time the Bolshevists had pulled themselves together. When the Whites first offered resistance, the Government of Soviet Latvia had addressed an urgent call for help to the Kremlin. In response to this

THE FIRST RESISTANCE

Trotsky had in all haste despatched several Russian regiments to Courland. They had arrived just at the time of the fall of Mitau, and were at once thrown into the front line, under the command of Latvian Communists and "gunwomen."

We did not know to what circumstances to ascribe this sudden halt of the White Army—almost within sight of the towers of Riga. Did it feel itself not yet strong enough for the final assault? Was it collecting its forces in Mitau? Or were there some other reasons at the back of it? Some political influence of which we were ignorant? Whatever the case may have been, the fact remained that the Whites were either unwilling or unable to take our town by storm in one rush. They were advancing only in fits and starts. We had to be content with that.

The Reds made use of this breathing-space to take drastic measures for the defence of Riga. The new blows fell in swift succession.

To begin with, a proclamation of the Government ordered the mobilization of all men between the ages of twenty-five and thirty-five. On presenting themselves, a great many of these men were declared fit for military service and enrolled in the Red Army. My own class—I was only twenty-three—was not yet called up. But many of my friends now had to go to the front and fight against their own brothers and allies, against the very men from whom they were daily and hourly expecting the deliverance of their native town. . . .

In addition to the mobilization of ten classes, a "registration" of *all* men between the ages of seventeen and seventy was ordered. This regulation seemed to the

Reds to be so urgent that they announced it by means of hastily multiplied posters. The object of this measure the Soviet power declared laconically to be a "statistical revision of the population." But everybody knew that this was quite untrue, and that the registration was ordered exclusively with a view to carrying off prominent bourgeois as hostages to the interior of the Muscovite Empire.

For the Reds, faithful to the retrograde, Asiatic character of their methods of government, used to seize as many hostages as possible in all the towns and villages they entered, either for the purpose of exchanging them later for Red prisoners of war, or with a view to shooting fifty or more of them by way of a reprisal for any reverse they might suffer. The moral principle respected throughout the world, that no person should suffer for an act which he has not himself committed, was quite unknown to the Reds.

On account of this prospect of being taken as hostages, neither my father nor I obeyed this latest Soviet ukase. But the overwhelming majority of the male population considered that it was out of the question to ignore the command. They carried it out submissively: like cattle being branded for the slaughter-houses, thousands of men obeyed the order and had their names entered on the fateful lists. Thenceforward they could expect from day to day to be dragged off with the retreating enemy into the wildernesses of the Siberian steppes.

Among those who had obeyed this malignant order of the Soviets were my friend Somoff and his old father. But Somoff's father was one of those people who, with their ideas rooted in a past age, invariably obeyed the orders of "the Government," whatever it might be, and had therefore persuaded his son to enter their two names in the Red lists. This I learned one day after the fall of Mitau, when Somoff had last visited us. Since then I had not seen him again. I anticipated no good for him and his father from the ill-considered step they had taken.

There were numerous indications that the Reds would hardly be content with "theoretical measures." They had other plans.

Even President Stutchka, who till now had always been considerably more moderate than such rabid extremists as Simon Berg, Endrup, Danishevsky, the President of the Revolutionary Tribunal and most of the other Bolshevist leaders, and had acted to some degree as a brake on their frantic zeal, now changed his tone—doubtless from fear that he would lose his popularity and that the control of the movement would slip out of his hands. He became less and less of the good-natured and friendly theorist and professor we had formerly known; he displayed a new roughness and irritability, and indulged more and more frequently in demagogic utterances, from which he had hitherto completely abstained.

"The bourgeoisie," he now declared, in his latest speech delivered after the fall of Mitau, "must not only be degraded; it must be annihilated as a class." The hatred of the Reds for the bourgeoisie swelled more and more with every new set-back at the front. And when at last the news of the heavy defeat at Mitau arrived, it seemed that now a real lust for blood and vengeance had taken possession of them.

This emotion was reflected, as usual, in the contents of the *Red Flag*. "The revolutionary proletariat is unfortunately often too merciful," it now declared; "the Soviet Government of Latvia also has been merciful for a long time, far too merciful. But away now with these illusions! A painless proletarian revolution there has never been and will never be. Even the first attempts towards it have always been bloody. And still more blood will flow in the streets of Berlin, Vienna, Rome, Paris, London and New York. There is only *one* choice: either a bourgeois dictatorship or a dictatorship of the proletariat and a Red terror of the masses. Then forward to the class war, the merciless class war! The bourgeoisie of Riga must pay with its blood for the Red warriors who have fallen at the front!"

Even the poems in the Soviet paper now breathed blood-lust. A few days after the fall of Mitau, in the same corner for poetry in which Heine's poem about the "Paradise on earth" had appeared on the first day of Soviet rule, there was now printed quite a different type of poem, a warlike hymn of hate. The following is a free version:

WE WILL NOT YIELD!

We will not yield!
Though we should have to pile the corpses up to Heaven!
And ye shall never snatch the Red Town from our grip,
The Town so closely bound to us working-people
By our innumerable bleeding wounds.

And if in the worst case ye drive us out,
We swear that then not one stone will remain standing
  on the other—
We will rather let ourselves be buried under the ruins,
But ye shall never have Riga!

THE FIRST RESISTANCE

So, if we collapse, we drag you with us—
Every step will be a thousand times bloody
Which ye take towards our gates—
And if we—then ye also shall be lost.

Despair drives us to gigantic fury—
And though we must wade through seas of blood,
And though we should have to tear out our own heart,
Never—the Red City for the Whites!

Come everyone, and take your arms in your hands
And cast the brand in the enemy's face—
The brand of our hate! We will not yield,
Though the corpses should pile themselves up to Heaven!

These cries for blood were no empty words. They were soon replaced by deeds.

In Mitau, it now became known, the Bolshevists had perpetrated a regular massacre. In spite of the rapidity of the White advance, they had found time before their flight to despatch about 100 people confined in the local prison. The remainder—in all some 351 men and women of the middle classes and the nobility—they had driven with them along the road towards Riga as they retreated.

A Bolshevist Commissary had led the convoy, sitting comfortably in a cart—a man who was conspicuous because he had a club foot. The other Reds were on horseback and rode at a quick trot; they knew the White cavalry was behind them, and were horribly afraid that they might be caught up and overwhelmed. With rifle-butts and blows of the whip they drove on their prisoners, who had to run along on foot.

A stretch of about twenty-five miles had to be covered. Many of the prisoners, most of them elderly and all ailing folk, could not stand this inhuman hardship. From time to time they sank exhausted to the ground, struggled to their feet again, and stumbled on. In the end only 284 out of the original 351 prisoners arrived in Riga. The escorting Red soldiers had shot dead on the way no fewer than 67 of the prisoners, among them the aged marshal of the Courland nobility, Baron von der Ropp-Brixten, on the high road. They were left lying in the ditches. Their bodies were never buried.

In Riga itself, directly after the first advance of the Whites had begun near Libau on the 11th of March, there began a long series of reprisals which continued for many weeks.

Hardly had the news of the Red retreat arrived than the President of the Revolutionary Tribunal ordered an examination of the lists of all citizens in prison at the time. From the list of some hundreds of "specially dangerous" citizens submitted to him he selected in the first instance 110 persons with names well-known in Riga and sentenced them to a "conditional death penalty": they were all to be executed if further bad news came from the front.

And when a few days after that the news of the fall of Tuckum arrived, sure enough the Commissary handed over to his minions for execution 63 men and women out of these 110 specially distinguished hostages. A few hours later, during the night of March 15–16, the sentence on these "reprisals victims" was carried out.

In this way three whole weeks passed. For every defeat suffered by the Reds during the White advance they wreaked vengeance on the defenceless population of Riga. Vengeance for Tuckum, vengeance for Schlock,

THE FIRST RESISTANCE

vengeance for Mitau, vengeance for every little town or village torn from their grasp!

On the following night, the 16th–17th of March, 21 more people were shot. On the 19th of March, 30 more; on the 20th of March, 50; on the 21st of March, 42. On the 25th and 26th of March there were mass shootings of large numbers of citizens without any names or figures being given, simply with the remark: "to cleanse Riga thoroughly from counter-revolutionary elements." On the 3rd of April there were 60 further shootings, this time with names of the victims, as reprisals for "atrocities" which the White troops were alleged to have committed against the Bolshevists who had been caught in the fall of Mitau.

The official *communiqués* announcing these executions giving the names, ages and sex of the victims, were published in Nos. 53–76 of the *Red Flag*.

It was only in the first week of April that the butchers seemed to grow weary of their work and there came a respite. In the short time between the 11th of March and the 3rd of April the Bolshevists had shot down in cold blood not less than from 350 to 400 citizens of Riga—solely in revenge for the defeats suffered at the front.

CHAPTER XIV

THE MASSACRE IN BICKERN WOOD

For over a week after the fall of Mitau my friend Igor Somoff, who up to then had been visiting us almost every day, had not put in an appearance.

On one of the first days of April, after the excitement in the town had somewhat abated, I betook myself to Somoff's house to obtain information about the reasons for his absence. But I found the house shut up and deserted. The neighbours seemed to be in a state of fright and disinclined to give me any news of the Somoffs.

It was only after persistent efforts that I succeeded in extracting from them what they knew and finally in finding out the truth.

Somoff and his father had been arrested on the 19th of March, the day after the fall of Mitau, and thrown into prison. One could only surmise what the causes had been: either the spy Yermoloff had denounced them to the Tribunal (doubtless to avenge himself on Somoff for his imprudent words during that memorable party), or the fact that they had previously belonged to a White organization had been fatal to them, once they had entered their names on the Red "Register." However that may have been, they were at once placed by the President of the Revolutionary Tribunal on a list of fifty "hostages" who were to be shot in retaliation for the loss of Mitau and "to cleanse Riga thoroughly from all counter-revolutionary elements." And at dawn on the very next day, the 20th of March, the execution had been carried out in Bickern Wood, the usual place of execution of the Reds.

By getting in touch with relatives of some of the victims who had gone to the prison warders for news, and by piecing together various fragments of information which filtered through from other quarters, I was able at last to obtain the full story of this peculiarly revolting massacre and learn the details of my friend's tragic end.

The relatives of the executed men, after the first disturbing rumours had begun to circulate, had assailed the prison warders with distracted questions about the fate of their kin. The warders' sole response was to pass on to the relatives the last farewell notes of the condemned men—little slips of paper with hastily scribbled words on them—and a few things that had belonged to them.

The warders, who mostly belonged to the old prison staff and were not themselves Bolshevists, told everything they knew: about the sudden appearance of the executioners and the hasty removal of the bewildered men, still half asleep. Also various persons were found who lived in the vicinity of Bickern Wood and, unnoticed by the Reds, had been involuntary witnesses, at a distance, of the gruesome happenings there. The statements of these people supplemented the information given by the warders. Finally, several months later, after the departure of the Reds, the common grave was opened and all the corpses of the murdered men were discovered. Most of the bodies were horribly mutilated, and the ghastly wounds visible all over them spoke eloquently of the agonizing death which the victims must have suffered at the hands of their murderers. . . .

The prison into which Somoff and his father had been thrown was the ill-famed "Citadel," one of the two largest prisons of the town, lying close to the river. This prison was remarkable in several respects. Once, more than half a century before, it had been a kind of fortress. In the last years of Tsarist rule it had stood unoccupied and unused. Immediately after the entry of the Reds, however, the building department of the Riga Soviet had turned its attention to the Citadel. It had evolved a "grandiose plan" (all Bolshevist plans were "grandiose"). The idea was that in the free Soviet State of Latvia there would in future be no death penalty or imprisonment, or, indeed, any prisons; and the Citadel was, therefore, to be pulled down "as soon as possible," in common with all the other prisons in the country.

According to the plan—for the publication of which the *Red Flag* considered the present moment a suitable one—a "gigantic people's palace" was to be erected on the space formerly occupied by the Citadel. It would contain "an assembly room to accommodate 50,000 persons, a people's theatre to seat 15,000 spectators, and a swimming-bath in which 3,000 Soviet citizens of both sexes could bathe at the same time; a huge orchestra, consisting of 300 Soviet musicians, would play the works of proletarian composers every evening in the roof-garden; and the promenading comrades, male and female, would from this roof-garden, the crown of the people's palace, have a view over all Red Latvia."

But things had not got so far at present. The Citadel still stood on its old site in its old form. Instead of being pulled down, it had, on the contrary, been put in order as speedily as possible to receive new guests. Instead of the 3,000 Soviet citizens of the future, promenading and listening to music, it now sheltered precisely that number of imprisoned "citizens of the 3rd Category."

Among them were the fifty hostages, including poor Somoff and his father. The Revolutionary Tribunal had sentenced them all to death immediately on their arrest. But neither they themselves nor the prison warders had known anything of the approaching execution. None of them had been given the possibility of bidding farewell to their closest relatives and friends, not even to their wives and children.

After their imprisonment on the morning of the 19th of March the condemned men had spent a most uneasy day, then, however, a rather more hopeful night; for the rumours of a further advance of the Baltic Volunteers, details of the capture of Mitau and reports of the Red preparations for a retreat had penetrated even behind the walls of this gloomy prison. Here, near the river, the dull booming of the guns from the front could be heard all day long, and the exciting drone of the White aeroplanes which hovered ceaselessly over the town seemed of good omen. To the men inside the prisons as well as to the rest of the population deliverance seemed assured and close at hand.

Thus it happened that towards evening, within the

cells occupied by the hostages, a fairly confident atmosphere had prevailed. Most of the prisoners had been strangers to one another up to the time of their incarceration. They had spent more than half the night in lively conversation. Not one of them had any presentiment of the gruesome end which awaited them all that very night.

In the cell in which the two Somoffs found themselves about 30 people were sitting or lying about, closely packed together. This room formed—unknown to its occupiers—one of the two "death cells": in these cells, which lay in a special corridor, only those prisoners who had already been condemned to death by the Revolutionary Tribunal were as a rule confined.

This little band of men who were thus, without knowing it, awaiting their last hour was a motley company, composed of men of all ages, classes and nationalities. The oldest among them were a Lettish merchant of seventy-six and a Balt clergyman of sixty-three, Eugen Berg, rural dean of Palzmar; the youngest a Lettish student and a Jewish shop-boy, both eighteen years old. There was also in the same cell a prominent citizen of Riga, John Cecil Armitstead; he had been included in the number of the "hostages" solely on account of his father's distinguished position and the fact that two of his cousins were serving in the White Army.

Among the inmates of the two cells were youths, men in the prime of life, and old men, noblemen and bourgeois, clergymen and land-owners, merchants and doctors, as well as agricultural labourers, artisans, factory hands and men belonging to the very poorest classes. Many of them were closely related: there were fathers and sons, grandfathers and grandsons, brothers and cousins. A number of nationalities were represented: Letts, Germans, Balts, Russians, Jews and Poles. The Reds regarded them all as "bourgeois," "enemies of the Soviet power," "counter-revolutionaries."

In one sense they were not mistaken: all these unfortunates, broken in body and spirit, had one thing in common: without exception and without distinction of age, class and nationality, they were united in their bitter hatred of the Red usurpers. There was not a single person in that crowd who, wavering between hope and fear, was not thirsting with all his soul for their final expulsion, not one who would not have regarded their complete extermination as an act of public salvation. This formed the chief topic of the conversation which went on all through the night and into the small hours of the morning.

Not till towards two in the morning did the prisoners fall into an uneasy sleep. Their rest was but a short one. About five they were awakened by a sudden noise. They heard the throb of motor engines outside, the sound of voices, a quarrel, shouts and cursing, and the laughter of drunken women; then footsteps, the clang of weapons on the stone floor, the rattle of keys in the corridor, and orders given by men approaching the cells. Then, through the gratings in the doors, the dazzling light of flickering lanterns shone into the blackness of the prisoners' dungeons. Almost immediately a horde of Bolshevist soldiers and "gunwomen," armed to the teeth and abominably drunk, burst wildly in.

"All out into the yard! Without coats, hats or

boots!" shouted a Red guard who seemed to be the leader, a man with a club foot and a typical criminal's face.

Still half asleep, the prisoners got to their feet, obeying the command mechanically, not realizing at first what it meant. But slowly the reality began to dawn on them. Meanwhile, levelling revolvers at their heads, the club-footed leader and his gang ordered complete silence.

One after another they left their cells. Pastor Berg led the way and the others followed him, mostly in couples, holding each other's hands.

In the courtyard the prisoners were herded into three or four closed motor-lorries already waiting for them. The leader got into a special car, while his followers swung themselves on to the backs of the rough Cossack horses jostling each other in the yard. The "gunwomen" clambered on to other lorries.

Complete silence reigned among the doomed men. Calm, outwardly composed, they climbed into the windowless lorries and let themselves be driven without resistance to the place of execution. The troop of riders and the other lorries carrying the women followed after them.

Day was breaking as the prison lorries, laden with their victims and their horde of escorting male and female Bolshevists, reached the distant Bickern Wood.

Although the sun, of course, had not yet risen, the landscape was illuminated by the early morning light—the still sleeping pinewoods, the cornfields, now almost bare of snow and pregnant already with germinating seed, and the humble peasants' cottages, half hidden in the distance, from whose chimneys rose the first smoke of the early morning fires.

On the place of execution a woman took over the command from the club-footed Commissary. She was young, but with cold and brutal features. Astride a white horse, theatrically clad in a voluminous black velvet cloak doubtless stolen from somewhere, she trotted from group to group giving orders in loud, imperious tones.

The club-footed man smoked a cigarette and watched the preparations, smiling. His men held themselves at a little distance, on the edge of the wood. There a large pit was to be seen, apparently freshly dug during the night. It was the grave, ready to receive the dead bodies after the execution. The task of burying the victims had been allotted to the men soldiers; the women had undertaken the other part of the work.

The "gunwomen" stood ready, waiting to carry out the orders of the amazon. They were a detachment of those Lettish Communist women, most of them former domestic servants or prostitutes, who had formed a special Women's Battalion immediately after the arrival of the Reds and had made themselves unpleasantly conspicuous, not only by the prominent part they took in domiciliary visits and arrests, but by their willingness to act as executioners, in which role they displayed a degree of cruelty and sadism to which men never attained.

Alarmed and exasperated by the latest bad news from the front, they seemed on this day to be particularly zealous and to be taking a peculiar pleasure in their work.

The victims were ordered to line up, with their backs to the wood. No sooner were they in their places than the relentless amazon raised her whip high in her gloved right hand.

The usual instruments of execution used by the Reds—machine-guns—were lacking, for they were all urgently needed at the front. Most of the female butchers were, therefore, armed only with revolvers, and one or two of them with rifles.

At the signal of their leader some forty or fifty of these women, with their loaded weapons in hand, advanced slowly towards the ranks of the prisoners. At first they moved forward hesitatingly and stopped, irresolute, a few paces away. Something very much akin to embarrassment was depicted on their coarse faces. . . .

But this hesitation and uncertainty lasted only for a few seconds. In obedience to the cries of the horse-woman exciting and urging them on, they suddenly opened a disorderly, erratic fire on the fifty unarmed wretches standing, barefooted and helpless, before them; still ill-trained in the use of firearms, they aimed badly, missed or wounded many of their victims without killing them outright; and they went on shooting and shooting, blindly, deliriously, like creatures possessed, into the defenceless mass of human bodies.

Piercing cries for help, despairing shrieks rent the air. It was as though the victims had only now awakened from their stupor. They huddled close together; the clergyman, erect in the midst of the throng, called on them loudly to submit to God's will.

Some of the prisoners—fathers and sons, brothers and

friends—clung together in groups of twos and threes, taking their last farewells, and trying to protect one another with their own bodies. Others stood upright in the midst of the rain of bullets, awaiting death with a quiet, cheerful countenance, saying "Our Father" to themselves. Some of the youngest died manfully, filled with an inward greatness. . . . Others broke into piercing cries, threw themselves to the ground and crawled towards their executioners to embrace their knees, clinging to life desperately in the face of death. Others again, already grievously wounded, attempted to save themselves by flight; they ran into the depths of the wood, hid themselves behind trees or flung themselves, as though seeking protection, into the slushy snow.

But their murderesses, now drunk with blood, rushed after them, tore their half-dead victims from their hiding-places, fired at them blindly, shooting them in the face, in the body, in the legs, till only a heap of mutilated quivering corpses lay before them.

In spite of the clumsiness of the female butchers the carnage lasted no longer than ten or fifteen minutes. A final shot here or there, and all was over.

The club-footed Commissary hobbled from body to body to see which were still alive, and wherever he saw any sign of movement fired his revolver into the body to be on the safe side. Then satisfied that the work had been well done, he nodded to the mounted woman. Laughing and screeching, the "gunwomen" then jumped into the lorries and were driven swiftly back to the town.

The soldiers, who had stood idly on one side during

the whole scene, now came forward. They threw all the bodies into the great pit which had been previously dug. The grave was big; yet in order to get them all in the soldiers had to stack the bodies in layers one on top of the other, like cargo in the hold of a ship.

Soon the grave was filled to the brim. Then the soldiers shovelled over it some of the yellow sand, mixed with snow and blood. But they did it so hastily and carelessly that here and there a foot, a hand or even a head of one of the victims still projected.

As they went off, the soldiers noticed that the bushes, already in bud, in the surroundings of the fatal spot were sprinkled with curious white tufts, which had not been there before; they looked rather like silkworm cocoons and seemed to cling delicately to the twigs, as though made of cotton-wool. But, as soon as the men touched them, they had the disagreeable sensation of something wet and soft that ran slimily through the fingers. They were fragments of human brains. . . . With exclamations of disgust and swearing loudly, the soldiers hurried away.

Attracted by the shots and cries, some peasants had emerged from their cottages and had stood watching the massacre from a distance. Yet, even after the executioners had gone away, they dared not come nearer to that place of horror, where the blood of half a hundred murdered men had reddened the earth and the snow. They speedily withdrew, scared and bewildered, to the solitude of their cottages.

The whole day long a radiant spring sun shone down unceasingly upon the still woods, the fields instinct with new life, and the fresh grave. Towards noon a

THE MASSACRE IN BICKERN WOOD

White aeroplane again circled, long and leisurely, in the cloudless sky. In the trees the first starlings twittered greetings to the spring.

But underneath, from the half-open grave, there sounded all day long the groans of some of the victims in whom life still lingered. The dreadful sounds could be heard some distance away, and did not cease till gentle night had spread her veil of darkness over earth and all its cruelty.

CHAPTER XV

A VISIT FROM ANOTHER WORLD

On one of the first days of April, at about three o'clock in the afternoon, I was sitting alone in our flat when I heard an unfamiliar knock at the front door. It was a light, hesitating knock—not the imperious banging of Bolshevist raiders—and I was therefore surprised, on opening the door, to find a Red soldier standing before me. I was even more surprised when this soldier—in contrast to the usual behaviour of his kind—showed no sign of hostility in his attitude, but smiled amiably at me as he stepped into our sitting-room.

The stranger was tall and dark, with lively brown eyes and a conspicuously open, honest look on his face. The features seemed to be curiously familiar to me. But the enigmatic visitor was so effectively disguised, partly by a pair of roughly made soldiers' spectacles which he was wearing, partly by a sort of bristly moustache and short beard which covered his upper lip and chin, and partly by his deeply sunburnt and weatherbeaten skin, that I could not be sure whether he was an old acquaintance or a stranger.

The man kept looking straight at me with a fixed and questioning smile. More and more puzzled, I began to scrutinize his face more closely. And suddenly I recognized him: my visitor was none other than my long-lost friend whom, on that memorable January night, Somoff and I had accompanied to the boat when he had left Riga to join the Volunteer Corps—Roy Carlyle!

With a shout of astonishment, I was on the point of assailing my old friend with a flood of questions, when he silenced me with a warning finger, peered cautiously round the room and then, with the air of someone warned by experience, asked me whether there was not "anybody suspicious" living in the house.

I soon reassured him on this point. At that moment I happened by chance to be entirely alone in the flat; my sister was at school, the two ladies of the house had gone to see Walter again, and my parents were somewhere in quest of victuals. But Carlyle still remained unsatisfied. In a tone still not free from mistrust, he asked who that "suspicious person" was who had opened the door for him in our old flat downstairs where he had first knocked.

I pictured to myself the meeting of Carlyle with Comradess Balgal, who now reigned in our former home; I explained to my astonished friend this woman's role, and told him how we had been compelled to move. I related briefly all the details of our life during the occupation, informed him of the tragic death of so many mutual friends, and roughly described our present situation.

Carlyle listened with growing interest, now and then shaking his head incredulously. Then, noticing my impatience, he gave me the explanation of his sudden appearance.

"I've come straight from the other side!" he said, motioning with his head towards the window which looked in the direction of the river. "I'm reconnoitring

—slipped through the lines last night! The most incredible rumours are going round over there about your situation. Unfortunately, the reality seems to be even worse than we imagined. . . . But now it's only a matter of days or weeks at most. We'll soon have them on the run!" And, with his right hand, he made a bold gesture which might have been taken to indicate a blow, or else a rush forward.

"Speak! Tell me all you know! How do things look over there? Where did that ship take you to? What do people in Europe think of things here? Are you strong enough to advance farther and take Riga? When are you coming?"

I bombarded my visitor from another world with a hail of questions. The apparition of this fresh, cheerful man, who had spent in a world of freedom and plenty all these weeks and months that we had been suffering and starving, was such an improbable event that it seemed to me almost like a dream.

All through the weeks and months in which we had been cut off from the west, we had daily wondered what Europe thought of the fact that one of its largest seaports was, in the twentieth century, being brought to ruin in this appalling way. Did the western peoples feel the horror of our situation, or were they so preoccupied with their own troubles that they had no time to worry about us?

We had asked ourselves these questions time without number, but up till now no one had been able to answer them satisfactorily.

Carlyle remained silent for awhile, regarding me with his clear eyes. It seemed that he had not expected to have to answer such a mass of questions. He reflected for a moment, as if collecting his thoughts; and then he explained the situation to me as fully as possible, telling me everything he felt he could reveal concerning the Whites' plans for the immediate future.

The tumultuous irruption of this human flood from the east—Carlyle began his account—and, above all, the seizure of our great seaport by the Red armies, had been followed by the world with attention and interest, but chiefly—it could not be denied—with that vague curiosity which is aroused by the events in strange and distant theatres of war. The real gravity of the situation seemed hardly to be recognized in the west. Europe was wrestling with problems enough of its own. The world war had just ended. Now, the Red torrent immediately threatened the frontiers of Germany. If it was not to break down the barrier of the German frontier, and submerge the whole of Europe, Germany, now disarmed, would have to be given some fresh means of defending herself. But this was just what the powers which were then presiding over the destinies of Europe would not allow. While individual Allied statesmen, such as Mr. Winston Churchill and others, urged Germany in their speeches to protect Europe against the torrent from the east, the Allies actually *forbade* those German troops who had remained on Baltic territory to organize any resistance to the Red invasion! They demanded that these troops should return to their own country. Germany, not wishing to have further trouble with the Entente, obeyed and actually began to withdraw her troops. The result was that the Red forces, meeting with no opposition, went on advancing farther and farther westward. Civilized regions were overrun without the slightest difficulty by the Muscovite bands. The nationals of several European countries—Germans, Russians, Balts, Letts, Estonians, Poles—were robbed, kidnapped, massacred. Europe did not raise a finger. In East Prussia, in the immediate neighbourhood of the scene of these barbarous excesses, were stationed excellently drilled German troops. They were not permitted to stir. Forces of their own the victorious Allies would not, or could not, send. British warships anchored in various Baltic harbours had put out to sea at the critical moment.

Only a very small part of the inhabitants of Riga had been able, like Carlyle, to leave the town in refugee ships. The ships had reached friendly ports in Sweden, Germany and Denmark only after a long and very difficult voyage through the ice-bound Baltic, during which the refugees had suffered great hardships, frozen by the bitter cold and in constant fear of striking a mine. The vessels had been so overcrowded with refugees that the majority of them had had to camp out on the open deck; there had not been enough food on board to go round; and by the time the ships reached port, most of the refugees were in the last stage of exhaustion. Nevertheless, their first act on their arrival was to appeal to the European Powers to save their homes from Bolshevism. But London, Paris and Berlin merely consoled them with empty promises, and did nothing.

Meanwhile the invading tide from the east still continued to sweep forward. Leaving Riga and Mitau far behind it, it had already approached to within fifty miles of the German frontier. Its penetration into the very heart of Europe seemed inevitable, was perhaps only a question of weeks. No one seemed able to bar its progress. The local volunteer forces composed of Balts and Letts, raised in haste and lacking adequate material, were completely crushed by the numerical superiority of the Muscovites. The few German troops still remaining in Courland were seriously demoralized. By the end of January the Baltic Volunteer Corps had been practically wiped out. It numbered now no more than about 700 men.

In this hour of the gravest peril, a few of the leaders of the hard-pressed anti-Bolshevist troops determined to organize resistance to the Soviet hordes on their own account. If Europe could not help them, they would help themselves. They established a base at Libau, not far from the German frontier, and sent out thence appeals to their countrymen. From all sides there arrived those who, like Carlyle, had succeeded in escaping, and had been hitherto dispersed. These men and many new volunteers filled up the gaps in the ranks of the Baltic troops.

The command of the Baltic Volunteer Corps was taken over by a former officer of the German General Staff, Major Alfred Fletcher. A Russian division was reorganized and led by Prince Anatol Lieven. Colonel Ballod commanded a Lettish battalion. Finally, the remnant of the German Army which had remained in Courland since the war, the so-called "Iron Division" under the command of Major Bischoff, joined the Baltic Volunteers against the wishes of the Allies. Indeed, it was even found possible to bring up some German regular troops (the 1st Guard Reserve Division) from East Prussia and to prevail on one of the most brilliant German military leaders, General Count von der Goltz, to undertake the supreme command of the combined Balt, Lettish, Russian and German troops. The so-called "White Army" had been created!

It was a wonderful exploit, with few counterparts in the history of our time: a handful of selfless men made up their minds, in the face of the indifference and opposition of a blind world, to take their courage in both hands and throw themselves in the path of the invader—to risk their own lives for the salvation of their own country and the salvation of Europe. It was a moment of historical importance; for it was these men who, at the beginning of the year 1919, saved Central Europe from the horrors of a new Hun invasion.

The White leaders, however, Carlyle continued, before they could think of launching an offensive, had still to grapple with all kinds of difficulties. Inevitably, the supplies of arms, munitions and equipment were at first very limited. Moreover, the effective forces of the White Army did not come anywhere near the numerical strength of the Reds; they numbered barely seven or eight thousand men, spread over a front of 250 miles. Against them the Reds, besides their army in Courland, which now consisted of about 20,000 men, could bring all the reserves of their huge empire, that is to say, millions of men. Furthermore, the Reds, whose resources were comparatively inexhaustible, had no need to fear any lack of munitions. Indeed, incredible as it may seem, some European Governments

A VISIT FROM ANOTHER WORLD

allowed greedy profiteers to supply the Reds with arms—the Reds, whose one and only thought was to set Europe ablaze as quickly as possible!

Apart from the unhelpful and even obstructive attitude of the European Powers, the Whites had to contend with disintegrating influences among the troops themselves. In some German regiments there existed so-called "Soldiers' Councils," which from time to time entered into direct negotiations with the Bolsheviks and carried on all kinds of shady transactions with them. There were even cases in which a German battalion sold its artillery to the Reds. In certain villages just behind the front some of these troops abandoned themselves to a life of debauchery without worrying further about the enemy's advance. Dubious elements had made their way in everywhere, animated solely by the idea of engaging in shady transactions or even direct theft, whereby the fighting value of some of the White regiments was seriously reduced.

But all this, Carlyle said, was soon changed by the prompt and energetic measures which were taken by Count von der Goltz and his officers. They quickly and thoroughly rooted out all the pernicious elements. Under their leadership the "Iron Division" and the other German formations soon became exemplary troops. An even greater excellence was soon attained by the Baltic Volunteer Corps, composed of natives of the country. In this corps, consisting of not much more than 2,000 or 3,000 men, men of seventy fought side by side with their fifteen-year-old grandsons, boys from school together with their masters, former officers of the Russian and German Armies shoulder to shoulder with typical civilians who had never before held a weapon in their hands. The corps consisted almost exclusively of educated men; the Reds called it the "barons' army." And the officers, when issuing commands to their men, addressed these not simply as "men" or "soldiers," but said to them: "Gentlemen!"

In the route of the White Army were a few Balt gentlemen of English origin; the more prominent of these were Mr. John William Armitstead and Mr. Alfred Armitstead, nephews of the former Mayor of Riga and cousins of John Cecil Armitstead, one of the victims of the massacre in Bickern Wood.

By the middle of February the newly formed White Army had begun to offer resistance to the Muscovites. The methods of warfare used in these fights between Whites and Reds had nothing in common with those of the Great War which had just ended. They rather reminded one of the romantic combats of past ages. There hardly existed any continuous front. The Whites advanced in small, independent detachments. Trench fighting was rare. Flying assaults and cavalry skirmishes were the order of the day. Here individual courage and bravery had ample scope and were indispensable. The Reds and the "gunwomen" were hunted like wild beasts. Villages and small towns were stormed, imprisoned bourgeois freed, and merciless punishment inflicted on the Red butchers, whenever caught, as an example to the rest.

The White offensive, in which Carlyle had taken part, began to bear fruit from the first weeks. One of the first places captured was the seaport of Windau, to the north of Libau. The Reds had captured the town in January and had behaved with special barbarity there. Among others, the following episode had been enacted in this town. When the Bolshevists arrived there in January, they found a German garrison of about 100 men still remaining. The Germans entered into negotiations with the Reds, who assured them that they would be allowed to go free if they laid down their arms; but as soon as the soldiers had given up their weapons they were all locked into a shed, the doors were bolted and the wretched men were then mown down in one mass with machine guns from outside. All perished miserably with the exception of three men who were only severely wounded and managed to creep away by night; they were smuggled into hospital by compassionate people and later bore witness to what had taken place.

Windau was so situated that in the case of a further advance of the Whites it would necessarily lie in their rear. It was therefore essential to clear out the Reds as soon as possible. On the 23rd of February, Major Fletcher, hardly two weeks after he had taken over the leadership of the Baltic Volunteer Corps, gave the order for the capture of Windau. A portion of the Volunteer Corps had been formed of specially picked men, the cream of the little army, and was known as the "shock detachment." It was led by Baron Hans Manteuffel, a gallant young officer, and was always entrusted with the carrying out of specially difficult tasks. This "shock detachment" advanced on Windau from different directions, and a short but severe infantry engagement ensued, during which the men of the Volunteer Corps took part of the town by assault.

In the course of heavy street fighting the enemy was forced step by step out of the town.

After the Volunteer Corps had taken Windau and secured the rear, the whole White Army was free to embark on its general offensive. Riga was still in the far distance. But Count von der Goltz wished to push his troops so far forward that he would have a shorter front, and a larger area for the assembly of troops for the capture of Riga could be obtained. This "shorter front" was a semi-circular line round Riga, Schlock–Mitau–Bauske. Towards these points the Whites advanced in the middle of March. They did not advance in an unbroken line, but in many small, independent detachments. Some of the soldiers were mounted, others rode on peasant carts or sleighs, the rest were on foot. A band of crusaders!

During the short time they had been there, the Reds had laid waste the country in an unbelievable manner. Throughout their advance the deliverers had the opportunity of seeing with their own eyes the havoc wrought by the Muscovites. They were quite justified, at the sight of the devastation, in saying: "This would have been the fate of all the neighbouring countries—Lithuania, East Prussia, Germany and the whole of Central Europe—had not we come forward at the last moment and flung ourselves in the path of the Red hordes!"

Everywhere the Whites appeared—Carlyle told me—they were greeted with joy by the population and hailed as saviours. The rural population also, the Lettish peasants, had suffered heavily under the Red domination and showed unfeigned friendliness towards the

White soldiers. In many liberated places the inhabitants were in fear lest the Reds should return once more. For this reason hundreds of people, as soon as the Whites arrived, packed up their belongings; and, whilst the army continued its eastward march, these terrified men, women and children hastened away bag and baggage in the opposite direction. For, they said, it would be better to starve somewhere in a foreign land than to fall again into the Bolshevists' hands alive.

The preliminary object of the White offensive was achieved with the capture of Mitau. The town was taken only after very heavy fighting. Many hundreds of prisoners were taken as well as valuable material. Particularly hot fighting had raged round the station. Here, in the end, whole companies of Bolshevists gave themselves up, together with all their rifles and artillery. The victory of Mitau was a complete and brilliant one. But none of the Volunteers could help bitterly regretting that the Reds had been able to carry off in their retreat over three hundred citizens of Mitau and that the White cavalry, which had been sent after them, despite a desperate ride, had not succeeded in freeing the prisoners.

The strange fact that, in spite of the tales of horror which came through to them from Riga, the Whites had made a halt in Mitau and delayed a further push forward, Carlyle explained as follows. There were two reasons. The Governments of the Allied Powers and that of Germany had followed the White advance from a distance and now began to express their opinion as to whether further developments would be of a desirable nature. The Entente still saw with displeasure the participation of German troops. It would have been more agreeable to it to see the Bolshevists driven out by an army of Balts and Letts alone. The Baltic Volunteers were, however, much too weak to be able to renounce the support of the regular German troops, and a national Lettish army obviously could not be created in the twinkling of an eye. But despite these obvious facts, and the fact that the Reds were massacring dozens of innocent citizens in Riga every week and each minute was precious, the question of the employment of German troops was argued and discussed for weeks by the Governments concerned. . . .

Another reason was that the Whites had to re-form the ranks of their battalions, which had suffered heavy casualties in the rapid advance; they had to repair the deficiencies in munitions and provisions; they had, finally, to make all preparations to ensure that the decisive blow, once undertaken, should succeed at all costs. After the defeat at Mitau the enemy had pulled themselves together and obtained reinforcements from Moscow, and were still vastly superior to the Whites in numbers and equipment.

The chances were, therefore, very unequal as now, in the beginning of spring, the day of the final struggle drew nearer and nearer. On the one side—only a few thousand, for the most part untrained warriors, lacking provisions and equipment, and kept waiting weeks on end for "permission" to fight against the Bolsheviks. On the other side—an immense host of soldiers with war experience behind them, amply provided with arms and every necessity, and knowing only one command from their leaders in Moscow: to storm forward, to pour themselves in a Red deluge over Europe!

In spite, however, of the heavy odds and the disadvantages it had to face, this little band of fearless men, particularly the Balt Volunteers, felt rightly confident of victory and success; and this confidence they owed less to their better discipline and higher civilization than to the extraordinary degree of idealism which animated not only their officers but also the vast majority of the rank and file. They had but one thought, one purpose—the deliverance of the homeland; and they were determined, come what might, to achieve this object.

Such was the description which Carlyle, in his quiet and simple way, unfolded to me of the situation in the White camp. His account had at last given me a clear picture of all that had been going on "on the other side." He stopped speaking for a moment and seemed to be reflecting. Then he came to the last and most important thing that he had to tell me.

"Your rescue is now close at hand," he said in conclusion. "Our commander-in-chief has decided not to wait any longer for permission to advance. He intends to undertake the deliverance of Riga on his own responsibility. We think of nothing else day and night. The attack is being most carefully prepared. I must not tell you when it will take place, but certainly some time during April. It is only a matter of days, or, at the most, weeks. Hold out till then, and you will be free!"

Carlyle stood up. He held out his right hand.

"Good-bye," he said. "I have still other missions

to carry out in the town, and I have to get back tonight. . . . Good-bye, until we meet again . . . soon!"

I grasped the hand of this friend who had so faithfully fulfilled his promise to give us news of our liberation, and shook it heartily. Then I accompanied him to the door and, for the second time that year, bade him farewell. Once more I was letting him depart into the unknown. But this time, thank Heaven, it was with the hope of a far speedier and happier reunion than there had been at that former parting, on that cold January night which had been so black with gloomy foreboding.

Carlyle was gone. I was left alone in the empty house. My thoughts followed after the departed friend who, in a few hours, would again be "on the other side" with our men . . . while we remained here in this plague-ridden city. Never had I realized more clearly the tragic absurdity of our position than when this "messenger from another world" had appeared among us, radiating hope and comfort, and then vanished again.

Between us and them lay in reality nothing but a broken and, in parts, hardly traceable front. Yet this thin line formed of barbed wire, of trenches, and soldiers' flesh and blood, stretching from the Baltic Sea far down to the south, separated like a thick red streak, like an insurmountable Wall of China, our world of stagnation and death from another one filled with life and freedom. Against this wall, all our vital human impulses towards freedom broke and melted away like sea-foam against the rocks.

CHAPTER XVI

THE TRIUMPH OF THE MUSCOVITES

For some time following Carlyle's visit, a certain improvement of spirits was noticeable in our household. The uncertainty in which we had been living until then had partially disappeared. Now, whenever we met the unwelcome guests from Moscow, in the street or elsewhere, we murmured with secret conviction: "Your time will soon be up. . . ."

But this confidence was short-lived. First days, then weeks passed without the hour of liberation coming which Carlyle had declared to be so imminent. Instead of this, on one of the last days of April, news of quite a different character came from Western Europe—very bad news indeed. While we in Riga waited daily, hourly for an advance by the Whites who lay at our gates, Bolshevism had suddenly broken out in their rear, in the heart of Europe!

In Hungary and Bavaria, Soviet Governments had been proclaimed in swift succession. Not only this, but throughout Europe the situation was growing more critical every day. From several other countries came reports of menacing Communist activities and disturbances. Was the Red flood really going to pour itself over the whole of Europe?

The first news came in a wireless message from Budapest. It ran:

The United Socialist-Democratic and Communist Party has taken over the government of the country in the name of the proletariat. We send our greetings to the Soviet Republic of Russia and to Comrade Lenin. We declare ourselves affiliated to the Communist International. We shall summon the first congress of Hungarian Workers', Soldiers' and Peasants' Soviets without delay. Long live the dictatorship of the proletariat! Long live the world revolution!

A few days later a message in almost identical terms was received from Munich:

The Soviet Republic has been proclaimed in Bavaria. . . . From now onwards everything belongs to the community. A Bavarian Red Army is being organized. Bavaria will follow Russia's lead in everything. We believe in the day of international liberation. Long live the Communist International! Long live the world revolution!

At the same time as the sensational news from Hungary and Bavaria, reports of revolutionary unrest poured in from many other countries. The *Red Flag* was full of them.

From Austria came the information:

The position in Austria is becoming daily more critical. As a consequence of the lost war bitter want prevails throughout the whole country. The influence of the Communist groups is gaining strength every day. The returned soldiers vehemently demand an increase of unemployment relief. Speakers call for cheers for the Hungarian Soviet Government and advocate the proclamation of the Soviet in Austria. . . .

From Roumania:

In Roumania disturbances have broken out which resemble an open revolution. The King and Queen attempted to flee to Jassy, but were obliged to return to Bucharest, as the railway track had been destroyed in places. . . . Shouts were raised of "Down with the King! Long live the Republic!"

From Italy:

The Congress of the Italian Socialist Party has advocated the overthrow of the monarchy and the introduction of radical Socialist reforms.

From Poland:

In Warsaw an illegal Workers' Soviet has been founded; it has held an assembly and drawn up a resolution in which it assures the workers of Hungary and Bavaria of its proletarian solidarity with them.

From England:

The strike movement is beginning to produce chaos throughout England. In Glasgow and Belfast bloody clashes have taken place between troops and strikers. The strike movement has London also in its grip.

From Egypt:

In Egypt disturbances have broken out. Rebellious Bedouin tribes are seizing power in many places. Railway communication has been broken at different points. In Cairo, Alexandria and many provincial towns sanguinary conflicts have taken place between the natives and the British troops. . . .

To this last-mentioned report the *Red Flag* appended the following comment:

The Egyptian rising is the first threatening sign of the awakening of the East. This awakening can easily be more dangerous for world imperialism than the establishment of the Soviet regime in more European States. At this moment the world revolution is spreading in Central and Western Europe. Its further path leads it to Egypt and from thence via Turkey and Asia Minor to India. Afghanistan is already in full revolt. Afghanistan, which has always been England's most important bulwark against Russia! Until now it has guarded the road to India, to that forbidden land out of which the English vampire is mercilessly sucking the last drops of blood. What Russian Tsarism did not succeed in achieving will be accomplished now by Muscovite Bolshevism! The way from Moscow through Turkestan and Afghanistan to India is now open to the Bolshevist revolution! India must be our main goal. For a revolution in India would be a fact which would decide the question of the world revolution once and for all. . . .

All these events filled our Riga Bolshevists with indescribable enthusiasm. Their exultation knew no bounds. The *Red Flag* blew the trumpet of victory. It published the news of the proclamation of Soviet Republics in Hungary and Bavaria and the reports of the troubles in the other countries in huge letters running right across the page. A triumphant article bore the heading, "But it does go round all the same!" meaning the world revolution. This article ran:

Comrades! It does go round all the same—the world revolution! The news of the magnificent victory of the workers of Hungary and Bavaria will go through our ranks like a stimulating, strengthening waft of air. Let us now muster up all our strength to deal the enemy the final blow. German workers in soldiers' uniforms, who are fighting here against your Lettish and Russian brothers, read the news from Hungary and Bavaria! Read and blush for shame, those who are still able to blush! Throw down your weapons and come over to us! The revolution of the working-classes is advancing victoriously; nothing can now stop it from becoming a world revolution. Your lying prophets who have always declared that only in dark Russia could a Soviet Republic arise, have now been answered by—Hungary! Your social traitors who tell you that a Soviet regime is not suited to Germany are to-day refuted by—Bavaria! And to-morrow—Austria and Germany and Europe and the whole world! He who is not with us is against us. Long live the Soviet Republics of Hungary and Bavaria! Long live the Bolshevist revolution in Germany! Long live the world revolution!

Comrade Peter Stutchka, our native Lenin, sent out the following wireless greeting to Budapest and Munich:

The Soviet of Workers' Deputies of Latvia greets its natural allies, the Hungarian and Bavarian Soviet Republics. The working-people of Latvia, in its hard struggle against the united counter-revolutionary forces, impatiently awaits news of the

THE TRIUMPH OF THE MUSCOVITES

outbreak of the world revolution and receives with strength redoubled to every message of new victories for the European proletariat. P. STUTCHKA."

Pastor Model, more fanatical than ever, and more convinced that Bolshevism was sent to bring happiness to the world, likewise expressed his joy. "Who was right after all?" he cried jubilantly, and warned the Riga bourgeoisie, "one last time, before it was too late": "You would not understand what was going on in the world. Blows were necessary to make you understand. Blows with a hammer! They have fallen. What lesson does the great social revolution in Germany teach to us people in Riga? It teaches us: whoever will not change his ideas must die! Do you realize this? Ever mightier, ever more imperious, life conveys to us the one great truth: whatever is to remain alive and develop itself must accomplish the conversion to Communism as swiftly and as radically as possible!"

The supreme political chiefs in Moscow, in the meantime, decided that they ought not to rest satisfied with words. They issued appropriate directions to their vanguard in Riga. The latter, in their turn, made the necessary practical decisions with regard to their further procedure. At a sitting of the Riga Soviet the following "guiding lines for the Red Army in Latvia" were laid down:

Latvia is the gateway through which the Russian Revolution must invade Western Europe. Our duty now, after the proclamation of the Soviet regime in Hungary and Bavaria, is to reach the Prussian frontier as quickly as we possibly can. By doing this we can most effectively secure the spread of Bolshevism over Western Europe. The Soviet Government of Moscow informs us that at this moment it is redoubling its efforts towards carrying Bolshevism into Germany, and particularly into East Prussia. In the last weeks it has sent several hundred agents into East Prussia. The prospects for the Red agitators are very favourable there. The only salvation for Germany lies now in an acceptance of Russian Communism and in a revolutionary inundation of the Allied countries. The Entente, by the way it is treating Germany, is only playing into our hands. We must march into Germany and fight against the Entente shoulder to shoulder with the Germans. An advance of the Red Army into Germany promises to be most successful. Through the collapse of German Imperialism and the outbreak of revolution in Hungary the Red troops can now venture to push forward against Europe in the north and the south simultaneously. The divisions of the Red Army fighting in Latvia have to deliver the decisive blow!

The resolution concluded with the following words:

This is no time for weariness or resting! We can only rest when the Red flags of the victorious Communist International wave over Berlin, Rome, Paris and London. Ça ira! It will soon come! Hurrah for Communist Latvia! Hurrah for the Communist International!

The outbreak of Bolshevism in the very heart of Europe was particularly welcome to the Muscovites at the moment. It came just when their power—in Latvia as well as in Russia—was visibly tottering. Red misgovernment had so swiftly and completely ruined the territories of the former Russian Empire that serious discontent was already making itself felt even among supporters of the Soviet.

It was not only the bourgeoisie of Riga who were suffering acutely now. The working-class too were beginning to suffer from hunger. Except for a few hundred leading Bolsheviks, who were provided with everything, the "citizens of the 1st Category" were hardly better off than those of the 2nd and 3rd

Categories. (For instance, the family of the workman Balgal, which was lodged in our old flat and belonged to the 1st Category, had long ago ceased to enjoy an abundance of good things. They now began to grumble openly.) All the "small people," in short—the working-classes, hawkers, small tradesmen and artisans—who had registered themselves as proletarians and at the beginning of the Bolshevist reign had received certain advantages, were now going hungry. The enemies of the Soviet power were substantially reinforced from the ranks of these people.

It was the same with the peasants. They hated the Bolshevists perhaps even more than the townspeople. The Red Commissaries who went about the country searching for corn and food supplies everywhere met with stubborn resistance from the Lettish peasants. Not in the least tempted by the valueless Soviet paper money which was offered them, the peasants still refused to deliver up their produce.

But worse by far than the loud grumbling of the workmen and the stubborn resistance of the peasants was the fact that even the Red troops now began to manifest their discontent. There had already been several attempts at rebellion in their ranks, especially among the Russian regiments, and although these movements had been brutally repressed, the unrest increased. The troops objected to the hardships of this new campaign when the war was long over, and the Red leaders' promises of new victories in the west, rich booty, and so on, seemed unlikely of early fulfilment.

The unexpected turn of events in Central Europe,

therefore, came as a providential diversion for the Muscovites. Here was something to distract the masses from the contemplation of their own hunger and misery. "The world revolution is on its way!" they cried triumphantly. "Who can fail to see it? Look—Hungary, Bavaria, Austria, Germany! The masses will now regain their faith in the further development of Bolshevist ideas."

For the celebration of their triumphs the Bolsheviks chose the 1st of May, the "fête day of the world proletariat," which had arrived in the meantime. On this day the "entire proletariat" of Riga, together with all the troops stationed in the town, were aroused, and a great series of festivities was announced. The whole town was hastily decorated at great expense and with a vast consumption of red paint and made to look as "revolutionary" as possible for the occasion.

A large number of streets and squares, above all those through which the mass processions were to pass, had previously been given new "revolutionary names." Thoroughfares which up till then had borne the name of "Alexander," "Nicholas" or "Church," now became "Revolution Street," "Karl Marx Boulevard," "Third International Prospect," etc. The chief theatre of the Red triumphal festivities was destined to be the large square in the centre of the town, the Esplanade, which had already been graced with the new name of "Communist Square," to suit the conquerors' taste.

The Reds then set to work to fit this square up in a peculiar way for the celebrations. Right in the middle of the square they erected, in all haste, a crazy-looking plywood structure, supposed to represent a so-called "Temple of Reason." They then proceeded to encircle this edifice with about twenty wooden obelisks, each at least fifty feet high, which they set up at intervals round the edge of the square. Temple and obelisks alike were decorated in a sort of wild futuristic style, with gaudy red-and-white daubs and zigzags. As to the object and sense of these remarkable monuments and glaring decorations the organizers of the festival themselves did not seem to be exactly clear. But the whole effect was beyond doubt very "revolutionary," and that was the first requirement.

When the Red embellishments were complete, our good old bourgeois Riga made an even more barbaric and "Red" impression than in the previous months. By order of the Soviet authorities, most of the houses in the main streets, all the lamp-posts, the telegraph poles, the tramway posts and in fact all possible objects within reach, were daubed with bright-red paint or at least smothered with red cloth and ribbons. Wherever human strength was sufficient for the task, old "bourgeois" statues were thrown down from their pedestals and rough attempts made to set up in their places new effigies mostly representing prominent Bolsheviks, or as the *Red Flag* expressed it in a previous announcement of the festival, "the well-known features of our glorious leaders." These effigies, according to this paper, were "displayed everywhere, for the joy of the revolutionary masses and for the intimidation of the White Guard bands and enemies of the proletariat!"

These Red gods—in the first rank Karl Marx and Lenin, the "Red Tsar," and also Trotsky, Zinoviev,

Kamenev and a whole quantity of idols of secondary importance—were honoured and worshipped by our tyrants with grovelling servility. There were a number of different images of each "leader." They shot up out of the earth on all sides like mushrooms after the rain.

As the time available was so short, however, it had only been possible to make them in most cases of clay or plaster; in several cases, indeed, the worshippers had to be content to scrawl the "well-known features of the glorious leaders" slap-dash on pieces of cloth or cardboard and plant these quickly fabricated portraits on the vacant bases of the overturned statues of former times.

During the previous night there had been some rain; the products of proletarian art had already received a sharp shower. All the plaster busts, clay statues and water-colour pictures had, therefore, lost a good deal of their beauty even before the festivities had begun. A few passers-by, "not yet completely exterminated citizens of the 3rd Category," who hurried past timidly in the early morning in search of food, looked with curiosity at these pitiful placards, flapping untidily in the wind.

Then, at about nine o'clock in the morning, the show began. In some outer district half the town gathered for a solemn procession. The whole population had been ordered to take part in the "celebration of the victory of the proletariat." Anyone not putting in an appearance was to be excluded from the "workers' unions" and would lose his food-card. The threats produced their result. Over 50,000 half-starved, ragged

Soviet citizens collected at the assembling place and formed an "imposing procession." Right in front marched a few groups of "reliable Communists" with red flags, huge placards, blaring bands and other attributes of Bolshevist pageantry. Behind them followed, slowly and drearily, droning out songs, the main procession of Soviet clerks, workmen, artisans, soldiers and a herd of miscellaneous people raked together for the occasion.

After filing for about three hours through the chief streets of the town, the procession, hot, tired, dusty and hungry, arrived on the Esplanade towards noon. Most of the participants stared gloomily before them and maintained a dejected silence. Only the leaders, the Lettish Communists and the Russian delegates sent from Moscow, behaved noisily and vociferously. They carried red banners with such bloodthirsty inscriptions as the following: "Death to Capitalism!!" "Long live the Red Terror of the Masses!" "World Communism—Our Final Aim!" "Death to the Barons and to the White Guards!" The flag-bearers waved their placards and red flags in the air, and paraded several times round the "Temple of Reason," like heathen priests round a sacrificial altar.

Throughout the festivity the dull rumble of guns was heard from the front—an unfitting accompaniment. Several White aeroplanes cruised over the multitude, buzzing and inquisitive. Some left thin trails of white smoke behind them which formed curious hieroglyphics on the blue background. These remained visible for a long time above the heads of the demonstrators, like some strange writing on the wall.

Down in the square, the Red throng looked anxiously skywards. It was evident that the unwelcome visitors overhead acted as a damper on the officially prescribed enthusiasm. But the White airmen took pity on the poor devils. They described a few more graceful curves in the blue, and then disappeared westward.

The Red chief, Comrade Stutchka, had indeed taken special precautionary measures against "possible disturbances from White Guard quarters." There were a number of captured volunteers in the Central Prison, and the commander of the White Army had been informed by wireless that they would be executed "in the event of an enemy airman disturbing the festivity of the revolutionary masses by shots, bomb-dropping or similar incidents."

Further, Comrade Stutchka had taken care that only "reliable Communists" should be armed.

At the end of the Esplanade, where the plaster busts of Marx, Lenin and Trotsky stood, a platform had been erected. The President of Soviet Latvia, Peter Stutchka, the President of the Soviet of Workers' Deputies of Riga, Simon Berg, the Commissary of Supply, Endrup, a delegate from the Kremlin called Irklis, a representative of the German Communist Party and all kinds of other prominent Bolshevists had mounted it. At about midday the crowd assembled in front of this platform and Comrade Stutchka addressed it.

Those of us who had not seen Stutchka during the past months noticed immediately that he had aged. His hair, which four months earlier had been only greying, was now quite white. He looked weary and depressed. The good nature had almost entirely dis-

THE RED DEMONSTRATION ON THE ESPLANADE ON THE 1ST MAY, 1919
On the extreme left is the "Temple of Reason"; in the background some of the wooden obelisks

appeared from his face, and a new expression had come over it—pained, savage, stubborn. And when he began to speak, we heard not the warm, paternal ring of old days, but a hoarse, exasperated, angry voice, which he had difficulty in making audible.

"Comrades! Communists!" he cried at the top of his voice. "You have all seen it: mighty, grandiose, overwhelming is this our parade of the united working-people! The same enthusiasm prevails to-day, I am told, over there—in the trenches, at the front. There too the joyous tumult of the May festival has burst forth. The enemy, however, opened fire on the red flags with machine guns. The Whites wanted to drown the strains of the 'International' in gun-fire. Fools! Fools, who think they can choke the Communist idea in the smoke of gunpowder or annihilate the world revolution by poison gas. The world revolution is not to be arrested. The 1st of May, 1919, is the field-day of the world proletariat. The 1st of May, 1920, will be the festival of victory of the triumphant Commune of the whole world, the New Year's day of the victorious proletariat!"

Stutchka stopped for a moment. He stared blankly in front of him as though reflecting, and hesitated before continuing. But the mob before him, especially the "convinced Communists" in the front ranks, bellowed encouragement to him and pushed forward, waving their banners and placards. The weary, almost fainting orator was affected as by the touching of a spring. He pulled himself together with a jerk and gave vent to the revolutionary phrases that were expected of him.

"Comrades! Workers! Communists! You know it:

yesterday and this morning we feared that the White hordes, by dropping bombs from aeroplanes, might turn our May festival into a bloody massacre of peaceful demonstrators. It was not for nothing that as many as six White airmen flew over Riga this morning. But we let them know what we had decided: in case shots had really been fired or bombs dropped by one of the White airmen on the peaceful demonstrators, we would have executed this evening twenty-five hostages taken from the Baltic barons! Fortunately this did not prove to be necessary. It was a great relief to me that we were spared from having to mar this festival—even though it is a festival of ruthless class war—by such an extraordinary measure as the shooting of hostages. All the same, this grave threat with regard to the hostages holds good, of course, for the future as well...."

In the evening, after a regular deluge of further speeches had beaten down upon the defenceless crowd, the proceedings began to liven up somewhat. An "imposing firework display" was begun. A few rockets and other products of Muscovite pyrotechnics—five-pointed stars, hammers and sickles and the words "world revolution" in huge blazing letters—hissing and spluttering convulsively, surged into the sky with more stench than fairylike beauty.

After the fireworks the People's Government graciously distributed beer and vodka among the participants. But the "reliable Communists" received, in spite of the principle of equality and fraternity, more than the other Soviet citizens of lower categories. The reliable ones, therefore, were soon noticeably tipsy. They shouted, sang and cheerfully fired their rifles and revol-

THE TRIUMPH OF THE MUSCOVITES

vers into the air. A few of their fellow-demonstrators were accidentally wounded. But the reliable ones cared little for that. They executed wild, indecent dances and leapt round the "Temple of Reason" like creatures possessed.

To put a check to this merry-making, a strong west wind, blowing in violent gusts from the sea, began to sweep over the square, lit up by innumerable torches and lanterns. It beat persistently against a gigantic portrait of Lenin, the "Red Tsar," crudely painted on cardboard and fixed, visible from a long way off, on a building flanking the Esplanade, looking down with its sarcastic smile on the doings of the foolish herd below.

The wind shook the picture so violently that a loud banging and groaning was heard from time to time, and at times the Mongolian head of the Red "Tsar" seemed to be grinning and nodding to the crowd below.

But none of the demonstrators paid any attention to the uncanny lifelikeness of the Mongolian skull. They went on dancing and shouting. Excited by the events of the day and the copious consumption of wine, they plunged into a mad carousal which did not cease till dawn.

CHAPTER XVII

"BOURGEOIS TO THE FRONT!"

The first May days went by—the fifth month of Soviet rule had begun! We still waited for the great events predicted by Carlyle. All was quiet at the front. If anyone spoke of an offensive, it was the Reds, who had now taken fresh courage and were eager to press forward and unite as quickly as possible with the revolutionaries of Western Europe.

This was, to be sure, not so easily done as the Red chiefs tried to make their followers believe. The White Army was still lying in Mitau and the East Prussian frontier was much farther from the Reds than at the beginning of their invasion. But that did not signify much after what had taken place in Hungary and Bavaria. Riga and Latvia were now more securely than ever in Moscow's hands. In Riga and the surrounding villages they could make preparations at their leisure for the "great offensive against world imperialism" (via Courland) and simultaneously carry to completion the work of the Bolshevization of this "incorrigibly bourgeois town."

In inventing measures which could promote the realization of these aims our rulers were indefatigable. A few new decrees could occasionally work Red marvels! So, when the talk of the necessity of a new offensive began, they dropped dark hints about "measures for protecting the rear of the advancing Red Army" that would have to be taken.

What was meant by this soon became known: the Riga Soviet had decided that all streets and squares of Riga, through which the Red troops proceeding to the front had to pass, would first have to be purged of bourgeois inhabitants. Otherwise the perfidious bourgeois, malignant as they were by nature, might fire at the "gallant advance-guards of the world revolution" from the windows and cellar gratings and perpetrate all kinds of mischief. Therefore—out with them, before it was too late!

It was ordered that all "citizens of the 3rd Category," that is, all citizens who were not workers and not Soviet employees, and whose houses and dwellings were situated in certain central streets (in particular, what had been the most fashionable part of the town), were to leave their domiciles as speedily as possible, and to settle down in "proletarian districts."

It was exactly the same thing as the Reds had done some time before with our family and with many other Riga people, but this time it was done on a much larger scale. No fewer than 20,000 people (the *élite* of the Riga bourgeoisie) were affected by this new decree! There were not, however, in Riga, which had always been distinguished by a high level of prosperity, sufficient "proletarian dwellings" to accommodate such a vast number of people. The Reds at first did not know where to put them all. But then an idea occurred to them, and they adopted the following solution.

In the immediate neighbourhood of the town, in the middle of the River Dvina, there were two completely uninhabited islands, or rather large sandbanks, on which stood barely half a dozen dilapidated wooden sheds and poor fishermen's huts. In earlier times, when Russia still maintained a flourishing trade with the rest of the world, large quantities of timber, which were floated down the river to Riga to be sawn up and exported, used to be stacked on these islands. Now they lay completely empty and deserted. The very names of these islands—one of them was called "Hare Island"—indicated their wild and inhospitable nature. But this did not prevent the Soviet power from ordering that all those "citizens of the 3rd Category" whom they planned to expel from their homes were to move to these islands and the adjacent bare, sandy banks of the Lower Dvina, and to settle down there as pariahs of the Communist State, strictly separated from the rest of the population.

The decree legalizing this measure was worded in the following characteristic manner:

THE REVOLUTIONARY SOVIET OF THE RIGA WAR AREA
ORDER No. 8

In view of the happenings in other towns of Latvia, where the bourgeois have fired from cellars and windows of their houses at troops of the Red Army, we issue the following order:

1. All citizens who are not manual workers or dependants of manual workers or soldiers of the Red Army, or who are not employed in factories, works or Soviet institutions, and who live in the following streets: Suvoroff Street, Mitau Road, the Dvina Embankment from Mühlen Street to Elizabeth Street, Great Moscow Street, Alexander Boulevard, Petersburg Road, Todleben Boulevard and in all corner houses of cross streets running out of the above-named streets, must leave their present dwellings within 24 hours and transfer themselves to the following places:
From the VIth District—to Hare Island. From the

"BOURGEOIS TO THE FRONT!"

Ist and IInd Districts—to Kundsingsholm Island, and from the remaining districts—to the Lower Dvina.

2. On leaving their homes the above-named bourgeois are not to take with them any superfluous food supplies, nor any furniture, clothes, utensils or other kinds of belongings.
3. All the vacated houses are placed by the Soviet Government under the management of the caretakers.
4. All not obeying this command will be punished in accordance with revolutionary military law.

The Revolutionary Soviet of the Riga War Area,
(Signatures)

When this new regulation became known, the citizens who were affected by it were seized with despair. They rushed to the military officials and the higher Soviet officials, implored them to modify the order, asked that the evacuation might be postponed, begged that they should at least be allowed to take with them a few food supplies and belongings. But all these entreaties and complaints were of no avail. They were not even allowed to move into the houses of relations or friends in districts where bourgeois were still permitted to live.

A swarm of Red soldiers and "gunwomen" was at once despatched to the streets in question with instructions to see that the order was strictly carried out. As usual, they forced their way into every house (our family was spared this time, for our house luckily was not situated in the zone to be vacated) and urged the citizens to make haste as they tied up their packages. Neither the tears of old and ailing women nor the whimpering of small children torn from their beds could move them. "Out with you! out!"

Then an endless, pitiful procession was to be seen making its way through the empty streets of Riga. Men bent with age, weak, tired women, hosts of weeping, whimpering children, burdened with bundles and bedding, driven on by an escort of cursing "gunwomen," set out in the direction of the river and were given no rest until they had arrived on the islands assigned to them as their future abode.

On these desolate, treeless sandbanks they found no houses whatever beyond a few fishermen's huts and woodsheds. The 20,000 people who had been driven there found themselves completely without lodging. The majority of them had to camp out on the naked earth, under the open sky. A kind of gipsy camp was formed—but without tents or caravans. In small and large groups the members of the most respected Riga families sat or lay about on the ground, like nomads; they could see before them the fine, slender church spires of their native town and the homes from which they had been driven. Not for nothing had the decree expressly ordered that none of the exiles might take food supplies of their own with them. There was, it is true, a public kitchen on the island, from which they received the notorious Soviet soup free of charge. But this Soviet soup meant gradual starvation. The inhuman sanitary conditions under which the exiles had to live here brought mass epidemics in their train. Diseases soon began to spread. Nobody attended to the sick. People died like flies. The Soviets saw the object of their measure fulfilled: they were not put to the necessity of shooting the bourgeois, but succeeded in killing them off by hundreds "peacefully and without bloodshed."

The Soviet chiefs invented yet other ways and means

to achieve the "complete physical destruction of the bourgeoisie," which was their "ideal and ultimate goal." Comrade Danishevsky, the People's Commissary for War, came forward with various fresh proposals. At a sitting of the Riga Soviet he delivered a speech devoted to the preparation of the Red offensive, and concluded (according to a report published in No. 106 of the *Red Flag*) with the following exhortations:

"In the immediate future," said Comrade Danishevsky, "fresh fighting awaits us. We must therefore not only make our Red Army as efficient as possible in battle, but also seriously consider the position of the bourgeoisie behind the front, in order that they should not commit any kind of harm, and in order that the able-bodied bourgeois young men should not remain behind in the threatened districts. This does not at all mean that the bourgeois should be killed off to the last man. The revolutionary spirit of the Soviets is not to be measured by the number of shot bourgeois. Not by any means! That is not absolutely indispensable. What is really necessary is that the bourgeoisie should be mobilized in working gangs. The bourgeois must be put to some practical use. Above all, they must be sent to the front to dig trenches for our army and lend it assistance in other ways!"

This idea appealed at once to the Reds, and it was promptly put into practice. Henceforward, if the Bolshevists got hold of any citizens who possessed no "certificate of work," or if fresh compulsory labour had to be provided for those languishing in prison, they sent them to the front to dig trenches.

In this fifth month of Soviet rule existence became

utterly unbearable for the bourgeois of Riga. A bourgeois family was not safe for one minute of the day from the Red intruders. Every day they were ordered to do something, forbidden to do something else, or threatened with something.

"The bourgeois must go and dig trenches at the front. . . . The bourgeois must go out and sweep the streets. . . . The bourgeois must not be allowed a moment's peace. . . . The bourgeois must be given as bad a time as possible. . . ."

• • • • •

For the young men among the population there was reserved yet another disagreeable eventuality, which hung perpetually over their heads like a sword of Damocles. It was the prospect of being enrolled one day in the Red Army.

As early as March and April, after the first White resistance at the front, the Soviet power had mobilized a certain number of Riga bourgeois. These conscripts, however, had all been of a class which was older than mine. But I knew that the turn of my class would come soon. I too might be called up for military service in the Red Army any day.

This eventuality was disagreeable from more than one point of view. Service in the Red Army was almost equivalent to a death-sentence. A "bourgeois" who entered the ranks of the Muscovite troops, where politics, propaganda and espionage were rife, found himself faced with two alternatives: either "to run with the hounds" with a more or less successful effort at dissimulation, or otherwise to be denounced as an opponent and counter-revolutionary and treated as such. But what he could count upon most certainly was to be despatched, only a few weeks after his enrolment, to fight against the White Army, and thus be forced to bear arms against his own friends and brothers.

My feelings were accordingly far from agreeable when one May morning, as I perused my *Red Flag* over a frugal breakfast, I discovered that my class was being called to the colours.

There it was, written down in black and white. "Point 4" of the mobilization order ran as follows:

Anyone not presenting himself, without valid reasons, within the fixed lapse of time will be handed over to the Revolutionary Tribunal and most severely punished (shooting not excluded).

I read the mobilization order carefully through several times. I considered what was now to be done. As I was not independent, I could hardly think of refusing to present myself or, indeed, attempting to escape and join the Whites. Repulsive though the idea was, I was compelled to obey. Perhaps I should be declared unfit. But in any case I would have to present myself at the recruiting office.

The news was a most painful surprise to my parents. They were most distressed at the prospect of being separated from me, perhaps for a long time, in the midst of the uncertainty then prevailing; they were old people, and regarded me as a kind of protection. Yet they realized that I would have to go, and resigned themselves to the inevitable.

The recruiting office of the Red Army was installed in an old patrician house, almost a palace, which had been the property of one of the most distinguished families of the town. I had been there quite often in past years, for the son of the house had been a school friend of mine. All the furniture had been removed, and the aristocratic dwelling had assumed a completely foreign aspect, disorderly and dilapidated.

The recruiting office was on the second floor; but the crowd of men who had been called up formed a long queue which stretched right out into the street—Russians and Germans, Balts and Letts, townsmen and peasants, workers and bourgeois. None of the faces displayed anything resembling enthusiasm for or even normal pleasure at the prospect of incorporation in the Red Army. On the contrary, it can be stated definitely that all these young conscripts felt the strongest repugnance at the thought of what was before them and made little attempt to hide their feelings.

Slowly the queue advanced, climbed the stairs and penetrated the room where the commission was sitting. At long tables were seated a number of well-known doctors of the town, flanked by quite an equal number of Soviet Commissaries of "revolutionary" appearance. These eyed the doctors mistrustfully and threateningly, as if they suspected them, now and again, of using the recruits with excessive indulgence.

The poor doctors, indeed, found themselves in an extremely delicate position: on one side the Commissaries urged them to declare the greatest possible number of recruits fit for service; on the other side, all these recruits were equally desirous of being exempt from military service and expressed this desire by looks and gestures which were almost supplicating.

Nevertheless, throughout the whole examination the doctors' faces remained like masks, inscrutable to the conscripts who, one after the other, filed past the fateful table. With the utmost conscientiousness, with an almost exaggerated care, they examined the young men, listened to their hearts, tapped their chests, explored them meticulously from head to foot.

As the result of their examination only one quarter of the men presented was declared unconditionally fit for service; another quarter was classed as unfit and was immediately dismissed, while the rest, that is, half, were sent to the military hospital for "further examination." For these last this practically meant salvation, for the "further examination" might take several weeks, and "to gain time," as we said then, "was to gain everything."

Whether the Commissaries saw through the doctors' manœuvre nobody ever knew. In any case the doctors had conformed so strictly to the clauses of the recruiting regulations that no objection could be raised, and the Commissaries were forced to ratify their decisions willy-nilly. It turned out later that the good doctors of our town, at this critical time, had by their little stratagem saved the lives of many of their fellow-citizens.

While I was awaiting my turn, I had time closely to observe the procedure. Nevertheless, when my name was called, I approached the table with some anxiety, for, endowed to my misfortune with a perfectly healthy constitution, I had not the slightest infirmity on which I could fall back for an excuse.

I was very near to answering the question "What's wrong with you?" put to me by one of the doctors in an encouraging voice and accompanied by a suggestive look through his glasses, with the word, "Nothing"; but at the last moment I remembered an affection from which I had suffered in the earliest years of my childhood—an injury to the ear-drum—and, confessing to this "physical defect," I entrusted my fate to the group of doctors and Red Commissaries sitting in front of me.

The result was miraculous. Hardly had I, somewhat embarrassed, stammered out the words "Interior of the ear . . . inflammation . . . ear-drum . . ." than the doctor breathed with evident relief and began to test my ear with an air of wisdom. He examined me, tapped me and listened to me with exhaustive care, and then pronounced the saving oracle:

"Internal injury to the ear. . . . Doubtful case. . . . For further examination in the military hospital. . . . Next, please!"

. . . . .

The military hospital, to which I betook myself the very next morning, was situated on the other side of the river, the west bank, on the Mitau road. The way from Nicholas Street, in which we lived, to the river led me across the Esplanade, where the "Temple of Reason," the twenty obelisks and all the other Bolshevist monuments were still standing. Between these monuments I saw a few dozen men marching briskly backwards and forwards: recruits being drilled. They must have been some of those citizens who had been conscripted earlier, in April.

With them were drilling the soldiers of the "1st Riga

"BOURGEOIS TO THE FRONT!"

Workmen's Regiment." This regiment consisted of men sent by the Communist trade unions to the Red Army as "volunteers." They were either middle-aged men or young lads, whom the members of the Committees, themselves remaining at home, had sent up for service. For example, the Communist (and anti-Semite) committee of the "clothing union" had sent a number of elderly Jewish tailors, who had joined the union from motives of self-preservation. In variegated civilian clothes and goloshes, with gloomy and complaining faces, all these Red soldiers were carrying out, under the command of Red officers, all kinds of manœuvres, and applying themselves to complicated rifle exercises.

"This pleasure may soon be in store for you too," I murmured to myself at the sight of the poor devils, and continued my way in no very cheerful mood to the military hospital.

I reached it towards noon. The hospital, an enormous building, was still managed by the former medical personnel of the town (that is, by the same doctors who had carried out the examination of the recruits). It made an impression of cleanliness and tidiness which struck me from the first very agreeably. The recruits sent "for further examination" were lodged in large light rooms. From the moment I was admitted I somehow felt comfortable and "at home."

From more than one point of view the hospital possessed advantages over the "outside world," the town apartments and private houses, which were continually invaded by the Reds. As it belonged to the military authorities, its inmates received the same nourishment as the Red Army, that is to say, more or less decent food. (The Reds did not conceal the fact that they had no intention of sharing the fate of the bourgeois, whose speedy death by starvation was their "ideal ultimate goal.")

The second and perhaps even greater advantage which internment in the military hospital brought to the "Red conscripts" was that all of them, so long as they remained there, were secure against any further arbitrary interference by the Soviet authorities. It was perhaps the only place in the whole town which was spared the dangerous attentions of the Red police. Many of the "patients," for this reason alone, made every effort to prolong to the utmost extent the duration of their stay.

The dictum: "He who gains time, gains everything," was here observed in its widest meaning. A man, for instance, who had been sent to hospital for "further examination" of his "visual faculty"—which could have been carried out in a few minutes—lay in bed for weeks, wearing hospital clothing, having his temperature taken several times a day, receiving good food and attention, and would tax all his ingenuity, after his sight had at last been recognized as normal, to discover in himself some other "physical defect" for "further examination."

The doctors, the hospital staff and the patients formed one great family in conspiracy against the Red power. They were continually gathering in little groups, sitting and standing and whispering. They read the *communiqués* from the front together, studied the maps of the theatre of war, and openly calculated how long, at the very most, it could be before the Whites started their advance for the liberation of Riga.

The nurses, who went every day into the town on errands and always returned full of news, took a most active part in our debates. These kind, womanly creatures, clean, smelling slightly of disinfectant, dressed in slightly starched overalls with blue and white stripes, glided from bed to bed, even at night, to whisper in the patients' ears the latest sensational political news. It would nearly always be something of this sort: "The Red troops have retreated another six miles!" Or: "A secret messenger has said that the advance will begin the day after to-morrow. . . ." Or else: "The Reds in Riga are packing up and clearing off . . ." and so on.

One other thing that comforted us was the fact that the dull bombardment from the front sounded slightly louder here than on the other side of the river.

This ceaseless bombardment was the only sound, sometimes almost imperceptible, then louder again and louder, which told us of the existence of another world outside our dead city. It told us that this lost world could still, from day to day, from hour to hour, open before our eyes, and that in order once more to take our place therein, it was worth while, after all, to bear all the Red torments in silence a little longer.

CHAPTER XVIII

AT THE LAST GASP

In the second week of May old Frau Walter died. Her strength had long been visibly slipping away. The sinister companion of the Muscovites—starvation—had at last claimed her as its victim. In the words of the death certificate which a Red militiaman, fetched by my parents, drew up, she had "died of under-nourishment."

When the news was communicated to me by telephone in the military hospital, I managed to obtain leave for one day in order to pay my last homage to the old lady, whom I had known from my earliest childhood. As I made my way to the town for the first time since my entry into the hospital my thoughts dwelt involuntarily upon the life of this unfortunate woman.

This human being who now, in a time of blackest distress, had vanished from the world without a sound, almost unnoticed by anybody, had once held a brilliant and universally envied position in our town. Frau Walter came of one of those old Balt families which with justified pride still called themselves "Hanseats." Her father had once stood at the head of the Riga business community; her dead husband had been Mayor of Riga for many years; she had lived, wealthy and esteemed, in one of the finest patrician houses; a numerous family and endless servants had always surrounded her; and in those days, as mayoress, she had been accustomed to drive through the streets—the inhabitants until the last used to whisper it to one another when they saw her—in a magnificent carriage with four horses, one of the richest, most noble, most admired women in Riga.

The decline of her fortune set in, swift and irresistible, immediately after the outbreak of the war. Frau Walter, who in peace-time had lived on the income of a handsome capital, was very soon forced to touch the capital itself. Then came the terrible increase in the cost of living and the devaluation of money.

Frau Walter gave up her old family house and went to live in a modest flat. The noble house where she had been born, had grown up and as mayoress had entertained the whole town was now occupied by a noisy military administration; and while the guns were thundering at the front, there resounded day and night in this once quiet and distinguished Hanseatic home the clatter and ringing of countless typewriters and telephones.

The war was followed by the Russian Revolution. Then came the final blow, sudden and catastrophic: the Red invasion, with its accompanying misery, slow starvation and sickness. This refined old lady, who once drove through the streets in a four-horse carriage, now knew starvation in the literal sense of the word. Of all her numerous family, only her son and her daughter-in-law remained. To the last she had given them all she possessed. She ate as little as she could in order to take her son some food in prison, until at last the limit was reached and death silently carried off this poor, wasted, long-suffering mortal. . . .

With my two parents, I followed her body as it was taken with all haste to the grave. It was a pitiful little troop that made its way almost unnoticed through the dead streets to the cemetery. A "3rd Category" funeral. . . .

Once half the town would probably have followed the bier. Now barely a dozen surviving friends appeared to accompany the dead woman on her last journey. In happier days, perhaps, black-plumed horses would have drawn a hearse draped with mourning slowly and solemnly through the streets. Now a simple stretcher, borne by a few unknown persons, was carried to the cemetery by the shortest way, almost at a run.

Not even a clergyman could be found to conduct the funeral. It was therefore one of the mourners, an old man who had once been in the service of the dead woman, who had the duty of pronouncing the farewell words at the cemetery: "Earth to earth, ashes to ashes, dust to dust. . . ." The grave was filled in hastily and inadequately; someone laid a modest bouquet of flowers upon it, and the ceremony was over.

Without losing any time we left the cemetery and returned to our homes. We could see Red soldiers a little distance away, supervising the work of a gang of prisoners, and no one wanted to approach them.

· · · · ·

A fresh surprise awaited us at home on our return from the cemetery. The door of our flat stood wide open, and in the middle of the sitting-room stood a Red militiaman and Comradess Balgal, arguing vehemently. The militiaman sulkily explained to me that it was he who had given the certificate of Frau Walter's death; he knew, therefore, that there was "one person less" living in our flat; he also knew that a second person of this household was being "supported in an institution at the expense of the State." In order to fill these vacancies, he declared, the military authorities had decided to install in our flat "two comrades, members of the Communist Party!"

It was to this proposal that the good woman was offering so vehement a resistance. She flung herself in the militiaman's path like a lioness defending her cubs. She called my mother "Comradess Popoff," and referred to the "high position" of her husband, who belonged to the "workmen's council" in a factory; in short, she made out such a powerful case for us that the militiaman soon gave way and dropped the proposal. Comradess Balgal looked round her with a triumphant air, spat vehemently on the spot where the man had stood, and rubbed the damp stain away contemptuously with her foot.

It was only after she herself had disappeared, having received our warmest words of gratitude, that my parents gave me the explanation of this remarkable and lucky intervention.

Comradess Balgal, who during the first weeks of Soviet rule had taken up a pronouncedly hostile attitude towards us, had for some time past become more and more friendly. As the blessings conferred by the Reds on their supporters—chiefly the abundant food rations—became more and more meagre, the revolutionary enthusiasm of the Balgal family had visibly abated. And now that the Reds had finally exhausted their store of economic wisdom, and working-class families too had been going hungry for sometime past, Comradess Balgal had turned from a Saul into a Paul. She now came up to our flat every day. She not only criticized the Reds every day more violently, but let fall from time to time such remarks as "I wish the devil would take the whole lot of them!" or "When is it all going to end?" Then she had volunteered to help my mother with her household duties. At first my mother would not let her. But Madame Balgal insisted, and at last my mother was completely reconciled with the woman who had ejected us from our home.

I took leave of my parents soon afterwards to return to the military hospital with a somewhat lighter heart. True, I had found my parents in a more deplorable situation than ever. But at least I knew now that they were under powerful protection; and I felt a certain justification in hoping that no further calamities would befall our home during my absence.

. . . . .

On my way back to the military hospital I was by chance to witness a singular event.

The Soviet campaign against religion which had been begun some months before was now—at the beginning of May—entering a new phase. Hitherto, for reasons of their own, the Reds had put a certain restraint on their persecution of the clergy and on their desecration of the churches. For, among those local Communists whose collaboration our tyrants had enlisted, many had remained favourable to religion; the Reds had deemed it prudent not to shock the ideas

AT THE LAST GASP

of these sympathizers too brutally at first. Nevertheless, there had been various indications of late that the Red tide would soon engulf even the churches.

All religious buildings were now, as the property of the Soviet State, administered by special Bolshevist Commissaries. The cathedral was no exception; it had been for some time under the management of a female commissary, a former working woman, who had taken the place of the church committee and supervised the actions of the vicar; she had the right to let the church, as she thought fit, for political meetings, theatrical entertainments, games and sports, Red soldiers' dances and "also for religious purposes."

For several weeks it had been reported that the Reds were planning a new blow against the Church. Yet, not only were the churches packed at every service; not only did innumerable persons seek consolation there; not only had many parents insisted that their children should receive daily in the churches the religious instruction which the Government forbade in the schools; but in many cases the clergy themselves, from their pulpits, at the risk of their lives, had upheld the freedom of belief and exhorted the faithful to hold out until the "day of deliverance."

All this the Soviet authorities were aware of, and day by day they became more incensed. For the launching of their new attack they had chosen that very Sunday on which I found myself walking from my home towards the "Mitau suburb" of Riga where the military hospital was situated.

Between the "Petersburg suburb"—the district in which we lived—and the bridge over the river (which

I had to cross on my way back to the military hospital), lay the oldest part of Riga, the so-called "City," or "Old Town."

In this quarter of the town, which is made up of a picturesque confusion of innumerable crooked streets and alleys, are situated not only the oldest buildings of Riga, such as the castle, the town hall, the House of the Black Heads and others, but also the most venerable churches of this always God-fearing city.

Here also, the most noteworthy and the largest of them all, stands the old Riga Cathedral. The cathedral had once been a Roman Catholic church, before it became Protestant. The pastorate and the series of other church buildings, arranged round a little rectangular garden, were in reality the remains of an old monastery. The garden was surrounded by one of those time-worn arcades, with crumbling pillars, grotesque roof-decorations and scarcely legible inscriptions, which are only met with in the vicinity of Catholic churches and cloisters.

It was already late in the afternoon as I approached the familiar square in front of the cathedral. The old cathedral and its cloisters were always, to me, the most beautiful and inviting places in my native town. And when I rounded the last street corner and suddenly saw the tall spire of the cathedral reaching skyward, I involuntarily slackened my pace, stopped and stood for a moment in silent admiration.

The soft strains of the organ were floating out. I saw one or two shrinking black-clothed figures disappearing in timid haste through the high portal; it was evident that evening service was in progress. I allowed myself to drift in also with the stream, entered on tiptoe, and having found myself a chair in one of the aisles, looked round in some surprise at the gathering of people so unusual in existing conditions.

The cathedral was filled with worshippers, sitting in long rows on the time-blackened benches. But how worn out they looked! One could read plainly on their faces all they had been through in the past months.

I had difficulty in recognizing even old acquaintances. They sat there motionless, gazing in a kind of rapture at the pulpit.

A comforting tranquillity hovered in the high nave and shed its soothing influence upon the multitude below. The old chants, sung by enfeebled voices, seemed to me to have a new, strange ring. The preacher in the pulpit was Pastor August Eckhardt, dean of the cathedral. An old man with silvery hair, bent with years and with the burden of his duties, he appeared quite changed; the conventional unctuous manner which many clergymen retain even in daily life had completely fallen away from him. He really looked, now, like a comforter of the weary and the oppressed. . . .

There he stood, clothed in his black robe, a smile on his thin lips, his old-man's hands resting on the open Bible before him, drawing to his face the looks of the whole congregation. In simple, homely words he spoke of the cross which should be "borne, not dragged," and of the moral, not physical resistance which must be offered to the torments of the day. The congregation listened to his words in silent reverence, and one could almost feel fresh will-power entering many an afflicted soul, and new courage inspiring the rows of sufferers.

But, before the service was over, before the minister, who had descended from the pulpit and was standing before the altar, had finished pronouncing the blessing, a savage uproar was heard; coarse shouts, the clatter of arms and the tramp of feet broke the peace of the church.

All eyes were turned to the entrance. Armed men, with excited gesticulations, rushed in, charged up the nave towards the altar, surrounded the clergyman as he stood Bible in hand, took him by the shoulders, and began to drag him away without a word of explanation.

The old man offered no resistance. But he addressed a few words to the Red soldiers in a conciliatory tone and asked for a brief delay. The soldiers hesitated; then they released him for a moment. The congregation followed the scene, speechless and breathless.

Once more the venerable pastor mounted slowly to the pulpit and faced the congregation. But he seemed to have grown in stature; it was no longer a bent old man who stood before them. Head erect, his hands stretched out over the congregation below him, he took leave of them in a firm, clear voice, begged them to remember his teachings, exhorted those who were still able to help and care for their poorer fellow-citizens and those in prison, and expressed his faith in better and happier times to come. Then he descended and walked with a firm step down the nave towards the exit.

But just as the old man had reached the open church door, the worshippers, recovering from their stupefaction, suddenly rose like one man and loudly and

AT THE LAST GASP

confidently sang Luther's old hymn of faith and trust:

> A safe stronghold our God is still,
> A trusty shield and weapon;
> He'll help us clear from all the ill
> That hath us now o'ertaken . . .

The effect was unexpected. Completely taken aback, the armed men stopped dead with uncomprehending, frightened faces, stepped timidly aside and withdraw their rough hands from the pastor. The old man stood for a moment framed in the doorway; his silver hair, touched by the last rays of the evening sunlight, formed a halo round his head.

The last verse of the hymn had died away. The guards awoke from their stupefaction. Hastily and confusedly, pushing and jostling one another, they surrounded their prisoner and pushed him out of the church. Docile and unresisting, his hands spread one upon the other flat upon his chest and a gentle smile on his face, the aged pastor let himself be conducted to prison.

. . . . .

In the course of the following days the Reds arrested nearly all the clergy of Riga who were still at liberty— mostly evangelical pastors, in all about thirty—and threw them into the notorious Central Prison, where they were confined not only with other "bourgeois" prisoners, but also with a large number of common criminals.

Men who had been in the Central Prison, but had been called up for service and released, and now arrived at the military hospital, gave us full details of the conditions in which the ministers of religion were living in captivity.

The state of the cells in the Central Prison defied all description. The walls were so wet that there was always a few inches of water on the floor. The prisoners' clothes were always sodden, and the air in the cells was unbearably stuffy from human exhalations and the smoke of cheap Russian tobacco.

The gaol, which had originally been built for 500 inmates at the most, now contained about 4,000. In each of the cells, intended to hold five or six men apiece, thirty or forty persons were now crowded, "political prisoners" and "criminals" together. Most of the prisoners were diseased and verminous. Half of them were in a high fever. But no one was ever taken to hospital. Some of them grew hysterical and howled for hours on end. The compassionate vainly attempted to console them; the brutal beat and kicked them.

Into this herd of hungry, mortally sick, half-mad creatures the clergymen were thrown. Never in their whole life had they had such an opportunity of assisting and comforting their stricken fellow-creatures. And they did what was expected of them. Like true Samaritans, they went from cell to cell, distributing among the hungry prisoners the food parishioners had brought them, and giving, as far as they could, medical aid to the sick.

Every morning and every evening the pastors held services in the cells, and the prisoners attended them in crowds. The fear of death had bound all these beings closely together and compelled them to seek the same refuge in religion and prayer. Common criminals, to whom the words "God" and "faith" had always seemed devoid of meaning, crept into the ranks of the faithful. Differences of creed were forgotten. Even some Jews and Mohammedans, grateful to the Christian servants of God who had helped them with word and deed in their distress, came and took part, if silently, in the prayers of the Christians.

The imprisoned clergymen were daily set to perform heavy forced labour in various places outside the town. The Reds humiliated them by compelling them to carry out the lowest and vilest tasks, obliging them, for instance, to clean out the prison lavatories, dig graves in the churchyards, and often bury the rotting bodies of their fellow-citizens who had died of contagious diseases, while the escorting soldiers stood by and jeered at them.

Pastor Oscar Schabert, one of the imprisoned clergymen, wrote later of his experiences in the Soviet prison: "What I found hardest to bear was not the rough treatment I received in prison, nor the degrading tasks we were compelled to perform—cleaning out the latrines, when spotted typhus and other diseases were prevalent, and drawing dung-carts through the town—nor blows or abuse. But it was this. After we had been searched in a most offensive manner in the prison office, those in control, a brutal collection of ruffians, wanted to take away my New Testament, which I always carried in my coat pocket. I valued it particularly because it had gone to Siberia with me [during the war]. And now it was to be taken away from me. I resisted, declaring that I would not give up my New

Testament, that I lived on it. At the mention of the Word of God there was such an outburst of diabolical mockery that I trembled all over. But God gave me strength to reply calmly and firmly to all their abuse, till at last the brute of a governor grew weary and flung me my New Testament with a gesture of contempt. . . . So I went into prison. In the dark unheated cell in which we were placed we prayed in common with the other prisoners, who always included some persons condemned to death. . . . What thrilling hours we spent thus before God's countenance! The love of the Crucified One created for us a world of beauty in the midst of a world of dirty prisons, rough warders, hunger, cold, lice and fleas. . . ."

Some of the clergy, from their cells, sent letters of comfort and consolation to their families, who eagerly copied them and circulated them among their friends. These documents, which thousands read, have been preserved. They are moving in the apostolic loftiness of the sentiments and the strength of the faith expressed in them.

"What a wonderful comfort is faith!" one of them (Erhard Doebler, vicar of St. James's) wrote to his parishioners. "It is in such a place as this, in the midst of such misery, that one grows rich in spirit and joyful. . . . Here we are naturally led to compare our own sufferings with those of Our Saviour, and that is a most tranquillizing thought. How little, after all, do *we* have to bear! We have only to tell ourselves that, and everything becomes easy. . . . No power on this earth is capable of crushing us. My spirits are excellent, my head is always high. I shall hold out, for to-day

I know—only to-day—the meaning of this saying: 'I am capable of everything through Him who gives me power!' Faith is a real joy to all us prisoners in this trying time. . . . We clergymen are having to go through our real test of maturity, which must decide whether we are really worthy to be shepherds of mankind. And it is necessary that we come out of it triumphant—before God and before men. . . . And if our end must be near, then pray for us, that we may not weaken in the last hour of trial."

•   •   •   •   •

About this time the Easter festival came round—usually such joyful days for young and old! In Riga, where the orthodox influence had always been strong, Easter had always been celebrated with true Russian gaiety and pomp.

But who could think of festivities this year, when, according to the official lists, over 2,000 people had been shot: when from 7,000 to 8,000—a large proportion of the population of the town—were behind bolt and bar; when some 20,000 others, forcibly ejected from their homes, were in concentration camps on the islands in the Dvina; when most of the clergy of Riga had been robbed of their freedom, and the city, once so gay and prosperous, was empty and dead?

On Easter Sunday, instead of the usual crowds of churchgoers, an endless string of people could be seen making their way towards the prisons—relations and friends of the prisoners, bringing them gifts. At noon they crowded in hundreds round the doors. There were many children among them; for in many families there were only children left to care for the prisoners.

Although almost all the clergy were in prison, the churches were not empty on the days when the Soviet allowed service to be held in them. As in the days of the earliest persecutions of the Christians, members of the congregation rose from the benches, ascended the pulpit, read chapters of the Bible and delivered impromptu sermons, formless, but giving eloquent expression to their feelings.

"We are journeying amongst the tribulations of this world; the yoke is heavy upon our neck," cried the wife of one of the arrested clergy from her husband's pulpit. "Yet, above this pain-racked life another life is now awakening for us, silent, grand, majestic, the like of which we have never known. It emanates from the darkness of the prisons, shines through mortar and stone, breaks through the walls and beams from the barred windows: is a life in eternal light. . . ."

One of the few Riga clergymen who still enjoyed the blessings of freedom was Pastor Edgar Model. He was obviously by now completely overwrought. With his slight, fragile figure, his huge projecting hook-nose, untidy reddish hair and wide, over-bright blue eyes, he was unquestionably a striking and in a way fascinating figure as he ascended his pulpit that Easter morning. In a hoarse voice, quivering with agitation, dribbling freely, and so deeply moved that his little red beard wagged and trembled in time with the words he uttered, he delivered his own "Red Easter message, the gospel of the emancipation of the proletariat!"

Hardly two dozen persons were there to listen to his sermon, and they drawn by curiosity. But they were enough for his purpose. Declaiming hysterically, the Red pastor affirmed that mankind had the joy of seeing in Bolshevism "a far more glorious Resurrection than that of two thousand years before."

"The great Resurrection foretold by Jesus Christ two thousand years ago," he cried, "is being fulfilled at this moment, and the Kingdom of this world is being erected before the eyes of this generation in such splendour as no one has ever dreamed of!"

CHAPTER XIX

RESURRECTION DAY

About the middle of May alarming rumours became current of strange happenings in the White camp; and on the strength of these the Bolshevist leaders decided to undertake in earnest the offensive against the west they had so long talked of.

These rumours, of which even the *Red Flag* took notice, were to the effect that in Libau, the chief headquarters of the Whites, a kind of *coup d'état* had taken place at the end of April. The "rump Government" of the Latvian democratic republic had fled to Libau when the Bolsheviks approached Riga. This Government, however, was not in agreement with the Balt and German leaders of the Volunteer troops. It was mainly its doing that the advance of the German and Balt troops had been continuously hindered; like the Entente, it wished to see the expulsion of the Bolshevists achieved by Lettish troops alone, without German-Balt help. Sufficient Lettish troops to undertake an advance were, however, not available. Nevertheless, the Libau politicians, although they were thus endangering the lives of innumerable people, adhered obstinately to their will.

In order to put an end to this impossible situation and clear away the last obstacles in the way of the advance, the Volunteer Corps had carried out a *coup d'état* at Libau: on one of the last days of April they had arrested all the Ministers of the old Latvian

Government and set up a new civil administration under their own control.

In these events the Bolshevists seemed to perceive a sign of approaching danger. They decided, therefore, to strike at once themselves. The moment for the launching of their great and decisive offensive against Western Europe, they said, had now arrived!

Between the Bolsheviks and the goal of their offensive —Libau, East Prussia, Germany—there still lay Mitau and the whole of Courland, both still in the hands of the Whites. But it was a matter of course that the Whites would be "crushed." This was confidently declared in a new Red Army Order published by the commander-in-chief with reference to the new offensive.

"The conquest of these lands so close to Western Europe," said he, "is the defence of our movement in all the countries of the world. Realize the historic, world-wide significance of your task. Obey without a murmur all orders that come from Moscow. . . . Terrible conflicts lie before us. But the victory of Moscow over Europe, and then over the whole world, is certain!"

The front, in the form of a wide semicircle, stretched away to the west of Riga, at a distance of barely twenty-five or thirty miles from the river. The hospital in which I was still confined lay on the main road to the west, along which the Red troops had to march in order to reach the front, and we had been waiting eagerly for twenty-four hours to see the world conquerors march by.

For hours on end column after column passed—

infantry with Red banners, cavalry mounted on shaggy Cossack horses, and artillery received from Russia—light and heavy guns in masses. The spectacle could not but have a discouraging effect on the inhabitants. The White Army, as everybody knew, was numerically very inferior; would it be able to hold its own against this Bolshevist steam-roller?

Our anxiety increased still further when, for two days, we heard the uninterrupted rumbling of guns in a westerly direction. The Bolshevist attack on the White positions had begun.

Would their efforts be crowned with success, or would they suffer a fresh defeat? Would they break through the White lines, capture Mitau, pour over Courland once more, or would they be beaten back?

With feverish excitement, during those two days and nights, we studied the maps of the theatre of war. We knew that the front was everywhere broken and disconnected; the ranks of the Whites could easily this time, as last time, five months before, be shaken, overwhelmed, annihilated. . . .

But if this tiny army entrenched before Mitau—the only one that was fighting against Bolshevism on real European soil—did not withstand the onslaught of the Muscovites, if it weakened, fell to pieces, what would happen then?

Would not the Red swarms arrive at the German frontier within a few days; then, as they were threatening, penetrate into Germany and carry Bolshevism into Europe with fire and blood? What consequences would such a flooding of Germany by the "modern barbarians" have for our old continent, for the life of every individual European, even if they did not succeed at once in bringing about a world revolution?

In the west, at the moment, nobody seemed to be thinking about the matter, although the possibility of such an outcome of this war that was going on in our country was now more imminent than it had ever been. . . .

Interminable hours, sleepless nights went by in tormenting uncertainty.

Then, at the end of the third day, it became noticeably quieter at the front. The booming of the guns became less continuous. Bolshevist motor ambulances came driving by at full speed. Some stopped at our hospital and wounded were unloaded. What had happened? Things were going badly, they whispered. With whom?

At last the truth came out; and we learnt the news, the joyful news that this last offensive of the Muscovites had been, contrary to all expectations, decisively repulsed by the enemy.

A few hours later we saw the greater part of the Red troops coming back from the front, covered with dust and mud, worn out and discouraged.

They had evidently no longer any taste for fighting. Having glutted themselves for months on the stores and the riches of our devastated country, they had become accustomed to an easy life. Like all the incursions of Asiatic hordes, their invasion had only kept its redoubtable penetrating force as long as they had found in their path the opportunity of looting, pillaging and using violence—above all, only as long as no real resistance was offered to them.

And now that the Red attack had failed, what was going to happen? There was no sign as yet of a White counter-attack. The thunder of guns from the front had again completely ceased; lorries full of wounded no longer passed. A week elapsed without any event whatever.

The 22nd of May, the 140th day of the Soviet domination, opened exactly like all the 139 days that had preceded it.

In the hospital that morning everything went on as usual; patients were brought in, new recruits arrived and so on, as on every day since I had entered it. For myself the day had begun dismally; the "further examination" of my fitness for military service had ended, the day before, in my being declared fit. The chief doctor had told me regretfully that a further postponement of my examination was impossible, for every day dozens of new recruits were pouring into the hospital for medical examination as well as patients, and room must be made for them. Accordingly he examined me once more, honestly doing his best to find a physical defect in me. Among other things he tested my hearing, and it actually appeared that I heard less well with one ear than with the other; but the defect was not sufficient to secure me exemption from military service. "Fit for service despite partial deafness," he said in a low voice; then he sat down at his desk, wrote his verdict on a sheet of official paper, and instructed me to take the document to the Red recruiting office.

I returned gloomily to my room and next morning —the 22nd—at about ten o'clock, I left the hospital to return to the town.

I set out from the hospital on foot. On my way I had to cross over the bridge which spanned the river Dvina. This bridge, which connected the western with the eastern part of the town, was at that time the only bridge in Riga. The other ones had been blown up two years before by the retreating Russian troops. To replace them the Germans had thrown this long bridge, built entirely of wood, over the broad river; it still bore the German name "Lübeck-Brücke" in memory of its constructors.

At the bridge-head were standing a few Red sentinels, and on the bridge itself a few soldiers were posted at intervals. That was all. Except for these fellows, not a soul was to be seen on the bridge (which in ordinary times, being the only connecting link between the two halves of the town, had always been crowded with traffic). I was the only person who was walking over the bridge; otherwise there was not a living creature, not a horse, not a cart, not a movement, not even a noise of any kind. The wooden planks resounded hollow under my footsteps.

It must have been about noon when I reached the opposite bank of the river, at the place where the markets were—once so busy and crowded, to-day completely deserted.

I had come thus far without being molested by anybody, and was preparing to plunge into the narrow winding streets of the Old Town, impatient to reach home, to see my parents again and to make sure that all had gone well with them during my absence.

I walked on, sunk in my thoughts, without looking either to right or to left, and least of all back towards the river.

But I had taken only a few steps across the quay in the direction of the Old Town when I became aware of an extraordinary noise behind me, proceeding from the other side of the river: loud shouts and cries and a succession of shots. I turned round swiftly and, standing on the quay, could see right across the bridge. And what I saw was so astonishing that I stood open-mouthed, rooted to the spot.

From the other bank of the river, from the quarter I had just left so peaceful, indeed as still as death, but which was now loud with shots, cries and other noises, I saw a number of men, galloping horses and rattling carts racing in complete disorder over the bridge. They were Red troops in flight! making straight for the town, shouting, gesticulating and from time to time, apparently without aiming at anything, shooting wildly behind them in the direction of the opposite bank.

Some invisible enemy on the other side was returning their shots. The bullets began to pepper the walls around me, here and there splintering a window-pane. Some of the fleeing Reds fell to the ground, wounded and groaning. I hastily took shelter in a large doorway leading into the courtyard of one of the houses on the quay.

But at this moment, just as suddenly as the skirmish had broken out on the bridge, the narrow alleys of the Old Town round about me came to life. As if they had

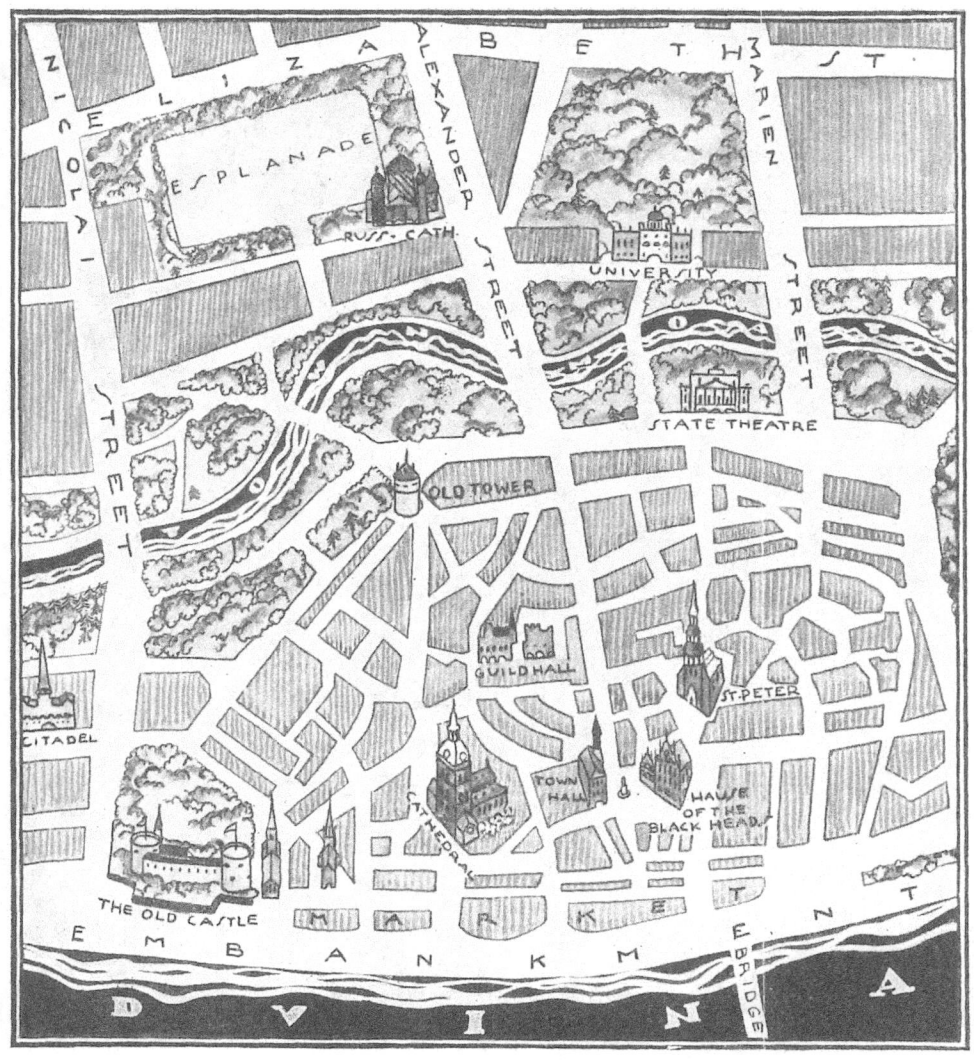

SKETCH-MAP OF THE CENTRAL PART OF RIGA

The house of the author's parents was situated in Nicholas Street, seen at the top left-hand corner of the map

grown up from the earth, Red soldiers sprang forth from all sides and rushed past me on to the quay. Many of them were buttoning up their uniforms as they ran, and putting their accoutrements straight. Others dragged a variety of chests and boxes out of the houses, but left them lying in the middle of the road and ran on to the quay. Meeting their fleeing comrades as they gained the near bank, they called on them to stop, entrenched themselves with them along the edge of the river, in groups behind heaps of stones lying along the quay, and all together they opened a vigorous fire against the enemy, who was still invisible but also kept up a heavy fire.

I took advantage of a pause in the shooting to look round for a better coign of vantage. The house in whose doorway I had been standing was one of the large blocks of flats on the quay from which the Reds had expelled all the inhabitants and which they had entirely looted. It was now completely unoccupied, with doors and windows standing wide open.

I climbed to the top story, entered one of the empty rooms, and chose a window fairly well protected from stray bullets. This observation post afforded an excellent bird's eye view over the river, both banks and the wooden bridge.

The bridge was quite empty now. All the fleeing Bolsheviks had reached the near bank. But no pursuers were yet in sight.

Yes, now they were! I had stood at my window for hardly five minutes, when I saw a second party of armed men come on to the bridge—only a few of them, not more than thirty or forty in all.

But they looked quite different from the Reds. They wore German steel helmets; their uniforms were not brown, like those of the Bolsheviks, but grey; and they were not fleeing in disorder, but moving forward in proper formation.

Not a doubt of it—it was they! The Whites! Our liberators! Their advance-guard! At last!

I followed their movements with bated breath. They came forward slowly and cautiously, step by step. In the middle of the bridge they halted. They had some machine-guns and one light field gun with them; they made these ready for action and opened fire on the Reds taking cover on the bank. Then they advanced a few paces farther, and then halted again.

Would not the Reds have time to blow up the bridge? Would the Whites' daring venture succeed? There were so few of them—what could they do against the hundredfold superiority of the Reds?

I did not know; nobody knew; I had only one feeling at that moment—at that moment when I, perhaps the only person in Riga who had that good fortune, saw that tiny band of liberators advancing towards me over the bridge; and that feeling was that I was witnessing a miracle.

Yes, a miracle had happened. The whole world round me was of a sudden wondrously transformed. All the dark shadows which had lain thick upon our town for five long months were dissolved at a touch. The crushing weight of silence and immobility was removed. There was light, sound, life—in everything and everywhere.

CHAPTER XX

OUR SAVIOURS

But what had happened at the front to enable the Whites to approach the town so suddenly and unnoticed? How had it been possible for them to reach the bridge almost simultaneously with the first Red fugitives? What was the explanation of this sudden appearance of the White advance-guard on the opposite bank of the Dvina?

Watching from my post of observation the still undecided contest at the bridge, I could only indulge in vague suppositions as to what had taken place. It was not till later that the true state of affairs was revealed.

The course of events in the White camp during the past weeks, right up to the morning of that day, the 22nd of May, had been, put briefly, as follows.

The new and docile Government set up by the White chiefs at Libau after the *coup d'état* aroused the displeasure of the Allied Commissions stationed at Libau. This "Barons' Government," they declared, was too much under German influence; an advance conducted by this Government would signify nothing less than a fresh armed action by Germany. They therefore forbade any of the White troops to advance, so long as the Germans were attached to them; and to lend force to their words, they pressed the Berlin Government more strongly to withdraw at once all the German volunteers from the White Army!

Thus the White Army—completely reorganized and ready for action—was not allowed to advance because the Powers for "political reasons" would not give permission. Foreign Governments withheld from natives of the country "permission" to rescue their nearest relations, hardly twenty-five miles away, from certain massacre. Faced by this senseless situation, the Volunteers were seized by a blind fury. They did not know what to do. Should they protest, resist the absurd demands of the Entente? Or should they allow the German troops to depart and, with reduced strength, but with the permission of the Allies, begin a perfectly hopeless campaign against the Bolsheviks? Or should they evacuate the battlefield altogether and definitely abandon their people to their fate?

The matter was decided by the Reds themselves. Their attack at the beginning of May had failed. But prisoners reported that a second offensive on a larger scale was soon to be undertaken with the help of new Russian regiments which were expected daily from Moscow. The Muscovites had taken the inactivity of the Whites as a sign of weakness.

That was decisive! The new Bolshevist onslaught had to be forestalled whatever happened. In any case, to remain in Mitau and carry on a protracted war with the Reds would be useless—indeed, was beyond the powers of the Whites; they were not in a position to maintain a regular campaign lasting for several months. The Entente Commissions might say what they pleased—they must fight now. Only an advance could rescue them from this desperate political and military cul-de-sac.

OUR SAVIOURS

In all haste negotiations were carried through between the leaders of the Baltic, Lettish and Russian Volunteer Corps and the officers of the German formations. After some hesitation the Germans declared their readiness to co-operate. They decided to strike on their own account without the permission of the Berlin Government.

Impelled by all these events and all these considerations, Count von der Goltz, commander-in-chief of the combined White Army, ordered that the attack, whose objective was the liberation of Riga, should begin on the night of the 21st–22nd of May.

It was a daring adventure. The blow must be delivered so as to make absolutely certain of success. The Red Army was fully twice as strong as the combined White forces. If our men were thrown back, the Reds in Riga would doubtless indulge in gruesome reprisals which would put all their previous atrocities in the shade; the consequence might very probably be something like a general massacre of the whole bourgeois population of the town. The storming of the town must therefore be carried out in such a way that the Reds would have no time for reprisals.

This task, by no means easy in itself, was rendered still more difficult by a natural circumstance: the river Dvina, many hundred yards in breadth in its lower course, where it passed through our town, separated the liberators from their goal. There was only one way across this river, and that was by the wooden and easily destructible "Lübeck Bridge." The little army possessed no engineering material. If the bridge were blown up, the whole enterprise would come to naught. To avoid the destruction of the bridge, it was necessary at all costs that the deliverers should reach it at the same time as the enemy and arrive together with them on the other bank. The opposite bank gained, all was gained.

Firmly resolved to conquer or perish, the combined White Army took the offensive on the night of the 21st–22nd of May and pushed forward towards the east. The attack was delivered along the entire front, which was in the form of a semicircle, with Mitau in the centre.

The bulk of the forces was divided into three groups: to the north, along the sea coast, Ballod's Lettish brigade and the Russian detachment under Prince Lieven; to the south, aiming at the river Dvina above the town, the German formations under the command of Major Bischoff; in the centre, straight towards Riga, the Baltic Volunteer Corps.

The tasks which each of these three divisions of troops had to carry out were allotted as follows.

The Letts and Russians, to the north, were to clear the sea coast and the approach to the lower course of the Dvina of Reds; they had to prevent the Bolshevists from taking the Volunteer troops in the rear as they advanced in the centre, and, in case the attack on the bridge failed, to try to get across the Dvina in boats.

The German formations to the south were entrusted with a specially important strategical manœuvre: they had to advance by forced marches, cross the Dvina above Riga, approach the town from the rear by executing a wide encircling movement, and so compel the whole Red Army to retreat. At the same time the action of the German troops was to make the frontal attack of the Volunteer Corps easier. Thus the Volunteer Corps would not have to fear the danger of being cut off by Red flank attacks, or of falling into a trap when they reached the town.

The Baltic Volunteer Corps had taken upon itself the task of carrying the town by a frontal assault, if necessary without support from the other divisions. These troops, consisting almost entirely of relatives of those languishing in Riga, were convinced, and rightly, that only an overwhelmingly rapid assault could prevent the Reds from perpetrating a general massacre of the population before their departure.

For this specially difficult task the Volunteer Corps had chosen from among its ranks a small picked force numbering only a few hundred men, which consisted of the very best and bravest of its soldiers. This was the "shock detachment" which has already been mentioned. The shock detachment was again commanded by Baron Hans Manteuffel, the same dashing young cavalry officer who had already distinguished himself so brilliantly at the capture of Windau. Baron Manteuffel, though of slight and almost delicate build, was a man of incomparable courage and contempt of death. He belonged to a noble Balt family, which had been settled in the land for centuries and had more than once defended its soil with the sword in their hands. A magnificent fellow! His soldiers revered him beyond all measure and followed him blindly wherever he chose to lead them.

One of the two Armitsteads (John William) was also

a member of the shock detachment; his brother had died some months before at the beginning of the White campaign.

The Reds, although surprised by the suddenness of the White attack, had nevertheless been warned by their spies of the impending offensive. They had in consequence fortified the ground lying between the front and the town, about a hundred miles long and thirty miles wide, with barbed wire, earthworks and machine-gun nests. They also had the use of heavy artillery and were far superior in numbers to their adversaries; to the 7,000 men of the combined White Army were opposed at least 12,000 Reds.

The night of the 21st–22nd of May was bright and clear. At zero hour—1.30 in the morning—light signals were sent up all along the line. It was the signal for the beginning of the attack. A relentless bombardment of the enemy lines began. The clatter of the machine-guns mingled with the droning of the German aeroplanes co-operating with the army and with the curt orders given in undertones.

For a time the troops advanced in the dark; then it grew light by degrees. Thick mist arose, but soon dissolved, and the sun came out brightly. The Volunteers advanced the whole morning, fighting without interruption. Their moral was extraordinarily high. Most of them even sang lustily as they advanced. The blood throbbed impatiently in their veins.

First they had to march over wooded sand-dunes, and then over difficult, swampy ground. The enemy were pelting this area with heavy shells; but it was obvious that they were shooting at random, with no definite target. The projectiles fell into the spongy plain near the advancing Whites and threw up fountains of black mud.

The Volunteers pursued the fleeing Reds hard; they were always at their heels. This was no monotonous trench warfare, but a real man-to-man struggle. Without a single look behind them, the troops advanced straight towards their objective. Before them galloped light cavalry with their blue and white pennons fluttering at the end of their lances. These gay colours, contrasted with the dirty red badges of the Muscovites, seemed extraordinarily bright and clean.

The Muscovites fell back before the fierce assault of the Whites, doing as much damage as they could in their retreat. But the country people everywhere turned against them and welcomed their liberators with shouts of joy. Peasant women brought out milk and bread from their cottages and gave them to the hungry, thirsty, dusty Volunteers.

One of those who took part in the campaign (Captain Wagener) thus gives his impressions of the advance:

"The rescued country breathed again with joy and sought to manifest in every way its gratitude towards us. Only then did we realize how terrible the Red scourge had been. A few months before, when, at the termination of the war, the German troops had evacuated this territory, industry and prosperity still reigned there. In the villages and farms there was a sufficient quantity of horses, cattle and poultry; on the large estates the barns were still filled with all the corn of the last autumn. But now! . . . Poverty and distress marked the trail of the Reds. Ruined houses, burnt cottages, bore witness to the 'new era of happiness' they had brought with them. The terror of their regime was still written upon the faces of the inhabitants who had had to live through it. The many Balt estates which until then, thanks to their organization and their powerful means, had given support to the small owners, fed the agricultural labourers and, for centuries past, raised the standard of civilization of the whole country, were now completely ravaged. The barns packed with grain had been a prey to fire; the stables and cattle-sheds no longer existed; the cattle had been slaughtered or driven away; the dwelling-houses and furniture shot to pieces, smashed up and burned. And everywhere in the courtyards of country houses and small farms lay the bleeding, horribly mutilated bodies of the owners. . . ."

In the later hours of the morning, the Reds, having recovered from the shock of the first attack, put up a much more obstinate resistance. Wherever officers of the old Russian Army, compulsorily mobilized, commanded them they defended themselves vigorously. To each of these old Tsarist officers was attached a Bolshevist Commissary, who forced the poor fellows, at the point of the revolver, to do their duty in the service of the Red Army.

Their resistance was most stubborn in the southeastern and most important sector of the front, on the upper course of the river near Friedrichstadt, where they found themselves at grips with the German Volunteer Corps. Here, where the German troops had at all costs to force the passage of the Dvina, a most sanguinary battle developed. It raged from five o'clock in the morning until two o'clock in the afternoon, and contributed in a very large measure to the success of the general offensive. The main forces of the Reds were decisively beaten by the war-experienced German troops; their left flank having been completely cut up, they were forced to recross the river below Riga, and order their comrades who were defending the town to withdraw in haste.

None the less, towards noon an armoured train, directed by former officers of the Russian Army, ran along the Mitau-Riga railway line, which cut through the front, and maintained itself there for some time, bombarding the attackers. But the other Red troops in that sector, commanded by less capable Red Commissaries, were falling back farther and farther, so that the armoured train, after some resistance, was abandoned by its crew and at last fell into the hands of the Whites.

The common soldiers of the Red Army, among whom were half-wild sons of the steppes, hardly knew why they were fighting. They were not inspired by the slightest enthusiasm. Suddenly finding themselves face to face with an adversary fully conscious of its goal and strongly determined to attain it, they turned about and began to flee in wild disorder towards the east, whence they had come hardly six months before, burning, plundering and massacring.

But even more swiftly than the Bolsheviks had fled, the shock detachment of the Volunteers had advanced. Indeed, with such terrific speed had the vanguard pressed forward—about a hundred men in all, led by Manteuffel himself—that it found itself suddenly in the midst of the enemy's area. From the woods in which they had concealed themselves the Volunteers could plainly see the columns of Reds retreating along the high road towards Riga.

They themselves were surprised by their rapid advance. What were they to do? Go back? Impossible! Wait till the bulk of the White Army came to their support—perhaps not for hours? Wait *now*? That would be even more unbearable; no one would consider it.

There was only one thing to be done—to go on! On to Riga! Even if they were only a hundred strong, they would risk it!

Filled with irrepressible eagerness, full of inward excitement, they hurried on. In the distance they saw some Reds, and they themselves were seen; but they were so covered with dust from head to foot after their ten hours' forced march that the Reds, in the excitement of the flight, took these men hurrying in the same direction as themselves for one of their own fleeing columns, and paid no further attention to them.

Hardly an hour later, immediately behind the first fleeing Reds, the men of the shock detachment reached the western bank of the Dvina.

Before them, across the river, for the first time since those dismal January days, they could see the well-known roofs and spires and towers of Riga: the venerable cathedral, the churches of the Old Town, the four-square castle, and behind the green roof of the Citadel. . . .

The Citadel, which was now a prison, in which at that very moment their relations and friends were suffering, were languishing in imminent peril of death.

The Volunteers knew that only the bridge separated them from those whom they had to save, that in order to accomplish the work of liberation, the bridge, above all, had to be conquered at all costs.

They saw the fleeing Reds rushing across the bridge in front of them, in tangled groups, yelling, gesticulating, in ever-growing numbers. What would they do when they got across? Would they dig themselves in on the other bank, blow up the bridge, and, before the main body of the Whites arrived, slaughter the hostages in the prisons?

No, not that! that must be stopped at all costs! The bridge, the bridge must be stormed! Not a moment must be lost, every minute now might be fatal. The assault *must* be attempted! Yes, even though they were only a hundred men, they would not wait for the others, they would go on alone, they would storm the bridge.

It was then there took place a matchless exploit, the story of which will for ever remain a glorious page in the history of the Balt people.

While the greater part of the little force was left behind to guard the western end of the bridge, a handful of men—thirty or forty at the most—at a sign from Manteuffel, plunged forward; their leader at their head, heedless of a violent rain of bullets from the Reds, who were now turning to face them, the little band, without a moment's hesitation, dashed forward to the bridge, and advanced along it at a run, without accompanying aeroplanes or by covering artillery fire—in short, without protection or help of any kind.

In the age of poison gas, tanks and airships, this little band of warriors, cleaving its way onward with sword and rifle in hand, were like knights storming the drawbridge of an ancient castle rather than soldiers of a modern army.

From my observation post, from the window of the riverside house in which I had taken refuge, I was able to follow events step by step: the flight of the Reds, the capture of the bridge, all the shifting fortunes of the battle. I was looking down from a considerable height, and river, bridge and assailants might have been toys; I had the feeling that I was watching the unrolling of a skilfully contrived film.

Only when, from time to time, one of the combatants fell, and a dull groan or sharp cry reached my ears above the clatter of the machine-guns, did I realize with a sudden shock the tragic reality of the scene before me.

The crossing of the bridge was accomplished! The Volunteers were over! Now they were on this bank, on the quay, directly below my window, so close that I would only have to lean out and call them to attract their attention. They were organizing the defence of the bridge-head.

But now part of the attacking force passed out of my field of vision. The small band of forty men which had crossed the bridge divided itself into two halves. Twelve or fifteen men, led by Manteuffel, dashed along the quay with two machine-guns. They were making straight for the Citadel, through the midst of the swarming Reds, to rescue the prisoners! Shooting ceaselessly all round them, they disappeared round the corner.

The others, now only just twenty men or so, remained in the market-place, around the bridge-head; they were now taking cover behind the heaps of stones which barely half an hour before had served as cover for their adversaries. They also used for cover all kinds of boxes and cases, overturned carts and market stalls, carcases of horses and dead bodies which were lying about in wild confusion.

They had now greater need of cover than before. More and more Reds had retreated into the houses on the quay and kept up a continuous fire upon the Volunteers. Their situation was becoming ever more critical. They had got across the bridge, but they could advance no farther; there were too few of them. The Reds had only to bring up small reinforcements, and they would be destroyed to the last man.

But why were the Reds not receiving reinforcements, when there were thousands of them? What was happening in the rear, in the town? And why had the rest of the White Army not yet come to the help of its comrades? Could its offensive have failed after all, been held up?

For a whole hour, an interminable hour, this strange combat continued on the river bank, without its being possible to foresee the issue. Then, at the very moment when the men of the shock detachment, who were obviously exhausted, seemed inclined to abandon the struggle, and there were indications that they were about to retreat again to the bridge, there was suddenly a fresh burst of machine-gun fire on the other bank, followed by cries of hurrah and the noise of marching troops. Friend and enemy looked across the bridge and saw a long column of fresh troops, with guns, machine-guns and motor-lorries, advancing, with slow and steady step, towards the town ... the main force of the Volunteer Corps!

The gallant men fighting on the quay, the town, the population—all were saved!

Thus the daring assault on the bridge executed by Manteuffel's small band of heroes had prevented the enemy from massacring thousands of inhabitants in their retreat. From a purely military standpoint other aspects of the battle of Riga may have been of greater importance. And the success of the whole campaign may justly be attributed to the fact that all nationalities in the country combined in the hour of need. But to eye-witnesses of those events, it is beyond doubt that the decisive moral effect—panic in the enemy's ranks, confidence among the liberators, joy among the population—was produced by the gallant action of Manteuffel's little band, and that these few men of the shock detachment whose deeds recall those of the famous heroes of classical antiquity, may be regarded as the true liberators of Riga from the Red yoke.

THE STORMING OF THE LÜBECK BRIDGE

A rare photograph taken by a White volunteer during the assault in the afternoon of the 22nd May, 1919; in the background is the building from which the scene was observed by the author

CHAPTER XXI

THE FLIGHT OF THE MUSCOVITES

As soon as the bulk of the Volunteers had arrived on the near bank and joined the small vanguard which had preceded it, the Whites prepared to penetrate farther into the town and complete the work of liberation.

Their first objective was the prisons. Baron Manteuffel with his fifteen men had already gone to attack the Citadel a good hour before. It was now necessary to follow up and go to his assistance. And as quickly as possible, in order that the Reds should have no time to do the prisoners any mischief at the last moment before they left, or, as they had often threatened to do, carry them off as hostages to the prison camps of Siberia.

The task of rescuing the prisoners was by no means simple. The two largest prisons were situated at opposite ends of the town. The Citadel lay on the riverside bank, in the immediate neighbourhood of the bridge which the Whites had just captured; the Central Prison, however, lay right on the opposite side, on the eastern edge of the town, where the high roads ran to Dvinsk and Pskov and right into the interior of the Soviet realm. If, therefore, both prisons were to be reached in time, there was not a second to be lost. While a large part of the newly arrived troops were rushed to the Citadel, the rest scattered and penetrated the many alleys which led from the Dvina into the Old Town, often only in twos and threes.

The moment the tide of battle had turned definitely in favour of the Whites, practically all the Bolsheviks entrenched on the river bank and in the houses along the quay had been seized by panic and vanished in the maze of winding streets of the Old Town.

As soon as I perceived that I was free, and at last relieved from my awkward situation, I rushed out into the open and ran towards the nearest White soldier I could see. How often had I dreamt of this moment during those weary months! How joyfully I would welcome the liberators, what fervent words of gratitude I would pour forth! And yet, now that this moment had come, I could hardly find one reasonable word with which to express my feelings—so strange, so unreal, so bewildering did all these events still appear to me.

The soldier whom I approached was a very youthful-looking, sunburnt fellow, with a serious expression on his face, and a redoubtable steel helmet on his head. He stood on the quay, not far from the house from which I had emerged, in an attitude of challenge, holding his rifle ready to shoot. He asked me who I was.

I explained my identity to him as best I could, and made to move on farther, to look for Roy Carlyle and other friends among the Volunteers. But the steel-helmeted lad looked me up and down mistrustfully and refused to let me pass. No doubt, shabby and untidy as I too had become in the course of the Soviet era, he took me to be a Bolshevik in civilian clothes. And not till several other Volunteers, who knew me, came up and spoke to me would he let me go on.

THE FLIGHT OF THE MUSCOVITES 307

"Tie something white round your arm!" one of them shouted to me. Then he hurried on, making signs for me to follow. They were all making for the Citadel.

We had not far to go. It was hardly ten minutes before we reached the gates of the prison. It was now about three o'clock. The doors stood wide open and joyful animation reigned outside, in the street, and inside, in the prison courtyard. The Citadel was already free!

One of those who took part in the assault on the Citadel, a Balt officer, Baron Walter von Medem, thus described what happened: "Bullets, fired treacherously from windows and hiding-places, whistled around us as we ran through the streets near the river. At last we were before the Citadel. A cry which seemed to issue from hundreds of throats echoed over our heads—a lusty hurrah. We looked up: at all the barred windows of the prison men were swarming, thickly packed, head against head, shouting, rejoicing, laughing, crying, as though crazy with joy that the incredible had happened —rescue! We pushed the machine-guns forward. But, if the guard at the bridge over the Dvina was an island, we ourselves, now completely isolated from our comrades on the bridge, were nothing but a rock in the sea of houses of Riga. The door of the prison was barricaded. We had to stay thus for an hour, unable to go forward or back. At the narrow windows of the four-storied prison the prisoners pressed their pale faces against the bars, shouting and crying. It was an ear-splitting tumult. Women came running up to us in spite of the bullets which swept the streets: 'My husband is in the prison; rescue him!' Heart-breaking scenes took place, with the inmates at the windows still before us. The prison *had* to be opened. Several of us went forward. The first bomb attack against the door failed. Shots rang out from the cellar windows. We had to retreat. Only three men still remained pressed against the wall to hear if the brutes inside were not beginning a massacre of their victims. As though coming from another world, beseeching female voices sounded faintly behind the barred windows. Forward once more! And then we broke the door in with bombs and axes and sprang, revolver in hand, into the prison yard . . ."

Thus the little band of Volunteers stormed the prison door and rushed into the inner courtyard.

The Reds, not knowing that there were only about forty of the enemy on this side of the river, lost their heads. Many of them were shot down. The rest, however, including the chief warder, recognizable by his club foot, scrambled over the stone wall, climbed to the roofs of neighbouring houses, and so made their escape. The inner town was still in the hands of the Reds, and the Whites were for the moment less bent on pursuing the guards than on setting free the prisoners. This comprehensible omission proved later to have had the most disastrous consequences.

The rapid storming of the Citadel had been dearly paid for with the life of Baron Manteuffel himself. As he rushed across the prison yard revolver in hand to free the prisoners he was suddenly laid low by a bullet from an enemy in ambush. The victors lost in him one of their very best leaders. Destiny had allowed him to fulfil his mission of liberation; but he would not see the joy of the people to whom he had just restored life; he would not hear their words of gratitude....

This reward was reserved for the troops whom he had so gallantly led thus far. These men had saved the prisoners at the last moment, for it turned out that the Red prison Commissaries had already brought bombs with which to kill the prisoners before they left. It was only the swiftness with which the rescuers advanced that prevented the Reds from carrying out their design.

One of our soldiers picked up a bunch of keys dropped by the fleeing Reds. They were the keys of the various cells. Several men took the keys, and hurried from cell to cell, opening the heavy iron doors. At the moment of our arrival the prisoners were just emerging.

What a joyful and at the same time heartrending spectacle!

Many came running out into the daylight full of eagerness, uttering loud cries of joy and happiness. "How beautiful the sun is!" they cried in delight, and drew deep, long breaths. Then they rushed up to their liberators and clutched at their hands to press them, shake them, kiss them.

Others crept out slowly and hesitatingly, dazed by the sunlight and blinking, apparently unwilling to believe that what had happened was real. Their minds, it seemed, could not yet shake off the sombre nightmare of captivity. In their miserable rags of clothes, with their pallid, shrunken faces and dull eyes, they really hardly resembled human beings; they were creatures for whom the world of freedom had already become something strange.

Some miserable creatures, imprisoned for many months, did not dare to come out of their cells at all. They remained sitting, in a dull brooding, on their wooden benches, mumbling unintelligible words to one another. It looked as if their unexpected deliverance had totally deprived them of their reason.

There were lively scenes in the prison courtyard. More and more White infantrymen arrived; a detachment of cavalry, too, rode in. Many of the liberated prisoners hurried up to their deliverers, and engaged in talk, telling them all they had suffered.

In the courtyard lay the corpses of the Reds killed during the assault on the prison—creatures who a few moments before had been the terror of the unhappy prisoners. They lay stretched just as they had fallen, some of them all twisted up by the last convulsions, others lying on their backs with limbs outspread and glassy eyes staring at the sky; others with their faces buried in the earth, as if seeking something.

Round the bodies were dark pools of blood. Many of the people who were now passing through the yard had trodden in these pools, and everywhere curious footsteps, wet and black, were visible in the sand. Somebody came and threw cloths and articles of clothing over the bodies and stiffened limbs, leaving only the arms and feet uncovered. Nobody wished to see those faces again which they had hated so bitterly for long weeks on end.

Among the rescued prisoners was a clergyman. He collected some of his comrades in suffering in the prison lobby, and suddenly a hymn burst forth in the damp, windowless room—a hymn never heard there before:

> Now thank we all Our God,
>   With hearts and hands and voices,
> Who wondrous things hath done,
>   In Whom His world rejoices.

The clergyman said a prayer; then most of the liberated men hurried away into the town, impatient to greet their relatives once more, to see their homes again. In their haste they stumbled against the dead bodies. But they paid no heed to these corpses. What had they to do with death? They had returned to life.

· · · · ·

Everyone was burning with eagerness to be present at the liberation of the town, to help the Volunteers in any way possible, to see his friends and relations again as quickly as possible.

I was anxious too, now that the day of deliverance had become a wondrous reality, to see, greet and speak to the man who had predicted it all to me with such confidence—Carlyle! He had been there for certain, perhaps he had been one of the first to enter the town. But where could he be? I had not seen him yet.

I asked the Volunteer cavalrymen who were still in the prison yard if they could tell me anything about him. Yes, of course they knew Carlyle. Who did not know him? Yes, he was there, had gone on ahead long before with the shock detachment, and was in the middle of the town by now, for certain. When we went on we should certainly find him somewhere.

Forward, then. I, too, was anxious to see my parents again as quickly as possible. I wondered how they had fared in my absence, and whether anything had befallen them.

The Volunteer cavalrymen came trotting out through the prison gates. The riders shouted that they were off to liberate the other citizens confined in the Central Prison. The good wishes of all accompanied them. Would they arrive in time? Or would all their self-sacrifice and energy prove to be in vain?

In the company of White soldiers mingled with freed citizens, I moved forward into the inner town. The surrounding neighbourhood had already been practically cleared of Bolsheviks by White troops who had passed through about half an hour earlier. But here and there shooting was still going on, as some of the enemy, whose retreat had been cut off, had remained hidden and were defending themselves. But heedless of danger, people were coming out of the houses everywhere and greeting the conquerors with shouts of joy and waving handkerchiefs.

The men knotted white handkerchiefs round their arms, as I had already done, and joined the rescuers, offering them their support and assistance. The whole population united itself with the liberators as one man.

In about half an hour, unmolested, I reached Nicholas Street, where my home was.

To the people inside the town, who, of course, had not been able to follow the development of all these events, as I had done on the river bank, the White victory had come, we were told, as an even more dramatic surprise.

At one o'clock in the afternoon, that is, when the bridge had already been forced and a regular battle

THE FLIGHT OF THE MUSCOVITES 313

was raging on the river bank, nobody in this part of the town had the slightest suspicion of what was going on, or knew anything of the advance of the Whites. The inhabitants and—what was still more astonishing —the Reds themselves were perfectly calm, engaged in their daily occupations, utterly ignorant of what was impending. Nothing, absolutely nothing, told them that less than an hour later the situation would be so completely reversed.

The simple explanation of this strange phenomenon was that the General Staff of the Red Army, which observed and superintended the events at the front, had informed no one but the "Council of People's Commissaries," that is, the highest members of the local Soviet Government, of the rapid advance of their enemy. And they, cowardly and treacherous, considering only the safety of their own skins, had deemed it prudent to hide the dangerous turn that things had taken until the last moment from their supporters, from the multitude of petty Soviet employees, and from the other members of their own party. Coolly and cynically abandoning the herd of dupes to their fate, they had made haste to get away to safety as quickly as they could.

During the morning, before the assault on the bridge had taken place, they had ordered a special train under military guard to be made up quickly at the East Station. In this train the head of the Latvian Soviet Republic, Peter Stutchka,—now completely shattered and apathetic,—Mangul, the commander of the Red Army, the anonymous President of the Revolutionary Tribunal, with his mistress, a former Riga prostitute,

Simon Berg, the President of the Riga Soviet, Endrup, the Commissary of Supply, Danishevsky, the Commissary for War, and various other Red oligarchs had taken their seats.

All these preparations had been made with the utmost speed, even hurriedly, but in the most complete secrecy. And when the clock had struck twelve, the train had steamed out eastward towards Moscow, bearing those mainly responsible for the Red Terror away from the city which had been the scene of their baneful activities.

So it was that no one in the town—not even the Red soldiers, so shamefully betrayed by their leaders—had any idea of what was happening on the banks of the river. While fighting was going on along the quay, on the bridge and on the other side of the river, no one in the eastern suburbs heard ever the clatter of the machine-guns.

Thus the midday hours passed without any sign announcing the decisive events which had already taken place in other parts of the town.

In the early hours of the afternoon the streets presented their accustomed picture. A few miserable figures crept timidly from house to house with their bowls of horrible Soviet soup. Here and there a surly-faced Red soldier was standing on guard, asking the infrequent passers-by to show their papers and carrying off "non-workers" to forced labour. From time to time one or two grimy newspaper boys appeared on the scene selling the *Red Flag*, which on that day was full of its usual contents. Even the dung-cart, dragged by citizens of Riga and escorted by "gunwomen," was making its accustomed way at its usual snail's pace through the silent streets, the sound of the clogs audible far off in the stillness.

And then all at once, at about two o'clock in the afternoon, the whole scene changed. All of a sudden, from the direction of the river, a few Red horsemen, military wagons and lorries came hurrying in wild disorder.

These first fugitives sat with clenched teeth and compressed lips on their shaggy little Tartar horses and on their lorries. Their amazed comrades shouted questions to them as they passed, but they answered only with a few curt, unintelligible words and hurried on eastward without checking their flight.

But that was enough; the miserable soup-carriers slackened their steps and, already less frightened, followed the fugitives, joyful surprise in their eyes; the Red guards disappeared and no longer molested the passers-by; the little newspaper boys ceased to shout the name of the *Red Flag*, but threw the whole bundle of papers into the nearest yard; the "gunwomen" escorting the procession of prisoners deserted their task, leaving their modern galley-slaves stranded in the middle of the street, leapt on to one of the military lorries as it passed and were no more seen. The skinny white-bearded drawers of the cart, left to themselves, gazed in stupefaction after their decamping torturers, not knowing what to do with their sudden and unexpected freedom.

The streets now became livelier every minute. The number of Muscovite fugitives swelled unceasingly.

The town of Riga is laid out in such a way that a

series of parallel streets cross it from west to east. To the west lies the river, to the east begin the great roads which lead into the interior of the Russian Empire. A few months earlier, when this army of barbarians made its entry into the town, it proceeded through these streets, in comparatively good order, from the east to the west. Now the Muscovites passed through the same streets, but in the opposite direction, from west to east, in confused, disorderly, scattered groups.

An extremely picturesque, almost grandiose spectacle of flight was offered to the citizens of Riga. Only vanquished barbarians, panic-stricken, trembling for their miserable lives, could flee so wildly. So must the Tartar hordes of Shich-Alai have fled when, centuries ago, they infested this same tormented Livonia, plundering and murdering.

On foot, on horseback, in vehicles, the routed Muscovite army hurried at breakneck speed along the straight roads that led to the east and safety. Some endeavoured to carry away with them anything they could lay hands on at the last moment: they piled on to their carts gold and silver objects, sacks of flour and sugar, pieces of furniture, mattresses, things of value and insignificant odds and ends picked up haphazard.

Others, on the contrary, in order to lighten themselves for flight, threw away all that they had on them—rifles, cartridge belts, food, alarm clocks, women's underwear —in short, everything that belonged to them and everything they had stolen was flung down in the streets.

Some of those who were fleeing on foot stood in the path of the rushing lorries and wagons to hold them up, and either sprang up or were thrust aside, pushed back, kicked away. They fell back sprawling into the roadway, and had to run after the carts that would not stop for them, uttering cries of despair.

One gun drawn by four horses was assailed by such a crowd that it could not get on, and the crew had to shoot with revolvers at their own comrades. Several machine-guns were flung from a lorry on to the paving stones and lay there unheeded, while a party of fleeing soldiers dashed at the lorry, scrambled on to it, and were carried away in the furious race.

From another wagon bags of sugar and flour fell, breaking open as they did so, and spread their precious contents over the roadway in long white smears. Immediately a mob of people assembled from right and left, poor hunger-stricken creatures, flung themselves greedily upon the food and at once began to eat. . . .

The flight lasted hardly more than half an hour. In the meanwhile, a strange storm from the south-west, of a kind unknown in those regions, burst over the town, blowing up clouds of dust and sand and flinging them at the backs of the fugitives, as though literally sweeping them out of the city. Then, when the mad race-past of the Muscovites had come to an end, the weather suddenly changed and a torrent of rain beat down on the streets, scattering the onlookers. It seemed that Nature herself was expressing her relief at the deliverance and, like some energetic charwoman, was washing away once and for all the loathsome traces the fugitives had left behind them.

Then the rain stopped, the sky cleared and the sun shone.

The streets were empty, but not dead. On either

side, in every house hundreds of heads were poking out and eyes were gazing westward. And their perseverance was rewarded. At last, at last, they saw what they were awaiting.

At the end of the street two soldiers appeared, at first two only. They walked on opposite sides of the street, holding their rifles in readiness to shoot. They were covered with dust from head to foot; but their whole aspect and demeanour were quite unlike that of the Reds who had just disappeared. The external difference between them and the Muscovites struck one immediately; properly clothed and equipped with steel helmets on their heads and wearing field-grey uniforms, they looked like the soldiers of any European nation on active service.

They advanced slowly, looking to right and left and up at the house-fronts, and shouted in German, politely but emphatically: "Shut all doors and windows! There is firing going on."

But a cry of wild enthusiasm, one "hurrah!" defying all possible danger, was the answer; and even the few doors and windows which had remained closed until now were opened wide.

Spontaneously, irresistibly, overcome by the glorious event, these people, who in five months of torture had almost forgotten how to breathe, emerged from their lairs, hailed their deliverers with shouts of joy, and, scarcely believing in the miracle which had just taken place before their eyes, threw themselves into one another's arms. . . .

. . . . . .

THE FLIGHT OF THE MUSCOVITES

In the meantime, while the arrival of our soldiers was thus spreading infinite joy throughout the town, a final act of horror was taking place in a remote eastern suburb.

The prisoners in the Citadel had already been set free. But in the Central Prison, the largest, which lay on the opposite side, in the east of the town, the captives were not yet released. It was here that most of the arrested churchmen were confined, as well as the majority of the imprisoned citizens.

The fear was expressed that the Commissaries who had fled from the Citadel had hurried straight to this other prison with the intention of perpetrating there one last act of vengeance.

Several parties of the shock detachment, some mounted, some in military lorries, hastened towards this more distant prison. To reach it they had to pass through districts which still swarmed with Bolsheviks. But they took no notice of the shots fired at them by enemies ambushed in cellars and other hiding-places. They reached their destination comparatively quickly. The prison doors were open; they dashed across the yard into the cells. . . . Too late! the atrocious deed had already been accomplished.

In this prison, just as in the districts of the town outside the field of battle, nothing had been known of the events of the day until the afternoon. All day the life of the captives had followed its normal course. That afternoon, more than thirty men were gathered together in the "hostages' cell," engaged in quiet conversation, while a few others lay asleep. Among them were Pastor August Eckhardt, the old clergyman whose arrest in the cathedral I had witnessed several weeks before, and seven other well-known preachers of Riga and neighbouring parishes: Erhard Doebler, of St. James's; Theodor Hoffmann, of St. Peters's; Eugen Scheuermann, of the Luther Church; Theodor Taube, of St. Martin's; Ernst Fromhold-Treu, vicar of Dickeln; Eberhard Savary, vicar of Ascheraden; and Hermann Bergengruen, vicar of Wenden; eight in all.

Then, shortly before four, the door of the cell was suddenly flung open and a Red Commissary burst in, in a state of visible excitement and suppressed fury; by the cringing haste with which the gaolers obeyed him, the prisoners recognized him as a chief. His special peculiarity was a club foot, and many believe that he was the same chief warder who had escaped from the Citadel and who had carried out the massacre at Mitau.

At this moment, when their own lives were in danger, he and his inhuman companions had but one thought: to satisfy their insatiable lust for vengeance.

The club-footed man and his fellow-murderers held revolvers in the faces of the bewildered assembly and called for twenty-three men whose names were on a list seemingly prepared a long time before. In another cell they demanded ten women captives, among them several young girls of barely twenty. But most of the thirty-three persons were old—about a third men over seventy. All without exception belonged to well-known and respected Riga families, the eight clergymen included among them, and all had been declared "hostages" weeks before by the Revolutionary Tribunal.

The club-footed man ordered silence, forbade them

SOME OF THE RIGA CLERGY KILLED BY THE BOLSHEVISTS IN THE LAST MOMENTS BEFORE THEIR FLIGHT

The first body from the right in the foreground is that of Pastor August Eckhardt, Dean of Riga Cathedral

THE FLIGHT OF THE MUSCOVITES

all communication with other prisoners, and ordered them to go out "without caps, coats or boots."

All realized what was going to happen. Yet not one of the victims, the women no more than the men, had shown a sign of weakness or uttered a word of protest. The silence of death reigned as the procession left the cell. Shoeless, with bare or stockinged feet, but proud and erect, as bravely as the noblest gentlemen in the French Revolution going to the guillotine, they went to their death.

Without being preceded by any of the escort, they were ordered to follow a long corridor as far as a cobbled courtyard. The yard was on a slightly lower level than the rest of the prison; it was reached by steps, and the leading prisoners had to descend these.

But before they had all descended, some of those behind gave sudden cries and fell down in the corridor, struck by bullets fired from behind. Then the club-footed man and his helpers flung a handful of bombs into the crowd in the yard. But when the smoke cleared away they saw that some of the victims were still alive, so they sprang down into the yard and killed the survivors with bayonet stabs, blows with the butts of their rifles, and kicks.

When the Volunteers arrived on the scene of this exploit, they found only a heap of mutilated, almost unrecognizable corpses. Many could be identified only by their clothes.

CHAPTER XXII

SHATTERED IDOLS

Rarely have I lived through hours crowded with such a variety of swiftly moving events as of May 22, 1919, between the moment I left the hospital and my arrival at my house.

I reached home not very long after the first White soldiers had passed through our street. Full of joy and excitement I bounded up the stairs, three at a time.

But before I reached the door of our flat, I was the witness of a little interlude which showed that in our house also the entry of the Whites had already turned life upside down and restored normality. On the staircase I came up against the Balgal family, who were moving out with all haste and obviously alarmed. It will be remembered that the Red Government had forcibly installed these poor people in our home several months earlier, after having first chased us out of it. To-day the re-establishment of order was being carried out with the same unreasonable haste which had characterized the previous revolution.

Hardly had the first White soldier appeared than the Balgals decided to leave our flat at once and return to their own working-class dwelling on the outskirts of the town. In a few minutes they had packed up all their belongings, and were hastily departing.

The quiet modest workman Balgal, his wife, who had lately been so close a friend of my parents, and their two rather frightened children were laden with all sorts of domestic articles and timidly creeping along the walls, as if some evil spirit were chasing them away.

I stopped on the stairs and pointed out that their haste was quite unnecessary and that they need not fear any kind of reprisals either from us or from the Whites. But the Balgals seemed to have had enough of the Red experiment; they did not listen to me, but hastily left the house with their belongings without saying a word.

After I had thus witnessed the panic-stricken flight of the Balgals, I was not very astonished to find my mother already in our old flat which had just been evacuated. My mother, a resolute woman, accustomed at all times to watch jealously over her household, had immediately reoccupied the domain so callously torn from its legitimate sovereignty.

Certainly she found it, thanks to the combined efforts of the four members of the Balgal family, in a somewhat filthy and disorderly state; but she could feel no more bitterness towards the once so unwelcome guests. She could only have sympathy for these people, who, after all, were just as much the victims of Bolshevism as we ourselves.

My mother seemed to be a new being: all her old cheerfulness and vigour had returned. She was in the best of humour, and even the colour had returned to her thin cheeks.

I found my father and the other inmates of the house in the other flat, a story higher, where we had lived through so many weeks of sorrow with the Walters. They welcomed me with exclamations of joy. But no one asked me how I had managed to find my way here from the other bank of the river safe and sound.

The fact was that they were all too busy. The silence, the semi-lethargy which had reigned in this house for so many months had vanished in a flash. And in our flat, as in those on the other floors, all was now movement and bustle. Furniture was being moved, all kinds of objects were being dusted and cleaned, and various articles of clothing, to which we had endeavoured to give as shabby and proletarian an air as possible, were being carefully brushed and cleaned and made to look presentable again.

My father surprised us all by producing from the remotest depths of a wardrobe—a top-hat, which no one knew he possessed, but which he had managed to preserve, in the hope of better times, from the clutches of the Reds. When I entered, the old gentleman was busily engaged in dusting up this precious but somewhat battered symbol of bourgeois respectability, and trying it on before the mirror. Like everyone else, he was making himself smart to go out and meet the liberators.

In the drawing-room I found young Frau Walter, now mistress of the house, chatting eagerly with a woman friend from another flat about all these events, the full significance of which her deafness had so far prevented her from grasping. Her friend, who had arrived full of news, was only able to communicate it to her with difficulty: she was obliged to shout several times into Frau Walter's ear things which everyone else knew all about by now.

"They've come! Yes, yes, *they've* come!" she cried

repeatedly. When at last the deaf woman understood, her very first act was to fling the working-class handkerchief which she wore on her head into a corner, produce a somewhat dilapidated but unquestionably smarter hat, and prepare to go out into the street in the hope of finding her husband.

But she had no need to do so; for at that moment Walter, just released from prison, burst into the room. Radiant with joy, he stretched out his skinny hands to his wife, who fell on his neck.

Walter's face was fringed by an untidy prison beard of a reddish hue, and his face bore unmistakable signs of his long captivity and the forced labour he had been compelled to undertake.

But his wife did not seem to notice it. With an expression of mingled happiness and fright she lay in her husband's arms and bombarded him with a thousand foolish questions—might not the Reds come back? would the Whites stay? and so on.

Her husband gave her gladly the answers she sought; but it was not easy to make her understand. And the poor fellow, between fits of violent coughing, had to bellow reassurances to her over and over again in a hoarse voice:

"No, no, they won't go away again! They're going to stay here now, always, always!"

. . . . .

Outside, the spectacle was indeed astonishing. While shots were still being exchanged here and there between Whites and Reds, the whole liberated population was already streaming in floods into the streets. Often people came under the fire of their own liberators; but seized by a kind of mad exultation only explained by the extraordinary character of the events, they seemed to be under the illusion that "bullets from our own men" could not hurt them; and they continued to run wildly through the streets, eager to see with their own eyes every detail of their long-awaited deliverance.

Through the midst of this crowd of excited people, I made my way to the gardens on the Esplanade, where the bulk of the army with its baggage and equipment was now making its entry.

In interminable ranks the troops arrived, on foot, on horseback, in lorries, on gun-carriages. All the soldiers, horses and carts were decorated with young sprigs of green leaves, lilac and wild flowers. The blue and white pennons fluttered gaily at the end of the cavalrymen's lances.

The faces of the youthful soldiers, prematurely aged by fighting and hardships, were still resolute and grave. The eyes that shone bright in their dark sun-burned faces told at once of bitter experience and joy in great deeds accomplished.

The crowd was still cheering the troops, throwing flowers to them and assailing them with questions. Many foolish citizens and still more foolish citizenesses persisted in asking them "why they had not come earlier," as if the great exploit of these men had been nothing but a pleasure-trip, the beginning, continuation and end of which could have been planned and arranged according to their whim and caprice.

Many people, particularly among the women, seemed to have lost their reason. Their eyes streaming with tears, they threw themselves upon the soldiers, embraced and kissed them, showered flowers upon them, pulled out all kinds of small presents from their bags and forced the men, too weary to resist, to accept them, and gave vent to their joy in the most childish and eccentric demonstrations.

But the troops too had gifts to distribute. The supply columns of the White Army had set up field-kitchens at several cross-roads, and were busy stirring delicious-smelling soup in large cauldrons for the hungry populace. Hundreds of people crowded round the cauldrons, eager for a share, till a positive riot ensued, and some trouble and the exercise of some military severity were required to restore order and see that the children and neediest persons were helped first.

I was continually jostled, accosted, greeted. People I had not seen for two or three months or more—Herbert Lang and his wife, for example, and the others who had been present at our memorable party—suddenly sprang out of the ground before one's eyes. But they became visible only for a lightning flash and disappeared again in the multitude of heads undulating along the streets, shouting and laughing like a wild carnival procession.

In liberated Riga it was as in one of those cities in the Middle Ages which had just come through an epidemic of the plague, and of which the old chronicles narrate:

"And when the distress had passed, men began again to dance and sing and be of good cheer. . . . ."

Never before had Riga known such a general gladness, such a rejoicing of the whole population, as in the afternoon of that memorable day. On every side were laughter, joyous cries, happy faces. Soldiers, proud and smiling, were talking with their friends, their families, their sweethearts. A chorus of bells pealed from every church tower. And over everything there was diffused a feeling of joy of which only those who experienced it can grasp the full meaning. . . .

. . . . .

Despite this universal joy, at every step one took through the streets one was reminded in the most unmistakable fashion of the past days of terror, of the battles which had raged but an hour or two before and were not everywhere completely at an end. Wherever I looked I saw smashed windows, broken doors, upset carts, and arms and ammunition lying about in confusion. In the streets where the fighting had been particularly heavy paving stones were torn up, chests and furniture, behind which the combatants had barricaded themselves, were lying about, and dark bloodstains were visible everywhere.

The most dreadful sight of all was that of the shot Bolsheviks and "gunwomen" who lay about the streets everywhere in masses. They had mostly been thrust off the pavement and flung into the roadway in heaps. Their Russian military overcoats were dingy and unclean, and gave the heaps of corpses, seen from a distance, the appearance of dark heaps of clothes.

More and more bodies were being flung upon these ghastly brown heaps. For the reckoning with the Bolsheviks was by no means ended. While most of the people gave themselves up to rejoicings for their deliverance a sentiment of vengeance and hatred gained the upper hand in others.

As soon as the first White soldiers entered the town, men and women, adults and children, called them, led them into houses and courtyards and showed them holes and corners where Bolsheviks were still in hiding. Immediately one of these laggards was discovered, there was neither trial nor mercy for him. He was at once dragged out into the daylight, pushed up against the nearest wall and shot down.

The fury of the population was above all directed against the feminine elements of the Red Army, the "gunwomen." Many of these had neglected to take themselves off with the rest, and now paid with their lives for their delay and for all their infamous doings. The judgment of the mob was swift and terrible.

The "gunwomen," most of whom were former Riga prostitutes, were coarse and shameless even in the last moments of their life. These fanatical women, glaringly powdered and rouged, dressed in Russian soldiers' overcoats, with dainty patent-leather shoes on their feet, behaved in the most contemptuous and provocative manner towards the Volunteers who seized them. They spat in their faces, put their tongues out and threw around them the most obscene curses and insults even when faced with immediate death. Some even pulled up their skirts and exhibited their bodies to the White soldiers who were firing on them.

It is strange how quickly human beings become brutalized. I myself saw so-called society ladies, who in normal times would have shuddered to see a beetle crushed, take part that day with obvious zest in the hunt for their former torturers and watch their execution without a sign of emotion.

In Church Street I saw two Volunteers dragging a man out of a house to shoot him. His face seemed familiar to me. It reminded me strongly of Yermoloff, the man who had betrayed my friend Igor Somoff to the Reds. His face was ashy and contorted. But he scarcely resisted. One of the men tore off his coat, the other knocked his head back with a punch under the chin. At that moment our eyes met. It seemed to me that he had recognized me, that he was going to say something to me. But already a shot had rung out.

The massive body subsided like a heavy sack and became suddenly limp; the head sank against the chest, and the eyes, remaining wide open and glassy, seemed to stare fixedly into space. The coat which had only just been torn off was thrown over this heap of still warm flesh; and, after this bloodthirsty revenge, the pitiless dispensers of justice passed on.

In Alexander Street, the main street of Riga, a number of White cavalrymen were trotting on the pavement in small parties. Each group was surrounded by a number of curious citizens listening eagerly to what the soldiers had to tell. They said they had been pursuing the Red fugitives along the road leading into the interior of Russia and captured a large number of them. I approached one of these groups, in the midst of which a Volunteer cavalryman sat on horseback, talking loudly—a man with a cheerful, open face, lively brown eyes, and a little black beard. When I came closer, I gave a sudden cry of joy—Roy Carlyle! It was he, still out of breath from swift riding, and full of excitement. And instead of greeting or questioning me, he began to tell me too where he had come from, what he had seen and done.

In hurried, disconnected sentences he told me that he and his comrades had pursued several fleeing Reds, including the club-footed man and other Bolshevist executioners. The Reds had run like hares, he said; but the Volunteer horsemen had ridden at full gallop, spurring their horses. "Hold on—don't let them go!" they muttered between compressed lips. After a furious ride they overtook the Reds, fell upon them like men possessed, and cut them down mercilessly to the last man. "They prayed, howled, whined—but that didn't help them! They were all for it, the dogs!"

He smiled all over his face, radiating cheerfulness and good-nature. In his left hand he held a formidable-looking Colt revolver, and he said, showing this and laughing carelessly and cheerfully, as though telling of some amusing experience:

"I myself have sent two Reds into the next world with this little toy. . . ."

He rode off with a friendly wave of his arm and disappeared.

I followed the rider with my eyes. I had known Roy Carlyle since my schooldays, since my earliest childhood. I had never noticed in him in the past the slightest sign of brutality or bloodthirsty instincts. On the contrary, he had always been a quiet, thoughtful and even unusually sensitive fellow. He used to write very fair verses, was keen on literature, an enthusiast for Goethe, and later he revealed himself as an excellent musician. And now Carlyle, the worshipper of Goethe,

the kind, harmless, sensitive fellow of years gone by, was experiencing an obvious pleasure in "sending two Reds into the next world," in shooting down his fellow-creatures like clay pigeons, as if he himself had come galloping out of these same Asiatic steppes whence those others had come who had disappeared eastward hardly an hour before, we hoped never to return. . . .

I now made my way towards the centre of the town, the Esplanade, where I had heard that there was to be a sort of *auto-da-fé*. As I passed through the crowded streets I was everywhere the witness of very strange and sometimes grotesque scenes.

Hitherto I had seen only people engaged in innocent rejoicing at their deliverance or in taking vengeance on the Reds. Now I saw a third type—people who seemed to have no other thought than the recovery of their stolen property, the speedy destruction of everything that could recall the vanished Bolshevik era, and the immediate, if only superficial, restoration of the old scheme of things and the former aspect of the town.

In one street I saw men and women invading Red warehouses and stores, seeking the belongings stolen from them. Many, indeed, actually found some of their own property, and I saw them, groaning under the burden, carrying away quantities of furniture, linen, etc., on their backs, or pushing it home in wheelbarrows.

At a street corner I saw caretakers, with ladders, hammers and pincers, busily engaged in removing, sometimes with difficulty, the "revolutionary" street signs which the Reds had nailed up on the walls, and in putting back the old signs, which had been carefully preserved. Streets, for example, which, previous to the invasion, were called Nicholas Street, Alexander Street, Church Street, and had been renamed by the Reds "World Revolution Boulevard," "Karl Marx Prospect," or "Third International Avenue," now had their old names restored to them.

Evening was approaching when at last I reached the Esplanade. Here before me, sure enough, was a spectacle which looked like a kind of final allegorical pantomime of all the fantastic events of that terrible but unforgettable time.

In the midst of the Esplanade still stood the "Temple of Reason," surrounded by a wide circle of twenty obelisks, all constructed, like the temple itself, of thin plywood. Here were also the so-called "Tombs of the Heroes," i.e. the sepulchres of the Red chiefs fallen in the course of the invasion.

The "Tombs of the Heroes" were still profusely decked with flowers and enclosed by a low wooden fence. A high platform, also wooden, had been placed close by, and behind a whole row of plaster monuments which the Reds had erected in honour of their dead divinity Karl Marx, as well as to the numerous living and lesser Buddhas (Trotsky, Zinoviev, Dzerzhinsky, etc.). From the roof of a neighbouring house the Mongolian countenance of Lenin still grinned down upon the Esplanade.

The crowd, composed here chiefly of children and youths, with a sprinkling of older men and women, swarmed onto the square with wild shouts, kicking and beating down everything that was not impregnably fastened.

Some lads had already climbed to the roof of the house where the huge picture of Lenin was displayed, and were tugging furiously at this crude representation of the "Red Tsar." They quickly succeeded in loosening the gigantic canvas from the scaffolding to which it was fastened. It fell with a loud crash and lay flat, face to earth. At once dozens of children and hooligans flung themselves upon it and smashed it into a thousand fragments. One holding an ear, another an eye, a third the nose, they all waved the painted strips of canvas in the air like sporting trophies.

Another group of youths made a rush for a colossal plaster bust of Karl Marx. This equally inartistic work was flung from its pedestal by a combined heave, and the assailants began to smash up the plaster into small fragments. Then they flung themselves with shouts on to the speakers' tribune and the wooden fence surrounding the "Tombs of the Heroes" and in a few minutes had hacked everything to pieces. In the meantime a crowd of women had hurried up, and—more practical-minded than the men—gathered up the broken pieces of wood which were all that remained of the platform and the palisades and carried them off hastily to their homes for fuel.

The men next razed the "Tombs of the Heroes" to the ground; and then the crowd, trebled in numbers, warmed up by its first work of destruction, moved towards the so-called "Temple of Reason," which still stood intact in the centre of the square, surrounded by its twenty plywood obelisks.

Somebody suggested that they should set fire to these flimsy monuments of an ephemeral regime; and in a trice the "Temple of Reason" was blazing, along with its twenty obelisks, like gigantic torches. The Temple collapsed into the fire in a great spurt of flames and sparks; the obelisks too tumbled down one after another, and an immense red glow filled the now darkening sky.

Standing a little distance away, I contemplated the strange spectacle of these tumbling "gods of the east," crackling like dry straw, annihilated with incredible ease and swiftness. Children and half-grown lads and girls danced round the blazing piles of wood, and each time one of the gigantic torches fell to the ground, howls of joy and exultant cheering burst forth.

Slowly the pyres burnt themselves out. Soon there was nothing left of them but a few miserable heaps of ashes, swiftly scattered by the wind.

Night fell, silent and gentle, over the town, sleeping peacefully again for the first time after months of torment.

EPILOGUE

The net result of less than five months of Soviet rule in Riga and Latvia, expressed in figures, was the following:

According to the official announcements published in the Soviet newspapers and various lists discovered at the Revolutionary Tribunal, the number of those executed during the Bolshevist regime was 1,549 in Riga itself and 2,083 in the country—in all 3,632 people.

Many people, however, were shot by the Reds without any record being kept of them. These persons, executed without an official death-sentence, can be estimated at another 1,400. The grand total of the people executed in Riga and Latvia during the Soviet era can thus be reckoned as at least 5,000.

In the same period, in Riga alone, no fewer than 8,590 persons died of starvation or of diseases caused by starvation. These data are derived from the Statistical Office of the City of Riga, which in giving them points out that the figures are not to be regarded as exhaustive. The mortality in Riga during the Bolshevist period reached 86 per 1,000 of the population, against 18 per 1,000 in normal times.

If we add to these 8,590 who died of starvation the 5,000 who were done away with by violence, we arrive at the result that in the five months of the Soviet domination in Riga no fewer than 13,500 human beings perished as the direct victims of the Bolshevist experiment attempted there.

Further, when the White Army entered Riga, it

liberated over 8,000 people, perfectly innocent men and women of all ranks and classes, who had been confined in the Riga prisons, mostly for months. Some 20,000 more had been removed by the Reds from the Inner Town and placed in a kind of concentration camp on the barren islands in the Dvina. In all Latvia over 30,000 persons were liberated from prisons and prison camps by the White advance.

Lastly, at the approach of the Bolshevists in January 1919, some 30,000 people fled from Riga into Estonia, Courland, Germany, Denmark, Sweden, etc. Only a few returned. Indeed, immediately after the liberation approximately 20,000 more people left the country from fear of a possible return of the Reds. So that the population of the city of Riga, which before the coming of the Bolshevists numbered some 200,000, was temporarily cut down by almost a third as a result of the Red invasion.

The material damage caused by the Soviets in Riga and Latvia, the unlimited destruction and burning of stores, carrying off of cattle and corn, requisitioning of the furniture and goods from hundreds of town dwellings, plundering of the banks and safes, consumption of the entire food stores of the town, etc., can hardly be calculated to-day in exact figures. However, according to the Statistical Office of Riga, the total material damage caused by the Bolshevist invasion of 1919 can be estimated without fear of exaggeration at about 200 million gold francs.

Further data illustrating the character of the Soviet era in Latvia could be quoted indefinitely. Accurate and carefully verified data testify to the ravages perpetrated, for instance in the schools, churches, charitable institutions, and in every sphere of public life; and also to the heavy losses suffered by the male population of the country in the fight against Bolshevism. But I think the figures I have quoted suffice.

They are the net result of an experiment which began with the boastful promise to establish a "heaven on earth," and ended—how differently!—with 5,000 people murdered, 8,500 dead of starvation, 8,000 in prison, 20,000 in the Dvina concentration camp; in all, some 30,000 persons deprived of their liberty. To this should be added millions upon millions of material damage through devastation, plunder and robbery.

Such was the ghastly outcome of this Bolshevist experiment carried out in a defenceless European country. It speaks for itself. And I can only wish that the truth of these experiences, which I have here set forth to the best of my ability, may be known and taken to heart everywhere in the world where people live and carry on the arduous struggle for existence.

BIBLIOGRAPHY

This book, as already pointed out in the Introduction, is based above all on my own experiences and on the notes which I myself made at the time of the events described.

I have used, besides, the following sources of references:

1. A complete collection of the "Red Flag" (Nos. 1-114) published in Riga during the Bolshevist period, from January 7 to May 22, 1919.

2. The diaries of the Baltic historian, Professor DR. A. VON HEDENSTRÖM, who was likewise a witness of the happenings, which he recorded day by day, and has kindly placed his notes at my disposal.

3. PETER STUTCHKA: "Five Months of Soviet Latvia," published by the Central Committee of the Communist Party of Latvia, Moscow, 1919. (In Russian.)

4. MONIKA HUNNIUS: "Pictures of the Time of the Bolshevist Domination in Riga," Eugen Salzer, Heilbronn, 1921. (In German.)

5. WOLFGANG WACHTSMUTH: "The Bolshevist Period in Riga," G. Lœffler, Riga, 1929. (In German.)

6. ALFRED ROSENBERG: "Plague in Russia," Dr. Ernst Boepple, Munich, 1922. (In German.)

7. Riga Town Mission: "Sayings of Baltic Martyrs," A. Grosset, Riga. (In German.)

8. PASTOR ERHARD DOEBLER: "Letters from Prison during the Bolshevist Period," Riga, 1919. (In German.)

9. The Baltic Volunteer Corps Headquarters: "The Baltic Volunteer Corps in the War against Bolshevism," G. Loeffler, Riga, 1929. (In German.)

10. JHNO MEYER: "The Iron Division in the War against Bolshevism," Hillman, Leipzig, 1920. (In German.)

11. CAPTAIN WAGENER: "Betrayed by the Fatherland," Ch. Belser, Stuttgart, 1920. (In German.)

12. PRINCE A. LIEVEN: "In the Southern Baltic Provinces," Berlin, 1927. (In Russian.)

13. The White Cause: "Concerning the Baltic Volunteer Corps," Berlin, 1927. (In Russian.)

14. COUNT R. VON DER GOLTZ: "My Mission in the Baltic Provinces," K. F. Koehler, Leipzig, 1921. (In German.)

15. MAJOR A. FLETCHER: "The Baltic Volunteer Corps," Riga, 1929. (In German.)

16. GENERAL RADZIN: "Latvia's Struggle for Independence," Gulbis, Riga, 1923. (In Lettish.)

17. COUNT ALEXANDER STENBOCK-FERMOR: "Volunteer Stenbock," J. Engelhorns Nachfolger, Stuttgart, 1929. (In German.)

18. COLONEL BOLSTEIN: "With the Iron Division in Courland," Rigasche Rundschau, Riga, 1927. (In German.)

19. CAPTAIN V. STEINAECKER: "At War against the Bolshevists," Budendey & Kober, Hamburg, 1920. (In German.)

Part of the statistical data has been taken from the "Statistical Annual of the City of Riga" of the year 1929. The rest was obtained for me and placed at my disposal by Mr. Herbert Pärn, Director of the Statistical Office of the City of Riga from 1920 to 1928.

Finally I would like once more to remind my English readers of the fact that throughout the whole duration of the Soviet rule in Latvia a considerable number of British subjects were living in Riga, and had exactly the same kind of experiences as the author. These people can easily be taken as witnesses of the events which I have related. Furthermore, there exists another group of English people who, although they were absent from Riga in the year 1919, are nevertheless permanent residents of that city and are consequently well acquainted with the principal facts described. They, too, can confirm in a very great measure the truth of what is written in this book. Considering that the names of all these people might be of some importance, I append a list of those which I have been able to ascertain:

Mr. W. D. Addison, Mrs. Lucy Addison, Miss Una Addison, Mr. H. Armitstead, Mr. J. W. Armitstead, Mr. Robert Ball, Mrs. Henrietta Ball, Mr. J. Barclay, Mr. Edward Berry, Mrs. Bessy Berry, Mr. Richard Bilby, Consul Bosanquet, Mr. John Bowell, Mr. Charles Ellis, Mrs. Charles Ellis, Mr. Thomas Ellis, Miss Ellen Ellis, Mrs. Edith Focht, Mr. Glyn Hall, Mr. Trevor Hall, Mrs. Eva Hall, Mrs. Walter Helmsing, Miss J. Helmsing, Mrs. Alexander Hill, Mr. Laurence Hill, Mrs. Margareth Hill, Mrs. J. Klemm, Mrs. Amy Langford, Mr. John MacIntosh, Mrs. N. MacIntosh, Miss Margareth MacIntosh, Mr. Leslie Marshall, Mrs. Ebba Mitchell, Miss Lucy Mitchell, Mr. J. Parkman, Mrs. Gladys Poskitt, Mr. William Posselt, Mrs. Mary Posselt, Miss M. Posselt, Mr. James Priestley, Mrs. Louise Priestley, Miss May Priestley, Mr. K. L. Robinson, Mr. Henry Sedcole, Mrs. Alice Sedcole, The Rev. J. Stuermer, Mrs. Stuermer, Mr. Alexander Taylor, Mr. Alfred Taylor, Mr. Arthur Taylor, Mrs. Alice Taylor, Miss Amy Taylor, Mrs. N. Trautman, Mr. R. O. G. Urch (Correspondent of *The Times*) and Miss Florence Waller, most of them resident in Riga.

For Product Safety Concerns and Information please contact our EU representative GPSR@taylorandfrancis.com
Taylor & Francis Verlag GmbH, Kaufingerstraße 24, 80331 München, Germany

www.ingramcontent.com/pod-product-compliance
Lightning Source LLC
Chambersburg PA
CBHW071758300426
44116CB00009B/1121